LETTERS
OF NOTE

LETTERS OF NOTE

CORRESPONDENCE DESERVING OF A WIDER AUDIENCE

COMPILED BY **SHAUN USHER**

CANONGATE

Edinburgh · London

This paperback edition published by Canongate Books in 2016

First published in Great Britain in 2013 by Canongate Books Ltd in conjunction with
Unbound

Canongate Books Ltd, 14 High Street, Edinburgh EH1 1TE
www.canongate.tv

Unbound, Unit 18, Waterside, 44-48 Wharf Road, London N1 7UX
www.unbound.co.uk

Based on an original design by Here Design

British Library Cataloguing-in-Publication Data
A catalogue record for this book is available on
request from the British Library

ISBN 978-1-78211-928-9

Repro: syntax21.co.uk

Printed in Italy by L.E.G.O. S.p.A.

For Karina

CONTENTS

Dear Reader,

The beautiful book you now hold in your hands is the culmination
of an unexpected but wholly enjoyable four-year journey through the
letters, memos and telegrams of the famous, the infamous and the
not-so-famous--an immensely gratifying project that first took shape
as a website but which now, thanks to the overwhelmingly positive
reaction to its online incarnation, takes on a physical form: a
carefully crafted, book-shaped museum of letters that will grip and
fling you from one emotion to the next, occasionally educate even the
most informed of minds and, I hope, perfectly illustrate the importanc
-e and unrivalled charm of old-fashioned correspondence just as the
world becomes digitised and the art of letter writing slips from view.
One thing that hasn't changed since Letters of Note began is
its main objective--that is, to showcase correspondence deserving of
a wider audience--and to say I'm pleased with the eclectic selection
with which you are soon to fall in love would be a huge understatement.
The highlights are endless, but let me pluck a handful from the bag to
whet your appetite. We have a letter from Mick Jagger to Andy Warhol
that contains a wonderfully laid-back design brief for a Rolling
Stones album cover; a handwritten note from Queen Elizabeth II to US
President Eisenhower which is accompanied by Ma'am's personal scone
recipe; a remarkable and masterful riposte from a freed slave to his
old master that will leave many of you punching the air; Virginia
Woolf's heart-rending final letter to her husband, written shortly
before taking her own life; a beautiful, delicate letter of advice
from Iggy Pop to a troubled young fan that could warm the coldest of
hearts; a truly incredible letter penned by scientist Francis Crick
to his son, in which he announces the discovery of the structure of
DNA; a harrowing account of a mastectomy performed without anaesthetic,
written by the 60-year-old patient to her daughter; and an extraordinary
job application letter from one of history's most celebrated minds,
Leonardo da Vinci. On your travels you will read love letters, rejection
letters, fan letters, apology letters; you will be saddened, maddened,
delighted and shocked. One of the letters, imprinted into a clay tablet,

dates all the way back to the 14th century BC; the most recent is just
a few years old. However, despite their many flavours, I am hopeful that
all will captivate you as they have me and whisk you to a point in time
far more effectively than the average history book--indeed, I can think
of no better way to learn about the past than through the often candid
correspondence of those who lived it.

Also important was to do these priceless time capsules justice
aesthetically; to make the book a visual treat. This was achieved by
working closely with the very best designers, to present each and every
letter respectfully and to its fullest potential. Where possible, we
have located and gained permission to reproduce facsimiles of the
original documents themselves, in doing so giving you the opportunity
to see the very material on which these messages were penned, typewritt
-en or even carved, not forgetting the various smudges, creases and
other imperfections that give these objects so much character; in cases
where this wasn't an option, we have instead sourced some gorgeous
photographs to accompany and complement the letters, a few of which
have never before been published. The end result is a book that I am
unspeakably proud to have compiled. My only hope is that it will take
pride of place on your bookshelf and be passed to your nearest and
dearest. Maybe, just maybe, it will inspire at least a few people to
put pen to paper, or even to dust off an old typewriter, and write
their own letters of note.

Yours in letters,

Shaun

SHAUN USHER
Letters of Note

ONE'S DROP SCONES

QUEEN ELIZABETH II to
US PRESIDENT DWIGHT D.
EISENHOWER
January 24th, 1960

In 1957, five years into her
reign, Queen Elizabeth II
made her first state visit
to the United States as a
guest of then US President
Dwight D. Eisenhower. The
favour was returned two
years later when, in August
1959, the Queen entertained
Eisenhower and his wife,
Mamie, at Balmoral Castle
in Scotland, a grand and
sprawling private estate of
the Royal Family's since
1852. What went on and
was discussed behind those
closed doors is unknown;
however, one thing we can
be sure of is this: President
Eisenhower was seduced
by, and fell in love with, the
Queen's drop scones. So
much so, in fact, that five
months after serving them,
she belatedly sent him her
personal recipe and an
accompanying letter.

BUCKINGHAM PALACE

Dear Mr. President,

Seeing a picture of you in today's newspaper standing in front of a barbecue grilling quail, reminded me that I had never sent you the recipe of the drop scones which I promised you at Balmoral.

I now hasten to do so, and I do hope you will find them successful.

Though the quantities are for 16 people, when there are fewer, I generally put in less flour and milk, but use the other ingredients as stated.

I have also tried using golden syrup or treacle instead of only sugar and that can be very good, too.

I think the mixture needs a great deal of beating while making, and shouldn't stand about too long before cooking.

We have followed with intense interest and much admiration your tremendous journey to so many countries, but feel we shall never again be able to claim that <u>we</u> are being made to do too much on our future tours!

We remember with such pleasure your visit to Balmoral, and I hope the photograph will be a reminder of the very happy day you spent with us.

With all good wishes to you and Mrs. Eisenhower.

Yours sincerely

Elizabeth R

MENU
DROP SCONES

<u>Ingredients</u>

4 teacups flour
4 tablespoons caster sugar
2 teacups milk
2 whole eggs
2 teaspoons bi-carbonate soda
3 teaspoons cream of tartar
2 tablespoons melted butter

Beat eggs, sugar and about half the milk together, add flour, and mix well together adding remainder of milk as required, also bi-carbonate and cream of tartar, fold in the melted butter.

<u>Enough for 16 people</u>

BUCKINGHAM PALACE

Dear Mr. President,

Seeing a picture of you in today's newspaper standing in front of a barbecue grilling quail, reminded me that I had never sent you the recipe of the drop scones which I promised you at Balmoral. I now hasten to do so,

and I do hope you will
find them successful.

Though the quantities are for
16 people, when there are
fewer, I generally put in
less flour and milk, but
use the other ingredients as
stated.

I have also tried using
golden syrup or treacle instead
of only sugar and that can
be very good, too.

I think the mixture needs
a great deal of beating
while making, and shouldn't
stand about too long before
cooking.

We have followed with
intense interest and much
admiration your tremendous
journey to so many countries,
but feel we shall never
again be able to claim
that <u>we</u> are being

5

made to do too much on
our future tours!

We remember with such
pleasure your visit to
Balmoral, and I hope the
photographs will be a
reminder of the very happy
day you spend with us.
With all good wishes to you
and Mrs. Eisenhower.
Yours sincerely   Elizabeth R

MENU

DROP SCONES

....

Ingredients

    4 teacups flour

    4 tablespoons caster sugar

    2 teacups milk

    2 whole eggs

    2 teaspoons bi-carbonate soda

    3 teaspoons cream of tartar

    2 tablespoons melted butter

Beat eggs, sugar and about half the milk together, add flour, and mix well together adding remainder of milk as required, also bi-carbonate and cream of tartar, fold in the melted butter.

Enough for 16 people

7632 G.87 2M 2/55 H & S Gp. 902

FROM HELL

JACK THE RIPPER to
GEORGE LUSK
October, 1888

On October 15th 1888, George Lusk, Chairman of the Whitechapel Vigilance Committee – a group of concerned citizens who actively searched for the person responsible for a spate of killings known as the "Whitechapel murders" – received this chilling letter from someone claiming to be infamous serial killer Jack the Ripper. It was sent along with a small box, the contents of which were later determined to be half a human kidney, preserved in wine. Catherine Eddowes, Jack the Ripper's fourth victim, was thought to be the organ's previous owner; according to the note, the remainder of her kidney had been fried and eaten.

From hell

Mr Lusk,

Sor

I send you half the Kidne I took from one women prasarved it for you tother piece I fried and ate it was very nise. I may send you the bloody knif that took it out if you only wate a whil longer

signed

Catch me when
you can

Mishter Lusk

From hell

Mr Lusk
        Sor
              I send you half the
Kidne I took from one women
prasarved it for you tother piece
I fried and ate it was very nise I
may send you the bloody knif that
took it out if you only wate a whil
longer

        Signed   Catch me when
                          you Can
                    Mishter Lusk -

9

WIND THE CLOCK

North Brooklin, Maine
30 March 1973

E. B. WHITE to MR NADEAU
March 30th, 1973

Author E. B. White won numerous awards in his lifetime, and with good reason. Born in 1899, he was one of the greatest essayists of his time, writing countless influential pieces for both *The New Yorker* and *Harper's*; in 1959, he co-authored the multi-million selling, expanded edition of *The Elements of Style* to much acclaim; he wrote children's books which have gone on to become classics, such as *Stuart Little* and *Charlotte's Web*. He was also responsible for writing hundreds of wonderful letters.

In March 1973, he wrote the following perfectly formed reply to a Mr Nadeau, who sought White's opinion on what he saw as a bleak future for the human race.

Dear Mr. Nadeau:

As long as there is one upright man, as long as there is one compassionate woman, the contagion may spread and the scene is not desolate. Hope is the thing that is left to us, in a bad time. I shall get up Sunday morning and wind the clock, as a contribution to order and steadfastness.

Sailors have an expression about the weather: they say, the weather is a great bluffer. I guess the same is true of our human society—things can look dark, then a break shows in the clouds, and all is changed, sometimes rather suddenly. It is quite obvious that the human race has made a queer mess of life on this planet. But as a people we probably harbor seeds of goodness that have lain for a long time waiting to sprout when the conditions are right. Man's curiosity, his relentlessness, his inventiveness, his ingenuity have led him into deep trouble. We can only hope that these same traits will enable him to claw his way out.

Hang on to your hat. Hang on to your hope. And wind the clock, for tomorrow is another day.

Sincerely,
E. B. White

I AM TO BE EXECUTED

MARY STUART to HENRY III OF FRANCE
February 8th, 1587

For the best part of 20 years until she died, Mary Stuart was either imprisoned or on trial in England at the behest of her first cousin, Elizabeth I. Her entire life was anything but normal, having been crowned Queen of Scotland at six days old, married and widowed by the time she was 17, and was even Queen of France for a short period. She also had her eye on the English throne and that cemented her downfall. This farewell letter was written by Mary, then aged 44, in the early hours of February 8th 1587 to the brother of her deceased first husband. Just six hours later, as mentioned in her letter, she was beheaded in front of 300 witnesses.

Reyne descosse
8 feu 1587

Monssieur mon beau frere estant par la permission de Dieu pour mes peschez comme ie croy venue me iecter entre les bras de ceste Royne ma cousine ou iay eu beaucoup dennuis & passe pres de vingt ans ie suis enfin par elle & ses estats condampnee a la mort & ayant demande mes papiers par eulx ostez a ceste fin de fayre mon testament ie nay peu rien retirer qui me seruist ny obtenir conge den fayre ung libre ny quapres ma mort mon corps fust transporte sellon mon desir en votre royaulme ou iay eu lhonneur destre royne votre soeur & ancienne allyee.

Ceiourdhuy apres disner ma este desnonsse ma sentence pour estre executee demain comme une criminelle a huict heures du matin ie nay eu loisir de vous fayre ung ample discours de tout ce qui sest passe may sil vous plaist de crere mon medesin & ces aultres miens desolez seruiters vous oyres la verite & comme graces a dieu ie mesprise las mort & fidellementproteste de la recepuoir innocente de tout crime quant ie serois leur subiecte la religion chatolique & la mayntien du droit que dieu ma donne a ceste couronne sont les deulx poincts de ma condampnation & toutesfoy ilz ne me veullent permettre de dire que cest pour la religion catolique que ie meurs may pour la crainte du champge de la leur & pour preuue ilz mont oste mon aulmonier lequel bien quil soit en la mayson ie nay peu obtenir quil me vinst confesser ny communier a ma mort mays mont faict grande instance de recepuoir la consolation & doctrine de leur ministre ammene pour ce faict. Ce porteur & sa compaigne la pluspart de vos subiectz vous tesmoigneront mes deportemantz en ce mien acte dernier il reste que ie vous suplie comme roy tres chrestien mon beau frere & ansien allye & qui mauuez tousiours proteste de maymer qua ce coup vous faysiez preuue en toutz ces poincts de vostre vertu tant par charite me souslageant de ce que pour descharger ma conssiance ie ne puis sans vous qui est de reconpenser mes seruiteurs desolez leur layssant leurs gaiges laultre faysant prier dieu pour une royne qui a estay nommee tres chrestienne & meurt chatolique desnuee de toutz ses biens quant a mon fylz ie le vous recommande autant quil le meritera car ie nen puis respondre Iay pris la hardiesse de vous enuoier deulx pierres rares pour la sante vous la desirant parfaicte auuec heurese & longue vie Vous le recepvrez comme de vostre tres affectionee belle soeur mourante en vous rendant tesmoygnage de son bon cueur enuers vous ie vous recommande encore mes seruiteurs vous ordonneres si il vous plaict que pour mon ame ie soye payee de partye de ce me que debuez & qu'en l'honnheur de Jhesus Christ lequel ie priray demayn a ma mort pour vous me laysser de quoy fonder un obit & fayre les aulmosnes requises ce mercredy a deulx heures apres minuit

Vostre tres affectionnee & bien bonne soeur

Mari R

Translated transcript:

Queen of Scotland
8 Feb 1587

Royal brother, having by God's will, for my sins I think, thrown myself into the power of the Queen my cousin, at whose hands I have suffered much for almost twenty years, I have finally been condemned to death by her and her Estates. I have asked for my papers, which they have taken away, in order that I might make my will, but I have been unable to recover anything of use to me, or even get leave either to make my will freely or to have my body conveyed after my death, as I would wish, to your kingdom where I had the honour to be queen, your sister and old ally.

Tonight, after dinner, I have been advised of my sentence: I am to be executed like a criminal at eight in the morning. I have not had time to give you a full account of everything that has happened, but if you will listen to my doctor and my other unfortunate servants, you will learn the truth, and how, thanks be to God, I scorn death and vow that I meet it innocent of any crime, even if I were their subject. The Catholic faith and the assertion of my God-given right to the English crown are the two issues on which I am condemned, and yet I am not allowed to say that it is for the Catholic religion that I die, but for fear of interference with theirs. The proof of this is that they have taken away my chaplain, and although he is in the building, I have not been able to get permission for him to come and hear my confession and give me the Last Sacrament, while they have been most insistent that I receive the consolation and instruction of their minister, brought here for that purpose. The bearer of this letter and his companions, most of them your subjects, will testify to my conduct at my last hour. It remains for me to beg Your Most Christian Majesty, my brother-in-law and old ally, who have always protested your love for me, to give proof now of your goodness on all these points: firstly by charity, in paying my unfortunate servants the wages due them – this is a burden on my conscience that only you can relieve: further, by having prayers offered to God for a queen who has borne the title Most Christian, and who dies a Catholic, stripped of all her possessions. As for my son, I commend him to you in so far as he deserves, for I cannot answer for him. I have taken the liberty of sending you two precious stones, talismans against illness, trusting that you will enjoy good health and a long and happy life. Accept them from your loving sister-in-law, who, as she dies, bears witness of her warm feeling for you. Again I commend my servants to you. Give instructions, if it please you, that for my soul's sake part of what you owe me should be paid, and that for the sake of Jesus Christ, to whom I shall pray for you tomorrow as I die, I be left enough to found a memorial mass and give the customary alms. Wednesday, at two in the morning

Your most loving and most true sister

Mari R

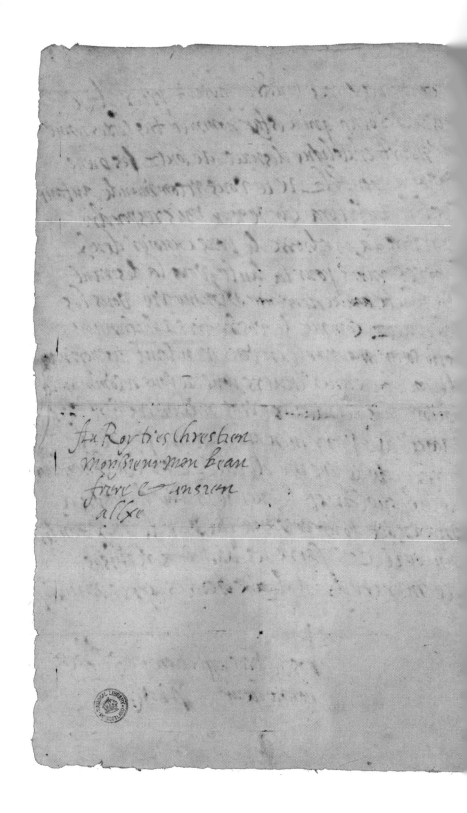

Au Roy tres Chrestien
Monsieur mon beau
frere et cousin
alixe

Royne d'escosse
8 feu 1587

Monsieur mon beau frere estant par la permission
de Dieu pour mes peschez comme ie croy venue
me rieter entre les bras de ceste Royne ma
cousine ou ray eu beaucoup dennuis et passe
pres de vingt ans ie suis enfin par elle et ses
estats condampnee a la mort et ayant demande
mes papiers par eulx ostez a ceste fin de fayre
mon testament ie nay peu rien retirer qui me
servist ny obtenir congé den fayre ung libre
ny quapres mamort mon corps fust transporte
sellon mon desir en votre royaulme ou ray eu
lhonneur destre royne votre soeur et ancienne
allyee

ce iourdhuy apres disner ma este denonse
ma sentence pour estre executee demain comme
une criminelle a huict heures du matin
ie nay eu loisir de vous feyre ung ample discours
de tout ce qui sest passe mays sil vousplaist
de croyre mon medecin et ces aultres miens
desolez serviteurs vous oyres la verite et comme
graces a dieu ie mesprise la mort et fidellement

proteste de la recepuoir innocente de la tax &
quant ie seroie leur subiecte la religion chatoliq
& le maynteen du droit que dieu ma donne a
ceste couronne sont les deulx poincts de ma
condamnation & toutesfoys ilz ne me veulle
permettre de dire que cest pour la religion cato
que ie meurs mays pour la crainte du chang
de la feur & pour preuue ilz mont oste mon
aulmonier lequel bien quil soit en la mayson ie
nay peu obtenir quil me vinst confesser ny
communier a ma mort mays mont faict grande
instance de recepuoir la consolation & doctrin
de leur ministre amene pour ce faict ce porteur
& sa compaignie la pluspart de vos subiectz
vous tesmoigneront mes desportementz en ce
dmyen acte dernier il reste que ie vous supplie
comme Roy tres chrestien mon beaufrere & ansien
allye & a qui mauiez toussiours proteste de
maymer qua ce coup vous faysiez preuue en
toutz ces poincts de vostre vertu tant par
charite me soulageant de ce que pour descha
ger ma consstrance ie ne puis sans vous qui
est de recompenser mes seruiteurs desolez leu

essant leurs gaiges la lettre faysant prier dieu
pour une d'oyne qui a esté nommée tres Chrestienne
et meurt Catholique desnuee de toutz ses biens
n'ayet a mon filz Je le vous recommande autant
qu'il le meritera car Je n'en puis respondre
ay pris la hardiesse de vous envoier deulx
pierres rares pour la santé vous la desirant
parfaicte avecq heureuse et longue vie vous les
receperez comme de vostre tres affectionnee
et plus soeur mourante en vous rendant tesmoignage
de son bon cueur envers vous Je vous recommande
encore mes serviteurs vous ordonnerez si il vous
plaict que pour mon ame ils soyr payee de
ce qui me debvez et que en l'honneur de
de Jesus Christ lequel Je priray demayn a
ma mort pour vous me laisser de quoy fonder
un obit et fayre les aulmones requises
ce mercredy a deulx heures apres minuict

Vostre tres affectionnee et bien
bonne soeur   MARI R

Campbell SOUP Company

❋ ❋ ❋ ❋ ❋ ❋ ❋ CAMDEN 1, NEW JERSEY ❋ ❋ ❋ ❋ ❋ ❋ ❋

May 19, 1964

Mr. A. Warhol
1342 Lexington Avenue
New York, New York

Dear Mr. Warhol:

I have followed your career for some time. Your work has evoked a great deal of interest here at Campbell Soup Company for obvious reasons.

At one time I had hoped to be able to acquire one of your Campbell Soup label paintings - but I'm afraid you have gotten much too expensive for me.

I did want to tell you, however, that we admired your work and I have since learned that you like Tomato Soup. I am taking the liberty of having a couple of cases of our Tomato Soup delivered to you at this address.

We wish you continued success and good fortune.

Cordially,

William P. MacFarland
Product Marketing Manager

I HEAR YOU LIKE TOMATO SOUP

WILLIAM P. MACFARLAND
to ANDY WARHOL
May 19th, 1964

As product marketing manager for Campbell's, William MacFarland must have been overjoyed with the incredible public reaction to Andy Warhol's first exhibition as a fine artist in 1962. Present at Los Angeles' Ferus Gallery was Warhol's now world-famous, unmistakable Campbell's Soup Cans piece: 32 silk screened portraits, each representing a different variety of the company's soup product, all arranged in a single line. These works helped bring the Pop art movement to the masses and provoked huge debate in all corners of the art world – all the while holding a certain soup brand in the limelight. In 1964, as Warhol's star continued to rise, MacFarland decided to show his appreciation to the artist by way of this letter, followed by some complimentary cans of soup.

BILL HICKS ON FREEDOM OF SPEECH

8 June 1993

BILL HICKS to A PRIEST
June 8th, 1993

As an outspoken stand-up comedian with strong, unbending views on the most divisive of subjects, the late Bill Hicks was no stranger to controversy during his all-too-brief career. In May 1993, less than a year before he succumbed to pancreatic cancer at the age of 32, a live recording of Hicks's *Revelations* show was broadcast on television in the UK. Shortly afterwards, deeply offended by its "blasphemous" content, a priest wrote to the broadcaster, Channel 4, and complained about the recent screening. After reading the complaint, Hicks, never one to avoid a discussion, replied to the priest directly by letter.

Dear Sir,

After reading your letter expressing your concerns regarding my special 'Revelations', I felt duty-bound to respond to you myself in hopes of clarifying my position on the points you brought up, and perhaps enlighten you as to who I really am.

Where I come from — America — there exists this wacky concept called 'freedom of speech', which many people feel is one of the paramount achievements in mankind's mental development. I myself am a strong supporter of the 'Right of freedom of speech', as I'm sure most people would be if they truly understood the concept. 'Freedom of speech' means you support the right of people to say exactly those ideas which you do not agree with. (Otherwise, you don't believe in 'freedom of speech', but rather only those ideas which you believe to be acceptably stated.) Seeing as how there are so many different beliefs in the world, and as it would be virtually impossible for all of us to agree on any one belief, you may begin to realize just how important an idea like 'freedom of speech' really is. The idea basically states 'while I don't agree or care for what you are saying, I do support your right to say it, for herein lies true freedom'.

You say you found my material 'offensive' and 'blasphemous'. I find it interesting that you feel your beliefs are denigrated or threatened when I'd be willing to bet you've never received a *single letter* complaining about your beliefs, or asking why they are allowed to be. (If you have received such a letter, it definitely did not come from me.) Furthermore, I imagine a quick perusal of an average week of television programming would reveal many more shows of a religious nature, than one of *my* shows — which are called 'specials' by virtue of the fact that they are *very rarely on*.

All I'm doing in 'Revelations' is giving my point of view in my language based on my experiences — much the same way religious broadcasters might organize their programs. While I've found many of the religious shows I've viewed over the years not to be to my liking, or in line with my own beliefs, I've never considered it my place to exert any greater type of censorship than changing the channel, or better yet — turning off the TV completely.

Now, for the part of your letter I found most disturbing.

In support of your position of outrage, you posit the hypothetical scenario regarding the possibly 'angry' reaction of Muslims to material they might find similarly offensive. Here is my question to you: Are you tacitly condoning the violent terrorism of a handful of thugs to whom the idea of 'freedom of speech' and tolerance is perhaps as foreign as Christ's message itself? If you are somehow implying that their intolerance to contrary beliefs is justifiable, admirable, or perhaps even preferable to one of acceptance and forgiveness, then I wonder what your true beliefs really are.

If you had watched my entire show, you would have noticed in my summation of my beliefs the fervent plea to the governments of the world to spend less money on the machinery of war, and more on feeding, clothing, and educating the poor and needy of the world … A not-so-unchristian sentiment at that!

Ultimately, the message in my material is a call for understanding rather than ignorance, peace rather than war, forgiveness rather than condemnation, and love rather than fear. While this message may have understandably been lost on your ears (due to my presentation), I assure you the thousands of people I played to in my tours of the United Kingdom got it.

I hope I helped answer some of your questions. Also, I hope you consider this an invitation to keep open the lines of communication. Please feel free to contact me personally with comments, thoughts, or questions, if you so choose. If not, I invite you to enjoy my two upcoming specials entitled 'Mohammed the TWIT' and 'Buddha, you fat PIG'. (JOKE)

Sincerely,

Bill Hicks

YOUR PAL, JOHN K.

JOHN KRICFALUSI to AMIR
AVNI
1998

In 1998, aged 14, aspiring
young cartoonist Amir Avni
decided to send a letter to
John Kricfalusi, creator
of the seminal animated
television show, *Ren &
Stimpy*, along with a few
cartoons he had drawn,
some of which contained
relatively unknown
characters of John's. To his
delight, Kricfalusi replied,
and not with a hastily
scribbled acknowledgement
of a few words.

"I think John puts a lot
of faith in the younger
generation of cartoonists,"
explains Amir, over a decade
later, "and wants to make
sure they are well educated.
He sees the younger
generation as the future of
cartoons, and that's why
he's so approachable and
good-willed."

An admirable stance
indeed, and one which has
inspired at least one fan to
follow his dream. Avni has
since studied and taught
Animation at Sheridan
College in Canada; in 2013
he was working on a new
show for Cartoon Network.

Dear Amir,

Thanks for your letter and all your cartoons to look at.

We're having trouble opening your flash-files, though; when I click the player it opens a blank screen. I have somebody trying to figure it out. If it doesn't work, maybe you can post them on the web and give me the URL.

Your comics are pretty good, especially your staging and continuity. You might have the makings of a good storyboard artist. I'm sending you a very good how to draw animation book by Preston Blair. Preston was one of Tex Avery's animators. He animated 'Red Hot Riding Hood' and many other characters.

His book shows you very important fundamentals of good cartoon drawing.

Construction. Learn how to construct your drawings out of 3-dimensional objects. Learn how to draw hands, so they look solid. I want you to copy the drawings in his book. Start on the first page. Draw <u>slow</u>. Look very closely. Measure the proportions. Draw the drawings step-by-step, just the way Preston does.

After you finish the d each drawing check it <u>carefully</u> against the drawing in the book. (if you do your drawings on tracing paper, you can lay the paper on top of the book to see where you made mistakes. On your drawing write the mistakes. Then do the drawing <u>again</u>, this time correcting the mistakes.

Here's another important piece of information for you:

<u>Good drawing</u> is more important than anything else in animation. More than ideas, style, stories. Everything starts with good drawing. Learn to draw construction, perspective.

Ok, now it's up to you.

Oh, by the way — OLD cartoons (from the 1940's especially are better than new cartoons. If you copy the drawings in new cartoons you won't learn anything — except how to get bad habits. Look at Tom and Jerry from 1947 – 1954 or Elmer Fudd + Porky Pig from the 40's + early 50's.)

I'm amazed at how much you know about us. How do you know about BOBBY BIGLOAF? and MILDMAN!

You can see Jimmy + George Liquor on the internet. Oh, I guess you know that.

ALLRIGHT Bastard, let's get to work. <u>Draw</u>! and <u>slow</u> now.

My email address is [redacted] if you have any questions — not <u>too</u> many I hope! I get a lot of email and it's hard to answer it all.

Your pal,

JOHN K.

Dear Amir,

Thanks for your letter and all your cartoons' to look at.

We're having trouble opening your flash-files, though; when I click the player it opens a blank screen. I have somebody trying to figure it out. If it doesn't work, maybe you can post them on the web and give me the URL.

Your comics' are pretty good, especially your staging and continuity. You might have the makings of a good storyboard artist.

/

I'm sending you a very good how to draw
animation book by Preston Blair.
Preston was one of Tex Avery's animators.
He animated "Red Hot Riding Hood" and
many other characters.

His book shows you very important
fundamentals of good cartoon drawing,
& Construction. Learn
how to construct your drawings
out of 3-dimensional objects.
Learn how to draw hands, so they
Look solid. → this

← not
this →

2

I want you to copy the drawings in his book. Start on the first page. Draw SLOW. Look very closely. Measure the proportions. Draw the drawings step-by-step, just the way Preston does!

ETc...

After you finish the d each drawing check it carefully against the drawing in the book. (if you do your drawings on tracing paper, you can lay the paper on top of the book to see where you made mistakes! On your drawing ₃ write the mistakes!

eyes too
high on head →

nose
too small

ear too big

head too thin

Then do the drawing again, this time correcting the mistakes!

Here's another important piece of information for you:

Good drawing is more important than anything else in animation.
More than ideas, style, stories.
Everything starts with good drawing.
Learn to draw construction,
perspective.

4

Ok, now it's up to you.

Oh, by the way — OLD cartoons (from the 1940's especially are better than new cartoons!.

If you copy the drawings in new cartoons you won't learn anything — except how to get bad habits! Look at Tom and Jerry from 1947-1954 or Elmer Fudd + Porky Pig from the 40's + early 50's.)

5

6

I'm amazed at how much you know about us'. How do you know about BOBBY BIGLOAF? and MILDMAN!

You can see Jimmy + George Liquor on the Internet. Oh, I Guess you know that.

7

ALLRIGHT Bastard, Let's get to work. Draw! and slow now.

My email address is CENSORED!@AOL.com if you have any questions - not too many I hope! I get a lot of email and it's hard to answer it all.

Your pal,

JOHN K.

THE ELEPHANT MAN

FRANCIS CARR-GOMM to *THE TIMES*
December 4th, 1886

In December 1886, the chairman of London Hospital, Francis Carr-Gomm, wrote to *The Times* newspaper and told of an unspeakably disfigured 24-year-old man whose appearance was so "terrible" that he was reduced to living in a small, isolated attic room at the hospital, hidden from view. Carr-Gomm was in fact describing Joseph Merrick – "The Elephant Man" – an unfortunate man born in 1862 in Leicester, England who began to develop abnormally as a child, resulting in enlarged limbs, lumpy skin and impaired speech by the time he was a teenager, not to mention an unimaginably difficult adolescence. A short-lived career as a living exhibit in London soon followed and then a trip to Europe during which he was robbed and beaten. On returning to England, jobless, penniless, sick and depressed, Merrick was admitted to London Hospital, at which point its chairman wrote to *The Times* and asked the public for assistance.

The positive reaction from the public – letters, gifts, money – was both overwhelming and unexpected, and essentially funded Merrick's stay at the hospital until his death a few years later. Shortly after he passed away, Carr-Gomm wrote one more letter to *The Times*.

From The Times, 4 December 1886

To the Editor of The Times

Sir, - I am authorized to ask your powerful assistance in bringing to the notice of the public the following most exceptional case. There is now in a little room off one of our attic wards a man named Joseph Merrick, aged about 27, a native of Leicester, so dreadful a sight that he is unable even to come out by daylight to the garden. He has been called "the elephant man" on account of his terrible deformity. I will not shock your readers with any detailed description of his infirmities, but only one arm is available for work.

Some 18 months ago, Mr Treves, one of the surgeons of the London Hospital, saw him as he was exhibited in a room off the Whitechapel-road. The poor fellow was then covered by an old curtain, endeavouring to warm himself over a brick which was heated by a lamp. As soon as a sufficient number of pennies had been collected by the manager at the door, poor Merrick threw off his curtain and exhibited himself in all his deformity. He and the manager went halves in the net proceeds of the exhibition, until at last the police stopped the exhibition of his deformities as against public decency.

Unable to earn his livelihood by exhibiting himself any longer in England, he was persuaded to go over to Belgium, where he was taken in hand by an Austrian, who acted as his manager. Merrick managed in this way to save a sum of nearly £50, but the police there too kept him moving on, so that his life was a miserable and hunted one. One day, however, when the Austrian saw that the exhibition pretty well played out, he decamped with poor Merrick's hardly-saved capital of £50, and left him alone and absolutely destitute in a foreign country. Fortunately, however, he had something to pawn, by which he raised sufficient money to play his passage back to England, for he felt that the only friend he had in the world was Mr Treves of the London Hospital. He therefore, through with much difficulty, made his way there, for at every station and landing place the curious crowd thronged and dogged his steps that it was not an easy matter for him to get about. When he reached the London Hospital he had only the clothes in which he stood. He has been taken in by our hospital, though there is, unfortunately, no hope of his cure, and the question now arises what is to be done with him in the future.

He has the greatest horror of the workhouse, nor is it possible, indeed, to send him into any place where he could not insure privacy, since his appearance is such that all shrink from him.

The Royal Hospital for incurables and the British Home for Incurables both decline to take him in, even if sufficient funds were forthcoming to pay for him.

The police rightly prevent his being personally exhibited again; he cannot go out into the streets, as he is everywhere so mobbed that existence is impossible; he cannot, in justice to others, be put in the general ward of a workhouse, and from such, even if possible, he shrinks with the greatest horror; he ought not to be detained in our hospital (where he is occupying a private ward, and being treated with the greatest kindness – he says he has never before known in his life what quiet and rest were), since his case is incurable and not suited, therefore, to our overcrowded general hospital; the incurable hospitals refuse to take him in even if we paid for him in full, and the difficult question therefore remains what is to be done for him.

Terrible though his appearance is, so terrible indeed that women and nervous persons fly in terror from the sight of him, and that he is debarred from seeking to earn his livelihood in an ordinary way, yet he is superior in intelligence, can read and write, is quiet, gentle, not to say even refined in his mind. He occupies his time in the hospital by making with his one available hand little cardboard models, which he sends to the matron, doctor, and those who have been kind to him. Through all the miserable vicissitudes of his life he has carried about a painting of his mother to show that she was a decent and presentable person, and as a memorial of the only one who was kind to him in life until he came under the kind care of the nursing staff of the London Hospital and the surgeon who has befriended him.

It is a case of singular affliction brought about through no fault of himself; he can but hope for quiet and privacy during a life which Mr Treves assures me is not likely to be long.

Can any of your readers suggest to me some fitting place where he can be received? And then I feel sure that, when that is found, charitable people will come forward and enable me to provide him with such accommodation. In the meantime, though it is not the proper place for such an incurable case, the little room under the roof of our hospital and out of Cotton Ward supplies him with all he wants. The Master of the Temple on Advent Sunday preached an eloquent sermon on the subject of our Master's answer to the question, 'who did sin, this man or his parents, that he was born blind?' Showing how one of the Creator's objects in permitting men to be born to a life of hopeless and miserable disability was that the works of God should be manifested in evoking the sympathy and kindly aid of those on whom such a heavy cross is not laid.

Some 76,000 patients a year pass through the doors of our hospital, but I have never before been authorized to invite public attention to any particular, case, so it may well be believed that this case is exceptional.

Any communication about this should be addressed either to myself or to the secretary at the London Hospital.

I have the honour to be, Sir, yours obediently,
F C Carr-Gomm, Chairman London Hospital.

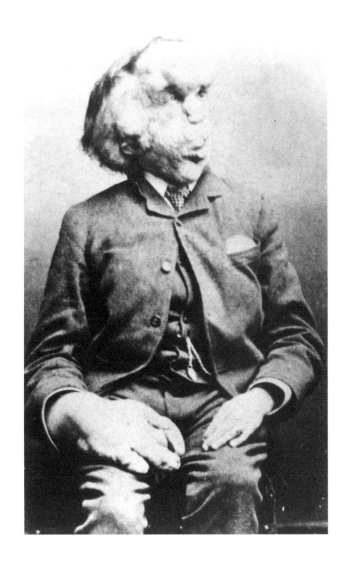

From The Times 16 April 1890

To the Editor of the Times

Sir, - In November, 1886, you were kind enough to insert in The Times a letter from me drawing attention to the case of Joseph Merrick, known as 'the elephant man.' It was one of singular and exceptional misfortune; his physical deformities were of so appalling a character that he was debarred from earning a livelihood in any other way than by being exhibited to the gaze of the curious. This having been rightly interfered with by the police of this country, he was taken abroad by an Austrian adventurer, and exhibited at different places on the Continent; but one day his exhibitor, after stealing all the savings poor Merrick had carefully hoarded, decamped, leaving him destitute, friendless and powerless in a foreign country.

With great difficulty he succeeded somehow or other in getting to the door of the London Hospital, where, through the kindness of one of our surgeons, he was sheltered for a time. The difficulty then arose as to his future; no incurable hospital would take him in, he had a horror of the workhouse, and no place where privacy was unattainable was to be thought of, while the rules and necessities of our general hospital forbade the fund and space, which are set apart solely for cure and healing being utilized for the maintenance of a chronic case like this, however abnormal. In this dilemma, while deterred by common humanity from evicting him again into the open street, I wrote to you, and from that moment all difficulty vanished; the sympathy of many was aroused, and, although no other fitting refuge offered, a sufficient sum was placed at my disposal, apart from the funds of the hospital, to maintain him for what did not promise to be a prolonged life. As an exceptional case the committee agreed to allow him to remain in the hospital upon the annual payment of a sum equivalent to the average cost of an occupied bed.

Here, therefore, poor Merrick was enabled to pass the three and a half remaining years of his life in privacy and comfort. The authorities of the hospital, the medical staff, the chaplain, the sisters, and nurses united to alleviate as far as possible the misery of his existence and he learnt to speak of his rooms at the hospital as his home. There he received kindly visits from many, among them the highest in the land, and his life was not without various interests and diversions: he was a great reader and was well supplied with books through the kindness of a lady, one of the brightest ornaments of the theatrical profession, he was taught basket making, and on more than one occasion he was taken to the play, which he witnessed from the seclusion of a private box.

He benefited much from the religious instruction of our chaplain, and Dr Walsham How, then Bishop of Bedford, privately confirmed him, and was able by waiting in the vestry to hear and take part in the chapel services. The days before his death, Merrick was twice thus attending the chapel services, and in the morning partook of the Holy Communion; and in the last conversation he had with him Merrick had expressed his feeling of deep gratitude for all that had been done for him here, and his acknowledgement of the mercy of God to him in bringing him to this place. Each year he much enjoyed a six week's outing in a quiet cottage, but was always glad on his return to find himself once more 'at home.' In spite of all this indulgence he was quiet and unassuming, very grateful for all that was done for him, and conformed himself readily to the restrictions which were necessary.

I have given these details, thinking that those who sent money to use for his support would like to know how their charity was applied. Last Friday afternoon, though apparently in his usual health, he quietly passed away in sleep.

I have left in my hands a small balance of the money which has been sent to me from time to time for his support, and this I now propose, after paying certain gratuities, to hand over to the general funds of the hospital. This course, I believe, will be consonant with the wishes of the contributors.

It was the courtesy of The Times in inserting my letter in 1886 that procured for this afflicted man a comfortable protection during the last years of a previously wretched existence, and I desire to take this opportunity to thankfully acknowledging it.

I am, Sir, your obedient servant,

F C CARR GOMM

House committee Room London Hospital, 15 April

I LIKE WORDS

ROBERT PIROSH to
VARIOUS
1934

In 1934, a New York
copywriter by the name
of Robert Pirosh quit
his well-paid job and
headed for Hollywood,
determined to begin the
career of his dreams as
a screenwriter. When he
arrived, he gathered the
names and addresses of as
many directors, producers
and studio executives as
he could find and sent
them what is surely one
of the greatest, most
effective cover letters
ever to be written; a letter
which secured him three
interviews, one of which led
to his job as a junior writer
at MGM.

Fifteen years later,
screenwriter Robert Pirosh
won an Academy Award for
Best Original Screenplay
for his work on the war film,
Battleground. A few months
after that, he also won a
Golden Globe.

Dear Sir:

I like words. I like fat buttery words, such as ooze, turpitude, glutinous, toady.
I like solemn, angular, creaky words, such as straitlaced, cantankerous, pecunious,
valedictory. I like spurious, black-is-white words, such as mortician, liquidate,
tonsorial, demi-monde. I like suave "V" words, such as Svengali, svelte, bravura,
verve. I like crunchy, brittle, crackly words, such as splinter, grapple, jostle, crusty.
I like sullen, crabbed, scowling words, such as skulk, glower, scabby, churl. I like
Oh-Heavens, my-gracious, land's-sake words, such as tricksy, tucker, genteel,
horrid. I like elegant, flowery words, such as estivate, peregrinate, elysium, halcyon.
I like wormy, squirmy, mealy words, such as crawl, blubber, squeal, drip. I like
sniggly, chuckling words, such as cowlick, gurgle, bubble and burp.

I like the word screenwriter better than copywriter, so I decided to quit my job in a
New York advertising agency and try my luck in Hollywood, but before taking the
plunge I went to Europe for a year of study, contemplation and horsing around.

I have just returned and I still like words.

May I have a few with you?

Robert Pirosh
385 Madison Avenue
Room 610
New York
Eldorado 5-6024

9

ÖJTCNAB
jRIKURS
ZOCNTAP
ESOSYNKE
SitY
VieNiGGRO
EALLUS
G
.
37

I CAN'T FIGHT ANY LONGER

VIRGINIA WOOLF to
LEONARD WOOLF
March, 1941

By the age of just 22,
influential novelist Virginia
Woolf had already suffered
two nervous breakdowns
– brought on, it's believed,
by the deaths of her mother
and half-sister in quick
succession, and then her
father some years later.
Unfortunately, the struggle
didn't end there for Virginia
and she fought off numerous
bouts of depression
throughout her lifetime,
until the very end.

One evening in March
1941, Virginia attempted
to end her life by jumping
into a river; however, she
failed and simply returned
home, sodden. Sadly, she
persisted, and a few days
later, on March 28th 1941,
she tried again and this time
succeeded in escaping a
lifetime of mental illness.

On the day of her
death, unaware of
her whereabouts,
Virginia's husband,
Leonard, discovered this
heartbreaking letter on their
mantelpiece. Her body was
found weeks later in the
River Ouse, the pockets of
her coat filled with heavy
rocks.

Tuesday.

Dearest,

I feel certain that I am going mad again. I feel we can't go through another of those
terrible times. And I shan't recover this time. I begin to hear voices, and I can't
concentrate. So I am doing what seems the best thing to do. You have given me
the greatest possible happiness. You have been in every way all that anyone could
be. I don't think two people could have been happier till this terrible disease came.
I can't fight any longer. I know that I am spoiling your life, that without me you
could work. And you will I know. You see I can't even write this properly. I can't
read. What I want to say is I owe all the happiness of my life to you. You have been
entirely patient with me and incredibly good. I want to say that – everybody knows
it. If anybody could have saved me it would have been you. Everything has gone
from me but the certainty of your goodness. I can't go on spoiling your life any
longer.

I don't think two people could have been happier than we have been.

V.

THERE IS NO MONEY IN ANSWERING LETTERS

GROUCHO MARX to WOODY ALLEN
March 22nd, 1967

In 1961, comedian Groucho Marx and filmmaker Woody Allen met for the first time and embarked on a friendship that would last 16 years. Marx – the elder of the pair by 45 years – reminded Allen of "a Jewish uncle in my family, a wisecracking Jewish uncle with a sarcastic wit", whilst Allen was, according to Marx in 1976, "the most important comic talent around". In March 1967, following a lengthy break in their correspondence that Allen found infuriating, Marx finally wrote him a letter.

Dear WW:

Goodie Ace told some unemployed friend of mine that you were disappointed or annoyed or happy or drunk that I hadn't answered the letter you wrote me some years ago. You know, of course, there is no money in answering letters—unless they're letters of credit from Switzerland or the Mafia. I write you reluctantly, for I know you are doing six things simultaneously—five including sex. I don't know where you get the time to correspond.

Your play, I trust, will still be running when I arrive in New York the first or second week in April. This must be terribly annoying to the critics who, if I remember correctly, said it wouldn't go because it was too funny. Since it's still running, they must be even more annoyed. This happened to my son's play, on which he collaborated with Bob Fisher. The moral is: don't write a comedy that makes an audience laugh.

This critic problem has been discussed ever since I was Bar Mitzvahed almost 100 years ago. I never told this to anyone, but I received two gifts when I emerged from childhood into what I imagine today is manhood. An uncle, who was then in the money, presented me with a pair of long black stockings, and an aunt, who was trying to make me, gave me a silver watch. Three days after I received these gifts, the watch disappeared. The reason it was gone was that my brother Chico didn't shoot pool nearly as well as he thought he did. He hocked it at a pawnshop at 89th Street and Third Avenue. One day while wandering around aimlessly, I discovered it hanging in the window of the hock shop. Had not my initials been engraved on the back, I wouldn't have recognized it, for the sun had tarnished it so completely it was now coal black. The stockings, which I had worn for a week without ever having them washed, were now a mottled green. This was my total reward for surviving 13 years.

And that, briefly, is why I haven't written you for some time. I'm still wearing the stockings—they're not my stockings anymore, they're just parts of my leg.

You wrote that you were coming out here in February, and I, in a frenzy of excitement, purchased so much delicatessen that, had I kept it in cold cash instead of cold cuts, it would have taken care of my contribution to the United Jewish Welfare Fund for 1967 and '68.

I think I'll be at the St. Regis hotel in New York. And for God's sake don't have any more success—it's driving me crazy. My best to you and your diminutive friend, little Dickie.

Groucho

From: Comedy Script Editor, Light Entertainment, Television

Room No. &
Building: 4009 TC   Tel.
                                             Ext.:   2900   date: 29.5.1974.

Subject: "FAWLTY TOWERS" BY JOHN CLEESE & CONNIE BOOTH

To: H.C.L.E.

I'm afraid I thought this one as dire as its title.

It's a kind of "Prince of Denmark" of the hotel world.   A collection of
cliches and stock characters which I can't see being anything but a disaster.

CF   (Ian Main)

AS/20

AS DIRE AS ITS TITLE

IAN MAIN to HEAD OF
COMEDY AND LIGHT
ENTERTAINMENT
May 29th, 1974

In May 1974, after reading through a pilot script written by John Cleese and his then wife, Connie Booth, a clearly unimpressed comedy script editor by the name of Ian Main sent this altogether disapproving memo to BBC Television's Head of Comedy and Light Entertainment. Luckily for the general population, and thanks in no small part to the persistence of Cleese and Booth, Main's opinion was ultimately ignored by his superiors: a year later, the script had evolved into a programme which to this day is considered one of the funniest ever to grace our screens. That show was *Fawlty Towers*.

Speaking in 2009, Cleese said of this very memo, "It just shows you people have no idea what they are doing."

I STAND ASTOUNDED AND APPALLED

CHARLES DICKENS to *THE TIMES*
November 13th, 1849

On November 13th 1849, an incredible 30,000 people gathered outside a prison in South London to witness the public execution of Marie and Frederick Manning, a married couple who had recently murdered Marie's wealthy former lover, Patrick O'Connor, buried him in the kitchen and then attempted, rather clumsily, to flee with his money. A married couple had not been hanged for over a century and so public reaction was feverish – the case was billed as the "Bermondsey Horror"; the execution itself became "the hanging of the century". The gruesome event even attracted the attention of Charles Dickens who, after studying both the execution and baying mob, wrote this despairing letter to *The Times*.

Devonshire Terrace,
Tuesday, Thirteenth November, 1849

Sir,

I was a witness of the execution at Horsemonger Lane this morning. I went there with the intention of observing the crowd gathered to behold it, and I had excellent opportunities of doing so, at intervals all through the night, and continuously from daybreak until after the spectacle was over. I do not address you on the subject with any intention of discussing the abstract question of capital punishment, or any of the arguments of its opponents or advocates. I simply wish to turn this dreadful experience to some account for the general good, by taking the readiest and most public means of adverting to an intimation given by Sir G. Grey in the last session of Parliament, that the Government might be induced to give its support to a measure making the infliction of capital punishment a private solemnity within the prison walls (with such guarantees for the last sentence of the law being inexorably and surely administered as should be satisfactory to the public at large), and of most earnestly beseeching Sir G. Grey, as a solemn duty which he owes to society, and a responsibility which he cannot for ever put away, to originate such a legislative change himself. I believe that a sight so inconceivably awful as the wickedness and levity of the immense crowd collected at that execution this morning could be imagined by no man, and could be presented in no heathen land under the sun. The horrors of the gibbet and of the crime which brought the wretched murderers to it faded in my mind before the atrocious bearing, looks, and language of the assembled spectators. When I came upon the scene at midnight, the shrillness of the cries and howls that were raised from time to time, denoting that they came from a concourse of boys and girls already assembled in the best places, made my blood run cold. As the night went on, screeching, and laughing, and yelling in strong chorus of parodies on negro melodies, with substitutions of "Mrs. Manning" for "Susannah" and the like, were added to these. When the day dawned, thieves, low prostitutes, ruffians, and vagabonds of every kind, flocked on to the ground, with every variety of offensive and foul behaviour. Fightings, faintings, whistlings, imitations of Punch, brutal jokes, tumultuous demonstrations of indecent delight when swooning women were dragged out of the crowd by the police, with their dresses disordered, gave a new zest to the general entertainment. When the sun rose brightly—as it did—it gilded thousands upon thousands of upturned faces, so inexpressibly odious in their brutal mirth or callousness, that a man had cause to feel ashamed of the shape he wore, and to shrink from himself, as fashioned in the image of the Devil. When the two miserable creatures who attracted all this ghastly sight about them were turned quivering into the air, there was no more emotion, no more pity, no more thought that two immortal souls had gone to judgement, no more restraint in any of the previous obscenities, than if the name of Christ had never been heard in this world, and there were no belief among men but that they perished like the beasts.

I have seen, habitually, some of the worst sources of general contamination and corruption in this country, and I think there are not many phases of London life that could surprise me. I am solemnly convinced that nothing that ingenuity could devise to be done in this city, in the same compass of time, could work such ruin as one public execution, and I stand astounded and appalled by the wickedness it exhibits. I do not believe that any community can prosper where such a scene of horror and demoralization as was enacted this morning outside Horsemonger Lane Gaol is presented at the very doors of good citizens, and is passed by, unknown or forgotten. And when in our prayers and thanksgivings for the season we are humbly expressing before God our desire to remove the moral evils of the land, I would ask your readers to consider whether it is not a time to think of this one, and to root it out.

I am, Sir, your faithful Servant.

FIFTY LADY SHARPSHOOTERS AWAIT

ANNIE OAKLEY to US
PRESIDENT WILLIAM
MCKINLEY
April 5th, 1898

As the Spanish–American War loomed in April 1898, celebrity sharpshooter Annie Oakley – a Buffalo Bill performer so famous that she was essentially the world's first female superstar – decided to donate her resources to the government by sending this letter to then US President William McKinley. The offer, written on a sheet of her magnificent stationery, was simple: Oakley would supply the military with a 50-strong army of "lady sharpshooters" so talented as to be indispensable at war, all equipped with enough ammunition to see them through. Much to her dismay, the powers-that-be politely declined. Undeterred and forever the patriot, Oakley later repeated the offer prior to World War I. The response was the same.

A SUCCESS IN ALL COUNTRIES
ANNIE OAKLEY
America's Representative Lady Shot

Nutley N J ap 5th

Hon Wm. McKinley President

Dear Sir I for one feel confident that your good judgment will carry America safely through without War.

But in case of such an event I am ready to place a company of fifty lady sharpshooters at your disposal. Every one of them will be an American and as they will furnish their own Arms and Ammunition will be little if any expense to the government.

Very truly Annie Oakley

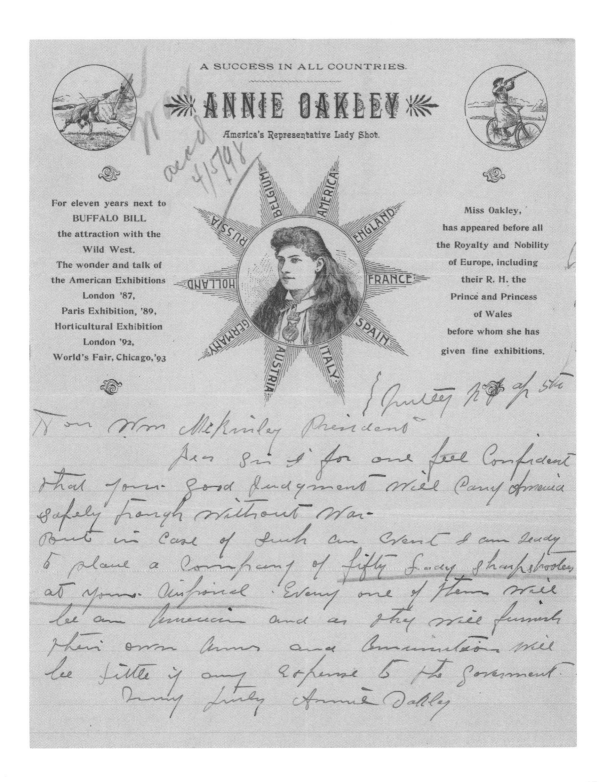

A SUCCESS IN ALL COUNTRIES.

ANNIE OAKLEY

America's Representative Lady Shot.

acd 1/5/98

For eleven years next to
BUFFALO BILL
the attraction with the
Wild West.
The wonder and talk of
the American Exhibitions
London '87,
Paris Exhibition, '89,
Horticultural Exhibition
London '92,
World's Fair, Chicago, '93

RUSSIA · BELGIUM · AMERICA · ENGLAND · FRANCE · SPAIN · ITALY · AUSTRIA · GERMANY · HOLLAND

Miss Oakley,
has appeared before all
the Royalty and Nobility
of Europe, including
their R. H. the
Prince and Princess
of Wales
before whom she has
given fine exhibitions.

Nutley N. J. ap 5th

Hon Wm McKinley President

Dear Sir I for one feel confident
that your good Judgment will carry America
Safely through without War.
But in case of Such an event I am ready
to place a company of fifty Lady Sharpshooters
at your Disposal. Every one of them will
be an American and as they will furnish
their own arms and ammunition will
be little if any Expense to the government.

Very truly Annie Oakley

TO HELL WITH HITLER

PATRICK HITLER to US
PRESIDENT FRANKLIN D.
ROOSEVELT
March 3rd, 1942

In 1940, a year after fleeing
Nazi Germany and setting
up home in New York,
the writer of this letter
attempted to enlist with the
US Armed Forces; however,
his application was denied
for one incredible reason:
he was the nephew of Adolf
Hitler. He wasn't deterred,
and two years later, a few
months after his uncle had
declared war on the US,
William Patrick Hitler tried
again to register for military
service by way of this written
plea, sent directly to the US
President. It was quickly
passed on to the FBI's
director, J. Edgar Hoover,
who then investigated
William and eventually
cleared him for service.

William Patrick Hitler joined
the US Navy in 1944 but was
discharged in 1947 after
being injured in service. He
passed away 40 years later
in New York.

March 3rd, 1942.
His Excellency Franklin D. Roosevelt.,
President of the United States of America.
The White House.,
Washington. D.C.

Dear Mr. President:

May I take the liberty of encroaching on your valuable time and that of
your staff at the White House? Mindful of the critical days the nation is now
passing through, I do so only because the prerogative of your high office alone can
decide my difficult and singular situation.

Permit me to outline as briefly as possible the circumstances of my position,
the solution of which I feel could so easily be achieved should you feel moved to
give your kind intercession and decision.

I am the nephew and only descendant of the ill-famed Chancellor and
Leader of Germany who today so despotically seeks to enslave the free and
Christian peoples of the globe.

Under your masterful leadership men of all creeds and nationalities are
waging desperate war to determine, in the last analysis, whether they shall finally
serve and live an ethical society under God or become enslaved by a devilish and
pagan regime.

Everybody in the world today must answer to himself which cause they will
serve. To free people of deep religious feeling there can be but one answer and one
choice, that will sustain them always and to the bitter end.

I am one of many, but I can render service to this great cause and I have a
life to give that it may, with the help of all, triumph in the end.

All my relatives and friends soon will be marching for freedom and decency
under the Stars and Stripes. For this reason, Mr. President, I am respectfully
submitting this petition to you to enquire as to whether I may be allowed to join
them in their struggle against tyranny and oppression?

At present this is denied me because when I fled the Reich in 1939 I was
a British subject. I came to America with my Irish mother principally to rejoin
my relatives here. At the same time I was offered a contract to write and lecture
in the United States, the pressure of which did not allow me the time to apply for
admission under the quota. I had therefore, to come as a visitor.

I have attempted to join the British forces, but my success as a lecturer
made me probably one of the best attended political speakers, with police
frequently having to control the crowds clamouring for admission in Boston,
Chicago and other cities. This elicited from British officials the rather negative
invitation to carry on.

The British are an insular people and while they are kind and courteous,
it is my impression, rightly or wrongly, that they could not in the long run feel
overly cordial or sympathetic towards an individual bearing the name I do. The

49

great expense the English legal procedure demands in changing my name, is only a possible solution not within my financial means. At the same time I have not been successful in determining whether the Canadian Army would facilitate my entrance into the armed forces. As things are at the present and lacking any official guidance, I find that to attempt to enlist as a nephew of Hitler is something that requires a strange sort of courage that I am unable to muster, bereft as I am of any classification or official support from any quarter.

As to my integrity, Mr. President, I can only say that it is a matter of record and it compares somewhat to the foresighted spirit with which you, by every ingenuity known to statecraft, wrested from the American Congress those weapons which are today the Nation's great defense in this crisis. I can also reflect that in a time of great complacency and ignorance I tried to do those things which as a Christian I knew to be right. As a fugitive from the Gestapo I warned France through the press that Hitler would invade her that year. The people of England I warned by the same means that the so-called "solution" of Munich was a myth that would bring terrible consequences. On my arrival in America I at once informed the press that Hitler would loose his Frankenstein on civilization that year. Although nobody paid any attention to what I said, I continued to lecture and write in America. Now the time for writing and talking has passed and I am mindful only of the great debt my mother and I owe to the United States. More than anything else I would like to see active combat as soon as possible and thereby be accepted by my friends and comrades as one of them in this great struggle for liberty.

Your favorable decision on my appeal alone would ensure that continued benevolent spirit on the part of the American people, which today I feel so much a part of. I most respectfully assure you, Mr. President, that as in the past I would do my utmost in the future to be worthy of the great honour I am seeking through your kind aid, in the sure knowledge that my endeavors on behalf of the great principles of Democracy will at least bear favourable comparison to the activities of many individuals who for so long have been unworthy of the fine privilege of calling themselves Americans. May I therefore venture to hope, Mr. President, that in the turmoil of this vast conflict you will not be moved to reject my appeal for reasons which I am in no way responsible?

For me today there could be no greater honour, Mr. President, to have lived and to have been allowed to serve you, the deliverer of the American people from want, and no greater privelege than to have striven and had a small part in establishing the title you once will bear in posterity as the greatest Emancipator of suffering mankind in political history.

I would be most happy to give any additional information that might be required and I take the liberty of enclosing a circular containing details about myself.

Permit me, Mr. President, to express my heartfelt good wishes for your future health and happiness, coupled with the hope that you may soon lead all men who believe in decency everywhere onward and upward to a glorious victory.

I am,
Very respectfully yours,
Patrick Hitler

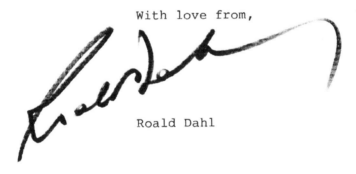

GIPSY HOUSE
GREAT MISSENDEN
BUCKINGHAMSHIRE
HP16 0BP

10th February 1989

Dear Amy,

I must write a special letter and thank you for the dream in the bottle. You are the first person in the world who has sent me one of these and it intrigued me very much. I also liked the dream. Tonight I shall go down to the village and blow it through the bedroom window of some sleeping child and see if it works.

With love from,

Roald Dahl

THANK YOU FOR THE DREAM

ROALD DAHL to AMY CORCORAN
February 10th, 1989

One rainy Sunday afternoon in 1989, with encouragement and much-needed help from her father, a seven-year-old girl named Amy decided to write to Roald Dahl, one of history's most successful children's authors and, most importantly for Amy, the person responsible for writing her favourite book, *The BFG* – the wonderful, magical story of a Big Friendly Giant who collects nice dreams and then blows them through the windows of sleeping children. With that in mind, and using a combination of oil, coloured water and glitter, young Amy sent to Dahl, along with a letter, a very fitting and precious gift: one of her dreams, contained in a bottle.

Judging by his response, the sentiment wasn't lost on Dahl.

HOW I WOULD LIKE TO WORK FOR YOU!

EUDORA WELTY to *THE NEW YORKER*
March 15th, 1933

In March 1933, in an attempt to secure some writing work, 23-year-old Eudora Welty sent this impossibly charming letter to the offices of *The New Yorker* magazine and gently laid her cards on the table. It's genuinely difficult to imagine a more endearingly written introduction to one's talents and for that reason it's both a surprise and disappointment to learn that her perfectly formed plea fell on deaf ears, initially at least. Thankfully, *The New Yorker* later rectified their error and Welty went on to write numerous pieces for the publication. Multiple awards followed including the Pulitzer Prize for Fiction in 1973 for her novel, *The Optimist's Daughter*, and seven years later, the Presidential Medal of Freedom.

March 15, 1933

Gentlemen,

I suppose you'd be more interested in even a sleight-o'-hand trick than you'd be in an application for a position with your magazine, but as usual you can't have the thing you want most.

I am 23 years old, six weeks on the loose in N.Y. However, I was a New Yorker for a whole year in 1930–31 while attending advertising classes in Columbia's School of Business. Actually I am a southerner, from Mississippi, the nation's most backward state. Ramifications include Walter H. Page, who, unluckily for me, is no longer connected with Doubleday-Page, which is no longer Doubleday-Page, even. I have a B.A. ('29) from the University of Wisconsin, where I majored in English without a care in the world. For the last eighteen months I was languishing in my own office in a radio station in Jackson, Miss., writing continuities, dramas, mule feed advertisements, santa claus talks, and life insurance playlets; now I have given that up.

As to what I might do for you — I have seen an untoward amount of picture galleries and 15¢ movies lately, and could review them with my old prosperous detachment, I think; in fact, I recently coined a general word for Matisse's pictures after seeing his latest at the Marie Harriman: concubineapple. That shows you how my mind works — quick, and away from the point. I read simply voraciously, and can drum up an opinion afterwards.

Since I have bought an India print, and a large number of phonograph records from a Mr. Nussbaum who picks them up, and a Cezanne Bathers one inch long (that shows you I read e. e. cummings I hope), I am anxious to have an apartment, not to mention a small portable phonograph. How I would like to work for you! A little paragraph each morning — a little paragraph each night, if you can't hire me from daylight to dark, although I would work like a slave. I can also draw like Mr. Thurber, in case he goes off the deep end. I have studied flower painting.

There is no telling where I may apply, if you turn me down; I realize this will not phase you, but consider my other alternative: the U of N.C. offers for $12.00 to let me dance in Vachel Lindsay's <u>Congo</u>. I congo on. I rest my case, repeating that I am a hard worker.

Truly yours,
Eudora Welty

'MUSIC IS 'LIFE IT'SELF

LOUIS ARMSTRONG to
LANCE CORPORAL VILLEC
1967

In 1967, jazz legend Louis
Armstrong wrote this
generous, heartfelt letter
to a US Marine stationed in
Vietnam who had recently
sent him some fan mail. You
wouldn't think they were
strangers as Armstrong's
favourite laxative, "Swiss
Kriss", is amusingly
mentioned in the first
paragraph – he then goes
on to reminisce about his
childhood and the music he
was exposed to; later on,
his wife, who had recently
had a tumour removed,
is discussed humorously
and affectionately. He even
ends with a song. All in all,
a wonderful letter from
a fascinating character,
further enhanced by
Satchmo's idiosyncratic
use of punctuation, which,
to the uninitiated, will no
doubt charm and confuse
in equal measure: for
reasons largely unknown,
he often peppered his
writing with an abundance of
capitalisation, apostrophes,
quotation marks, dashes
and underlining – more
often than not, in places you
usually wouldn't expect.
This particular missive is a
perfect example.

34—56—107 St.
Corona New York'
U.S.A.

Dear L/Cpl, Villec"

I'd like to 'step in here for a 'Minute or 'so' to "tell you how much—I 'feel to know that 'you are a 'Jazz <u>fan</u>, and 'Dig' that 'Jive—the 'same as '<u>we</u> 'do, "yeah." "<u>Man</u>—I carry an 'Album, 'loaded with '<u>Records</u>—'Long playing 'that is. And when I am '<u>Shaving</u> or 'Sitting on the 'Throne with '<u>Swiss Kriss</u>' in me— <u>That</u> Music 'sure 'brings out those 'Riffs' 'Right Along with 'Swiss Kriss, which I 'take 'every night or when I <u>go</u> to bed. '<u>Yeah</u>. I give myself a 'Concert with those 'records. 'Music is 'life it'self. What would this 'world be without 'good music? No matter 'what kind it is.

It 'all came from the Old 'Sanctified 'Churches. I can remember—'<u>way</u> back in the 'old days in 'New Orleans, La—'My home town. And I was a little Boy around 'ten years old. My Mother used to take me to 'Church with her, and the Reverend ('Preacher that is') used to '<u>lead</u> off one' of those 'good <u>ol</u> good '<u>Hymns</u>. And before you realized it—the 'whole 'Congregation would be "<u>Wailing</u>— 'Singing like 'mad and 'sound so 'beautiful. 'I being a little boy that would "Dig" 'Everything and 'everybody, I'd have myself a 'Ball in 'Church, <u>especially</u> when those 'Sisters would get 'So 'Carried away while "Rev" (the preacher) would be 'right in the 'Middle of his 'Sermon. '<u>Man</u> those 'Church 'Sisters would '<u>begin</u> 'Shouting 'So—until their 'petticoats would '<u>fall</u> off. Of course 'one of the 'Deacons would 'rush over and 'grab her—'hold her in his 'Arms and 'fan her until 'she'd '<u>Come</u> 'to.

Then there were those "Baptisms—that's when someone wants to be <u>converted</u> by Joining the 'Church and get 'religion. So they have to be 'Baptized. 'Dig this—I remember 'one Sunday the 'Church had a 'great big <u>Guy</u> they had to 'Baptize. So these 'Deacons all 'Standing in this 'River—in 'Water up to their <u>waist</u> in their 'white 'Robes. They had 'Baptized 'several 'women and a few 'Men—'saved their 'Souls. When in 'Walks' a '<u>Great</u> 'big' 'burly '<u>Sinner</u>' who came down the line. So—'these 'Deacons whom were 'very 'strong 'themselves, they grabbed 'hold of this '<u>Cat</u> and said to him as they 'ducked him down into the water, as they let him they asked him—"<u>Brother</u> 'do you 'Believe?" The Guy didn't say 'anything—Just looked at them. So they 'Ducked him down into that 'River again, 'only they 'held him down there a 'few minutes 'Longer. So when the 'Deacons looked in the guy's <u>eye</u> and said to him—"Do you 'Believe?" This Guy finally 'answered—he said "<u>Yes</u>—I Believe you '<u>Son</u> <u>of</u> <u>Bitches</u> trying to '<u>drown</u> <u>me</u>."

P.S. I guess you think I'm 'Nuts. 'Nay 'Nay. I only 'mentioned these incidents because it all was 'built around 'Music. In fact, it's 'All Music. "You 'Dig? The 'Same as we did in my 'Home Town 'New Orleans'—those 'Funeral Marches etc. "Why '<u>Gate</u>" '<u>Villec</u>, we 'played those 'Marches with 'feeling from our 'hearts. 'All the way to the Cemetery—'Brass Band of course. The 'Snare drummer would put a 'handkerchief under the 'snares of his 'drum to 'deaden the 'Sound while 'playing on the way to the Cemetery—"Flee as a Bird." But as 'soon as the 'preacher 'say "Ashes to 'Ashes—'Dust to 'Dust"—the "<u>Snare</u> <u>Drummer</u>

Commence 'pulling the handkerchief from his 'drum, and make a 'long roll' to 'assemble everybody, including the members of the 'dead man's 'Lodge—or 'Club. 'Then we'd 'return 'back to the 'headquarters 'playing "Didn't he 'Ramble" or "When the Saints Go Marching In." You 'See? 'Still Music."

I said 'All of that to Keep 'Music in your 'heart the 'same as 'you're 'doing. And 'Daddy—you 'Can't 'go 'wrong. 'Myself and my 'All Stars' are 'Playing here at the 'Harrods 'Club (Reno) for 'Three weeks. My 'wife 'Lucille as 'joined me here. The 'rest will do her lots of good. She was 'operated on for a 'Tumor, about the 'Middle of 'July. She's improving 'very 'Rapidly. Her 'Doctor who 'operated on her at the 'Beth 'Israel Hospital' in New York told her—'She could go to 'Reno and 'spend some time if 'you (Lucille) + your 'husband (Satchmo) 'promised to 'behave 'yourselves and 'don't try to 'do the "Vonce" ("meaning 'Sex). I 'Said—"Doc I 'Promise—But I'll 'Just 'touch it 'lightly every 'morning—to see if it's 'still 'there. 'Ha 'Ha. 'Life's 'sweet. 'Just the 'thought that 'Lucille is 'through with her 'little 'Hindrance—and "soon "be well and 'happy—'be 'her 'lil 'ol 'cute 'self 'again— 'Just "knock's' me out.

'Well 'Bre'r 'Villec, I guess I'll 'put it 'down, and get some 'shut eye." It's the 'Wee 'hours in the 'Morning. I've 'Just 'finished 'Work. I am too 'tired to 'raise an 'eye 'lid. Tee hee. So I'll leave this little message with you. "Here goes'.

> When you 'Walk—through a 'Storm—
> Put your 'Head—up 'high—
> And 'Don't be Afraid of the 'Dark—
> At the 'End of a 'Storm—
> Is a 'Gol-den 'Sky—
> And a Sweet Silver 'Song—
> Of a 'Lark—
> 'Walk—'on—through the 'Wind—
> 'Walk—'on—through the 'Rain—
> Though your 'Dreams be "Tossed and 'Blown—
> 'Walk—'on—'Walk—'on—
> With 'Hope in your heart
> And 'You'll 'Nev-er 'Walk 'A-'lone—
> You'll 'Nev-er 'Walk A-lone—
> (one more time)
> 'Walk—'on—'Walk—'on—with 'Hope in your 'heart—And 'you'll
> Nev-er 'Walk 'A-lone—'You'll 'Nev-er 'Walk—'A-lone—. "Savvy?

Give my regards to the fellows that's in your company. And the other fellows too. And now I'll do you 'Just like the 'Farmer did the 'Potato—I'll 'Plant you 'Now and 'Dig you 'later. I'll 'Close now. It's a real 'Pleasure 'Writing—'You.

"Swiss Krissly"

Satchmo
Louis Armstrong

56

TO MY OLD MASTER

JOURDON ANDERSON
to PATRICK HENRY
ANDERSON
August 7th, 1865

In 1864, after 32 long years in the service of his master, Jourdon Anderson and his wife, Amanda, escaped a life of slavery when Union Army soldiers freed them from the plantation on which they had been working so tirelessly. They grasped the opportunity with vigour, quickly moved to Ohio where Jourdon could find paid work with which to support his growing family, and didn't look back. Then, a year later, shortly after the end of the Civil War, Jourdon received a desperate letter from Patrick Henry Anderson, the man who used to own him, in which he was asked to return to work on the plantation and rescue his ailing business.

Jourdon's reply to the person who enslaved his family, dictated from his home on August 7th, is everything you could wish for, and quite rightly was subsequently reprinted in numerous newspapers. Jourdon Anderson never returned to Big Spring, Tennessee. He passed away in 1907, aged 81, and is buried alongside his wife who died six years later. Together they had a total of 11 children.

To my old Master, Col. P. H. ANDERSON, Big Spring, Tennessee.

SIR: I got your letter, and was glad to find that you had not forgotten Jourdon, and that you wanted me to come back and live with you again, promising to do better for me than anybody else can. I have often felt uneasy about you. I thought the Yankees would have hung you long before this, for harboring Rebs they found at your house. I suppose they never heard about your going to Colonel Martin's to kill the Union soldier that was left by his company in their stable. Although you shot at me twice before I left you, I did not want to hear of your being hurt, and am glad you are still living. It would do me good to go back to the dear old home again, and see Miss Mary and Miss Martha and Allen, Esther, Green, and Lee. Give my love to them all, and tell them I hope we will meet in the better world, if not in this. I would have gone back to see you all when I was working in the Nashville Hospital, but one of the neighbors told me that Henry intended to shoot me if he ever got a chance.

I want to know particularly what the good chance is you propose to give me. I am doing tolerably well here. I get twenty-five dollars a month, with victuals and clothing; have a comfortable home for Mandy,—the folks call her Mrs. Anderson,—and the children—Milly, Jane, and Grundy—go to school and are learning well. The teacher says Grundy has a head for a preacher. They go to Sunday school, and Mandy and me attend church regularly. We are kindly treated. Sometimes we overhear others saying, "Them colored people were slaves" down in Tennessee. The children feel hurt when they hear such remarks; but I tell them it was no disgrace in Tennessee to belong to Colonel Anderson. Many darkeys would have been proud, as I used to be, to call you master. Now if you will write and say what wages you will give me, I will be better able to decide whether it would be to my advantage to move back again.

As to my freedom, which you say I can have, there is nothing to be gained on that score, as I got my free papers in 1864 from the Provost-Marshal-General of the Department of Nashville. Mandy says she would be afraid to go back without some proof that you were disposed to treat us justly and kindly; and we have concluded to test your sincerity by asking you to send us our wages for the time we served you. This will make us forget and forgive old scores, and rely on your justice and friendship in the future. I served you faithfully for thirty-two years, and Mandy twenty years. At twenty-five dollars a month for me, and two dollars a week for Mandy, our earnings would amount to eleven thousand six hundred and eighty dollars. Add to this the interest for the time our wages have been kept back, and deduct what you paid for our clothing, and three doctor's visits to me, and pulling a tooth for Mandy, and the balance will show what we are in justice entitled to. Please send the money by Adams's Express, in care of V. Winters, Esq., Dayton, Ohio. If you fail to pay us for faithful labors in the past, we can have little faith in your promises in the future. We trust the good Maker has opened your eyes to the wrongs which you and your fathers have done to me and my fathers, in making us toil for you for generations without recompense. Here I draw my wages every

Saturday night; but in Tennessee there was never any pay-day for the negroes any more than for the horses and cows. Surely there will be a day of reckoning for those who defraud the laborer of his hire.

In answering this letter, please state if there would be any safety for my Milly and Jane, who are now grown up, and both good-looking girls. You know how it was with poor Matilda and Catherine. I would rather stay here and starve—and die, if it come to that—than have my girls brought to shame by the violence and wickedness of their young masters. You will also please state if there has been any schools opened for the colored children in your neighborhood. The great desire of my life now is to give my children an education, and have them form virtuous habits.

Say howdy to George Carter, and thank him for taking the pistol from you when you were shooting at me.

From your old servant,
JOURDON ANDERSON.

MY GOOD FRIEND ROOSVELT

FIDEL CASTRO to US
PRESIDENT FRANKLIN D.
ROOSEVELT
November 6th, 1940

In November 1940, 13 years
before spearheading the
revolution which would
ultimately see him replace
dictator Fulgencio Batista
as leader of Cuba, a teenage
Fidel Castro – aged 14, not
12 as he misclaimed – wrote
a somewhat cheeky letter
to the then President of the
United States, Franklin D.
Roosevelt and asked him
for some money – a $10 bill,
to be precise. Some time
later, he received a standard
reply from officials; sadly,
his request for cash fell on
deaf ears, as did his offer to
reveal the whereabouts of
Cuba's largest iron mines.
Young Castro's priceless
letter was rediscovered
in 1977 by specialists at
the National Archives and
Records Administration.

Santiago de Cuba

Nov 6 1940
Mr Franklin Roosvelt,
President of the United States.

My good friend Roosvelt I don't know very English, but I know as much as write to
you.

I like to hear the radio, and I am very happy, because I heard in it, that you will be
President for a new (periodo).

I am twelve years old. I am a boy but I think very much but I do not think that I am
writing to the President of the United States.

If you like, give me a ten dollars bill green american, in the letter, because never, I
have not seen a ten dollars bill green american and I would like to have one of them.

My address is:

> Sr Fidel Castro
> Colegio de Dolores
> Santiago de Cuba
> Oriente Cuba

I don't know very English but I know very much Spanish and I suppose you don't
know very Spanish but you know very English because you are American but I am
not American.

> (Thank you very much)
> Good by. Your friend,

> (Signed)
> Fidel Castro

If you want iron to make your ~~sheaps~~ ships I will show to you the bigest (minas) of
iron of the land. They are in Mayari Oriente Cuba.

Ack. 12/13/40 SoD cds

COLEGIO DE DOLORES
APARTADO 1
SANTIAGO DE CUBA

DIVISION OF
NOV 25 1940
THE AMERICAN REPUBLICS
DEPARTMENT OF STATE

811.001 Roosevelt 6957 Castro Fidel

Santiago de Cuba.
Nov 6 1940.
Mr. Franklin Roosvelt,
President of the United
States.

My good friend Roosvelt
I don't know very En-
glish, but I know as much
as write to you.
I like to hear the radio, and
I am very happy, because
I heard in it, that you will
be President for a new
(periodo)
I am twelve years old.
I am a boy but I think very
much but I do not think
that I am writting to the

President of the United S
tates.
If you like, give me a
ten dollars bill green american, in the letter, because
never, I have not seen a
ten dollars bill green american and I would like
to have one of them.
My address is:
        Sr. Fidel Castro
Colegio de Dolores.
        Santiago de Cuba
            Oriente. Cuba.
I don't know very English
but I know very much
Spanish and I suppose
you don't know very Spa-
nish but you know very
English because you
are American but I am
not American.

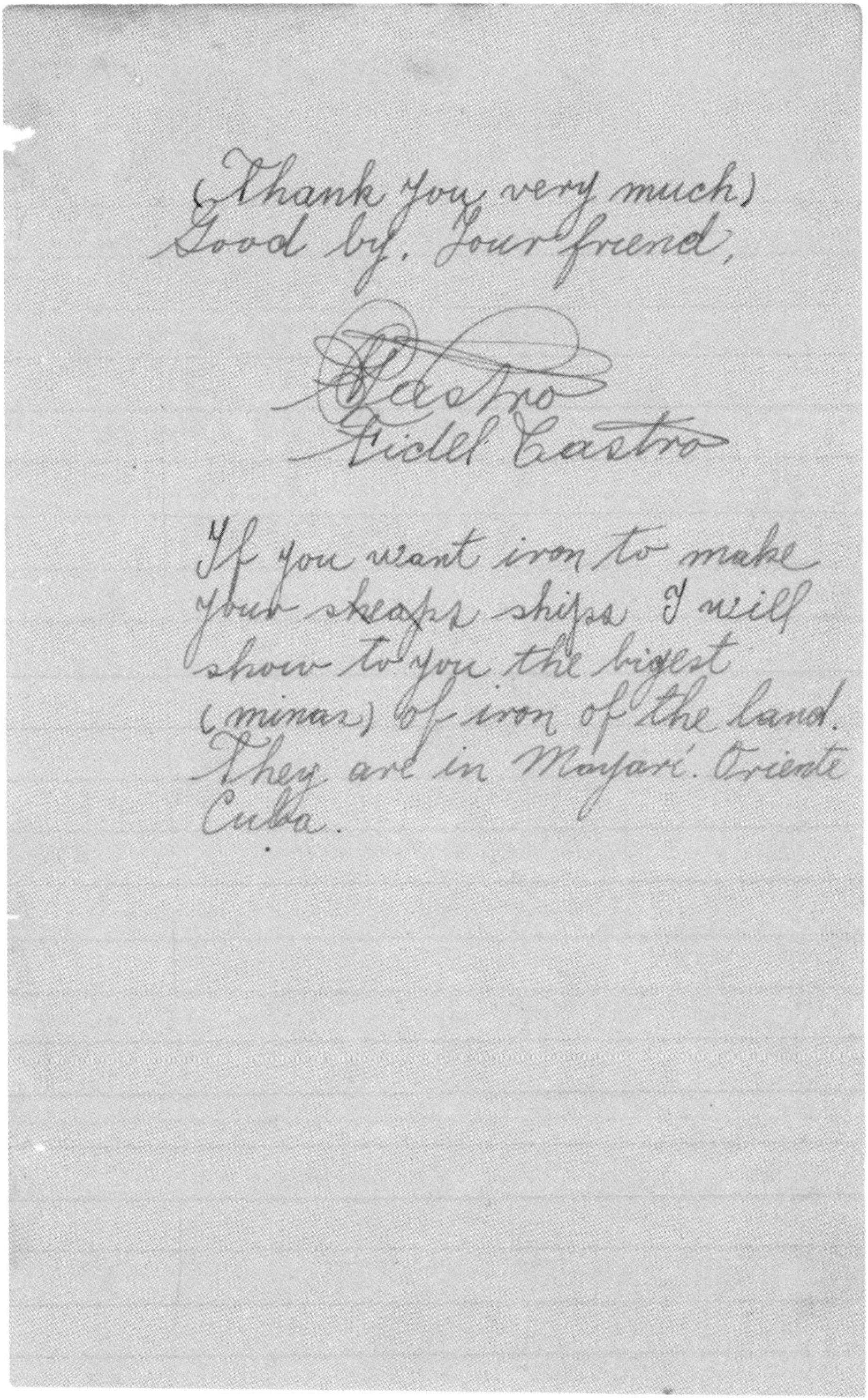

(Thank you very much)
Good by. Your friend,

Castro
Fidel Castro

If you want iron to make
your sheaps ships I will
show to you the bigest
(minas) of iron of the land.
They are in Mayarí. Oriente
Cuba.

April 22, 1958
57 Perry Street
New York City

A MAN HAS TO BE SOMETHING; HE HAS TO MATTER

HUNTER S. THOMPSON to
HUME LOGAN
April 22nd, 1958

The inimitable Hunter S. Thompson was just 20 years of age and still in the US Air Force when, in April 1958, he wrote this profoundly wise letter to his friend Hume Logan in response to a request for life advice. It would be another ten years until Thompson's own career gathered pace, due in no small part to a brave exposé of the Hell's Angels that he wrote after a year in their company. Arguably his most famous book, *Fear and Loathing in Las Vegas*, soon followed, as did much of the Gonzo journalism for which he is now known. In 2005, with his health in decline, he took his own life; he left a note for his wife titled, "Football Season Is Over", which read:

"No More Games. No More Bombs. No More Walking. No More Fun. No More Swimming. 67. That is 17 years past 50. 17 more than I needed or wanted. Boring. I am always bitchy. No Fun — for anybody. 67. You are getting Greedy. Act your (old) age. Relax — This won't hurt."

Dear Hume,

You ask advice: ah, what a very human and very dangerous thing to do! For to give advice to a man who asks what to do with his life implies something very close to egomania. To presume to point a man to the right and ultimate goal—to point with a trembling finger in the RIGHT direction is something only a fool would take upon himself.

I am not a fool, but I respect your sincerity in asking my advice. I ask you though, in listening to what I say, to remember that all advice can only be a product of the man who gives it. What is truth to one may be disaster to another. I do not see life through your eyes, nor you through mine. If I were to attempt to give you *specific* advice, it would be too much like the blind leading the blind.

"To be, or not to be: that is the question: Whether 'tis nobler in the mind to suffer the slings and arrows of outrageous fortune, or to take arms against a sea of troubles…"

(Shakespeare)

And indeed, that IS the question: whether to float with the tide, or to swim for a goal. It is a choice we must all make consciously or unconsciously at one time in our lives. So few people understand this! Think of any decision you've ever made which had a bearing on your future: I may be wrong, but I don't see how it could have been anything but a choice however indirect—between the two things I've mentioned: the floating or the swimming.

But why not float if you have no goal? That is another question. It is unquestionably better to enjoy the floating than to swim in uncertainty. So how does a man find a goal? Not a castle in the stars, but a real and tangible thing. How can a man be sure he's not after the "big rock candy mountain," the enticing sugar-candy goal that has little taste and no substance?

The answer—and, in a sense, the tragedy of life—is that we seek to understand the goal and not the man. We set up a goal which demands of us certain things: and we do these things. We adjust to the demands of a concept which CANNOT be valid. When you were young, let us say that you wanted to be a fireman. I feel reasonably safe in saying that you no longer want to be a fireman. Why? Because your perspective has changed. It's not the fireman who has changed, but you. Every man is the sum total of his reactions to experience. As your experiences differ and multiply, you become a different man, and hence your perspective changes. This goes on and on. Every reaction is a learning process; every significant experience alters your perspective.

So it would seem foolish, would it not, to adjust our lives to the demands of a goal we see from a different angle every day? How could we ever hope to accomplish anything other than galloping neurosis?

The answer, then, must not deal with goals at all, or not with tangible goals, anyway. It would take reams of paper to develop this subject to fulfillment. God only knows how many books have been written on "the meaning of man" and that sort of thing, and god only knows how many people have pondered the subject. (I use the term "god only knows" purely as an expression.) There's very little sense in my trying to give it up to you in the proverbial nutshell, because I'm the first to admit my absolute lack of qualifications for reducing the meaning of life to one or two paragraphs.

I'm going to steer clear of the word "existentialism," but you might keep it in mind as a key of sorts. You might also try something called *Being and Nothingness* by Jean-Paul Sartre, and another little thing called *Existentialism: From Dostoyevsky to Sartre*. These are merely suggestions. If you're genuinely satisfied with what you are and what you're doing, then give those books a wide berth. (Let sleeping dogs lie.) But back to the answer. As I said, to put our faith in tangible goals would seem to be, at best, unwise. So we do not strive to be firemen, we do not strive to be bankers, nor policemen, nor doctors. WE STRIVE TO BE OURSELVES.

But don't misunderstand me. I don't mean that we can't BE firemen, bankers, or doctors—but that we must make the goal conform to the individual, rather than make the individual conform to the goal. In every man, heredity and environment have combined to produce a creature of certain abilities and desires—including a deeply ingrained need to function in such a way that his life will be MEANINGFUL. A man has to BE something; he has to matter.

As I see it then, the formula runs something like this: a man must choose a path which will let his ABILITIES function at maximum efficiency toward the gratification of his DESIRES. In doing this, he is fulfilling a need (giving himself identity by functioning in a set pattern toward a set goal) he avoids frustrating his potential (choosing a path which puts no limit on his self-development), and he avoids the terror of seeing his goal wilt or lose its charm as he draws closer to it (rather than bending himself to meet the demands of that which he seeks, he has bent his goal to conform to his own abilities and desires).

In short, he has not dedicated his life to reaching a pre-defined goal, but he has rather chosen a way of life he KNOWS he will enjoy. The goal is absolutely

secondary: it is the *functioning toward the goal* which is important. And it seems almost ridiculous to say that a man MUST function in a pattern of his own choosing; for to let another man define your own goals is to give up one of the most meaningful aspects of life—the definitive act of will which makes a man an individual.

Let's assume that you think you have a choice of eight paths to follow (all pre-defined paths, of course). And let's assume that you can't see any real purpose in any of the eight. THEN—and here is the essence of all I've said—you MUST FIND A NINTH PATH.

Naturally, it isn't as easy as it sounds. You've lived a relatively narrow life, a vertical rather than a horizontal existence. So it isn't any too difficult to understand why you seem to feel the way you do. But a man who procrastinates in his CHOOSING will inevitably have his choice made for him by circumstance.

So if you now number yourself among the disenchanted, then you have no choice but to accept things as they are, or to seriously seek something else. But beware of looking for *goals*: look for a way of life. Decide how you want to live and then see what you can do to make a living WITHIN that way of life. But you say, "I don't know where to look; I don't know what to look for."

And there's the crux. Is it worth giving up what I have to look for something better? I don't know—is it? Who can make that decision but you? But even by DECIDING TO LOOK, you go a long way toward making the choice.

If I don't call this to a halt, I'm going to find myself writing a book. I hope it's not as confusing as it looks at first glance. Keep in mind, of course, that this is MY WAY of looking at things. I happen to think that it's pretty generally applicable, but you may not. Each of us has to create our own credo—this merely happens to be mine.

If any part of it doesn't seem to make sense, by all means call it to my attention. I'm not trying to send you out "on the road" in search of Valhalla, but merely pointing out that it is not necessary to accept the choices handed down to you by life as you know it. There is more to it than that—no one HAS to do something he doesn't want to do for the rest of his life. But then again, if that's what you wind up doing, by all means convince yourself that you HAD to do it. You'll have lots of company.

And that's it for now. Until I hear from you again, I remain,

your friend …
Hunter

I BEG YOU TO TAKE MY CHILD

VARIOUS MOTHERS to THE
FOUNDLING ASYLUM
1870s

In the late 1860s, in direct response to a sharp rise in the number of babies being abandoned in New York and an even more worrying increase in cases of infanticide, Sister Irene Fitzgibbon campaigned for and then founded The Foundling Asylum, essentially a house in Greenwich Village dedicated to taking in and caring for the city's unwanted babies. It opened to the public in 1869 with a single white cradle on its doorstep, and immediately began to give safe shelter to abandoned infants. In the first two years alone 2,500 children were taken in, often accompanied by handwritten letters of explanation written by distraught parents; many of the notes have since been preserved by the New York Historical Society.

The New York Foundling, as it is now known, is still operating 140 years later, offering foster care and other support services for local families.

New York Tuesday

Kind Sisters

you will find a little boy he is a month old to morrow it father will not do anything and it is a poor little boy it mother has to work to keep 3 others and can not do anything with this one it name is Walter Cooper and he is not christen yet will you be so good as to do it I should not like him to die with out it his mother might claim him some day I have been married 5 years and I married respectfully and I did not think my husband was a bad man I had to leave him and I could not trust my children to him now I do not know where he is and he has not seen this one yet I have not a dollar in the world to give him or I would give it to him I wish you would keep him for 3 or 4 months and if he is not claimed by that time you may be sure it mother can not support it I may some day send some money to him do not forget his name

Yours Respectfully

Mrs Cooper

1703
admitted as James Fish
2-21-71

New York Tuesday

Kind Sisters

you will Find a little boy he is a month old to morrow it Father will not do anything and it is a poor little boy it mother has to work to keep 3 other and can not do anything with this one it name is walter Cooper and he is not christen yet will you be so good as to do it I should not like him to die with out it his mother might claim him Some day I have been married 6 years and I married respectfuly and I did not think my husband was a bad man I had to leave him and I could not trust my children to him now I do not know where he is and he has not seen this one yet I have not a dollar in the world to give him or I would give it to him I wish you would keep him for 3 or 4 month and if he is not claimed by that time you may be sure it mother can not support it I may someday send some money to him do not forget his name

Yours Respectfuly

Mrs Cooper

Sister Superioress

I am a poor woman and I have been deceived under the promis of marriage; I am at present with no means and with out any relations to nurse my babes. Therefore I beg you for god sake to take my child until I can find a situation and have enough means so I can bring up myself. I hope that you will so kind to accept my child and I will pray god for you.

I remain humble servant

Teresa Perrazzo

New York, Dec. 3rd 1874

Sister Superioress.

I am a poor woman and
I have been deceived under the
Promis of marriage; I am at
Present with no means and without any relations to nurse my
baby Therefore I beg you for god
sake to take my child untill
I can find a situation and I have
means so I can bring up myself
I hope that you will so kind
to accept my child and I will
pray god for you
          I remain umble servant

          Teresa Peruzzo

          New york. Dec 3d 1874

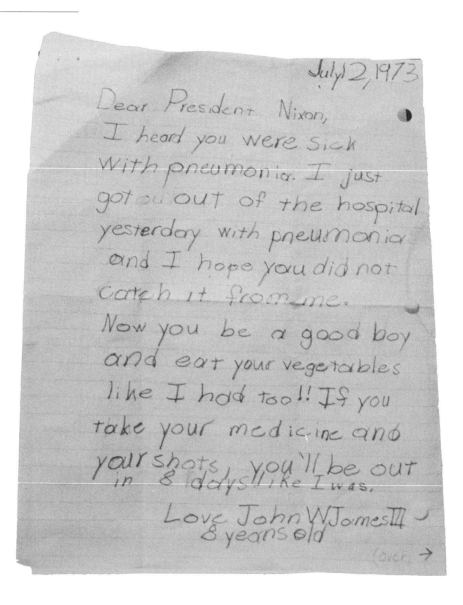

July 12, 1973

Dear President Nixon,
I heard you were sick
with pneumonia. I just
got out of the hospital
yesterday with pneumonia
and I hope you did not
catch it from me.
Now you be a good boy
and eat your vegetables
like I had too!! If you
take your medicine and
your shots, you'll be out
in 8 days like I was.
Love John W James III
8 years old
(over) →

EAT YOUR VEGETABLES!

JOHN W. JAMES III to US PRESIDENT RICHARD NIXON
July 12th, 1973

July 1973 wasn't the best of months for US President Richard Nixon. The Watergate scandal that would ultimately cost him his job was gathering steam, with the revelation that conversations in the Oval Office had been secretly recorded adding yet another twist to a murky tale that already had millions gripped. Then, mid-month, pneumonia arrived on his cluttered doorstep and a weakened Nixon was forced to watch the televised hearings helplessly from a hospital bed. Still, at least he had John W. James III on his side – an empathetic eight-year-old boy whose charming letter of advice reached the troubled President halfway through his recovery and so amused him that he read it aloud to the White House staff on his return.

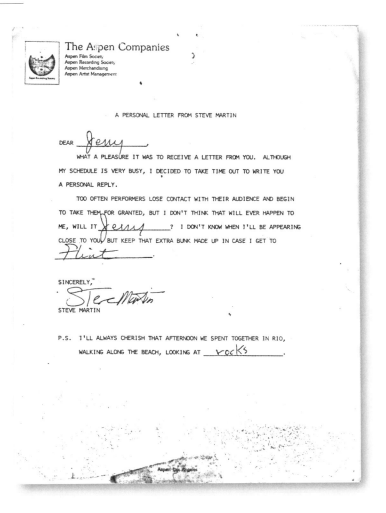

The Aspen Companies

Aspen Film Society
Aspen Recording Society
Aspen Merchandising
Aspen Artist Management

A PERSONAL LETTER FROM STEVE MARTIN

DEAR *Jerry*,

WHAT A PLEASURE IT WAS TO RECEIVE A LETTER FROM YOU. ALTHOUGH MY SCHEDULE IS VERY BUSY, I DECIDED TO TAKE TIME OUT TO WRITE YOU A PERSONAL REPLY.

TOO OFTEN PERFORMERS LOSE CONTACT WITH THEIR AUDIENCE AND BEGIN TO TAKE THEM FOR GRANTED, BUT I DON'T THINK THAT WILL EVER HAPPEN TO ME, WILL IT *Jerry*? I DON'T KNOW WHEN I'LL BE APPEARING CLOSE TO YOU BUT KEEP THAT EXTRA BUNK MADE UP IN CASE I GET TO *Flint*.

SINCERELY,

Steve Martin

STEVE MARTIN

P.S. I'LL ALWAYS CHERISH THAT AFTERNOON WE SPENT TOGETHER IN RIO, WALKING ALONG THE BEACH, LOOKING AT *rocks*.

A PERSONAL LETTER FROM STEVE MARTIN

STEVE MARTIN to JERRY CARLSON
1979

Celebrities are faced with a dilemma as their star ascends: the fan mail that used to trickle to the front door now needs its own home, and replying to those messages of support – a task that once took a couple of hours each week – is suddenly a full-time job of its own. A small few battle on valiantly, determined to respond personally to each and every piece of correspondence regardless of the trouble, expense or delay; most, however, take the easy, altogether more sensible route and produce a form letter, to be signed and used as a stock reply for every fan. Impersonal and slightly disappointing, yes, but a response nonetheless. Trust comedy legend Steve Martin to plump for the latter option but still, thanks to a dab of perfectly pitched humour, come out smelling of roses. Back in the day he replied to fan mail with "A personal letter from Steve Martin", a form letter in which just a few words were personalised for each recipient, and which was hilarious precisely for that reason. This particular example was sent to a 17-year-old fan named Jerry Carlson in 1979, the year *The Jerk*, arguably one of the funniest films Martin has ever starred in, was released.

IS IT A DISGRACE TO BE BORN A CHINESE?

MARY TAPE to SAN
FRANCISCO BOARD OF
EDUCATION
April 8th, 1885

In September 1884, San
Francisco residents
Joseph and Mary Tape did
something seemingly quite
ordinary: they attempted
to enrol their eight-year-
old daughter, Mamie, at
Spring Valley School, a local
school also to be attended
by Mamie's friends.
However, this was 1884,
and although born in the
US, Mamie was of Chinese
descent and the daughter
of immigrants – as a result,
she was quickly denied entry
by the school's principal,
Jennie Hurley. Furious, the
Tapes took the untested
route of suing the school
board and, against all odds,
won. Despite the decision,
the school board then
temporarily circumvented
what was a groundbreaking
ruling by establishing a
separate school for local
Chinese children, Mamie
Tape included. Progress
continued to be slow and
painful.

In April 1885, as the local
authorities continued to
duck and dive, Mamie's
mother wrote the school
board a letter.

1769 GREEN STREET,
SAN FRANCISCO, April 8, 1885.

To the Board of Education—

DEAR SIRS:

I see that you are going to make all sorts of excuses to keep my child out off the
Public schools. Dear sirs, Will you please to tell me! Is it a disgrace to be Born a
Chinese? Didn't God make us all!!! What right have you to bar my children out
of the school because she is a chinese Decend. They is no other worldly reason
that you could keep her out, except that. I suppose, you all goes to churches on
Sundays! Do you call that a Christian act to compel my little children to go so far
to a school that is made in purpose for them. My children don't dress like the other
Chinese. They look just as phunny amongst them as the Chinese dress in Chinese
look amongst you Caucasians. Besides, if I had any wish to send them to a chinese
school I could have sent them two years ago without going to all this trouble. You
have expended a lot of the Public money foolishly, all because of a one poor little
Child. Her playmates is all Caucasians ever since she could toddle around. If she
is good enough to play with them! Then is she not good enough to be in the same
room and studie with them? You had better come and see for yourselves. See if the
Tape's is not same as other Caucasians, except in features. It seems no matter how a
Chinese may live and dress so long as you know they Chinese. Then they are hated
as one. There is not any right or justice for them.

You have seen my husband and child. You told him it wasn't Mamie Tape
you object to. If it were not Mamie Tape you object to, then why didn't you let
her attend the school nearest her home! Instead of first making one pretense Then
another pretense of some kind to keep her out? It seems to me Mr. Moulder has
a grudge against this Eight-year-old Mamie Tape. I know they is no other child
I mean Chinese child! care to go to your public Chinese school. May you Mr.
Moulder, never be persecuted like the way you have persecuted little Mamie Tape.
Mamie Tape will never attend any of the Chinese schools of your making! Never!!!
I will let the world see sir What justice there is When it is govern by the Race
prejudice men! Just because she is of the Chinese decend, not because she don't
dress like you because she does. Just because she is decended of Chinese parents I
guess she is more of a American then a good many of you that is going to prewent
her being Educated.

MRS M. TAPE

O.M.G.

**JOHN ARBUTHNOT FISHER
to WINSTON CHURCHILL**
September 9th, 1917

John Arbuthnot "Jacky"
Fisher enjoyed an
illustrious, 60-year career in
the Royal Navy that began in
1854 – at which point he was
a 13-year-old naval cadet
– and peaked in 1905 when
he was appointed Admiral of
the Fleet, the Navy's highest
possible rank. All told, he
played an influential part in
four wars. By far his most
impressive achievement,
however, occurred in 1917:
in a letter to future Prime
Minister Winston Churchill,
Fisher wrote down the
now commonplace but
then unheard-of acronym
"O.M.G.". According to the
Oxford English Dictionary,
this was its first known
usage.

My Dear Winston,

I am here for a few days longer before rejoining my "Wise men" at Victory House—

"The World forgetting,
By the World forgot!"

but some Headlines in the newspapers have utterly upset me! Terrible!!

"The German Fleet to assist the Land operations in the Baltic."

"Landing the German Army South of Reval."

We are five times stronger at Sea than our enemies and here is a small Fleet that we could gobble up in a few minutes playing the great vital Sea part of landing an Army in the enemies' rear and probably capturing the Russian Capital by Sea!

This is "Holding the ring" with a vengeance!

Are we really incapable of a big Enterprise?

I hear that a new order of Knighthood is on the tapis—O.M.G. (Oh! My God!)—Shower it on the Admiralty!!

Yours,
FISHER.
9/9/17.

P.S.—In War, you want—"SURPRISE." To beget "SURPRISE" you want "IMAGINATION" to go to bed with "AUDACITY."

IT IS ONLY ADULTS WHO EVER FEEL THREATENED

URSULA NORDSTROM to A
SCHOOL LIBRARIAN
January 5th, 1972

When first published
in 1970, *In the Night
Kitchen*, the award-
winning children's book by
Maurice Sendak who also
wrote and illustrated the
magnificent *Where the Wild
Things Are*, caused quite
a stir for one particular
reason: its protagonist, a
young boy named Mickey,
was sometimes depicted
naked. Rather than ignore
the offending book, some
parents and librarians
chose to censor it by
drawing nappies on Mickey;
others thought it easier
and somehow safer to just
burn the entire book. Two
years after its publication,
as these acts of censorship
grew in frequency, Sendak's
editor, the wonderful Ursula
Nordstrom, wrote a letter to
a librarian who had chosen
the latter, hotter option.

January 5, 1972

Dear [Redacted]:

Your letter about Sendak's *In the Night Kitchen* was delayed in reaching my desk as you sent it to our Scranton, Pennsylvania, division. I am sorry not to have written you more promptly.

I am indeed distressed to hear that in the year 1972 you burned a copy of a book. We are truly distressed that you think it is not a book for elementary school children. I assume it is the little boy's nudity which bothers you. But truly, it does not disturb children! Mr. Sendak is a creative artist, a true genius, and he is able to speak to children directly. For children—at least up to the age of 12 or 13— are usually tremendously creative themselves. Should not those of us who stand between the creative artist and the child be <u>very careful</u> not to sift our reactions to such books through our own adult prejudices and neuroses? To me as editor and publisher of books for children, that is one of my greatest and most difficult duties. Believe me, we do not take our responsibilities lightly! I think young children will always react with delight to such a book as *In the Night Kitchen*, and that they will react <u>creatively</u> and <u>wholesomely</u>. It is only adults who ever feel threatened by Sendak's work.

I will send you a few positive comments on this book within the next few days, and I hope you will read them and that you will give the children in your school a chance to enjoy Mr. Sendak's book.

Yours sincerely,
(Signed)

GOD DAMN IT, I SPLIT IT SO IT WILL STAY SPLIT

RAYMOND CHANDLER to
EDWARD WEEKS
January 18th, 1947

In January 1947, renowned
novelist Raymond Chandler
wrote a letter to the editor
of *The Atlantic Monthly*,
Edward Weeks, primarily
with regard to the title of
a piece he had written for
the magazine which was
ultimately published the
next year, titled, "Oscar
Night in Hollywood". It is
the latter half of this letter,
however – a wonderfully
lyrical message to be
passed on by Weeks to the
publication's proofreader –
that has since become one
of Chandler's most famous
quotes. Indeed, Weeks did
pass on the message, to a
copyeditor named Margaret
Mutch. She then wrote a
letter to Chandler, to which
Chandler responded with
the delightful poem also
shown here.

6005 Camino de la Costa
La Jolla, California
Jan. 18th, 1947

Dear Mr. Weeks:

I'm afraid you've thrown me for a loss. I thought "Juju Worship in
Hollywood" was a perfectly good title. I don't see why it has to be linked up with
crime and mystery. But you're the Boss. When I wrote about writers this did not
occur to you. I've thought of various titles such as Bank Night in Hollywood,
Sutter's Last Stand, The Golden Peepshow, All it Needs is Elephants, The Hot
Shop Handicap, Where Vaudeville Went it Died, and rot like that. But nothing that
smacks you in the kisser. By the way, would you convey my compliments to the
purist who reads your proofs and tell him or her that I write in a sort of broken-
down patois which is something like the way a Swiss waiter talks, and that when I
split an infinitive, God damn it, I split it so it will stay split, and when I interrupt
the velvety smoothness of my more or less literate syntax with a few sudden words
of barroom vernacular, this is done with the eyes wide open and the mind relaxed
but attentive. The method may not be perfect, but it is all I have. I think your
proofreader is kindly attempting to steady me on my feet, but much as I appreciate
the solicitude, I am really able to steer a fairly clear course, provided I get both
sidewalks and the street between.

If I think of anything, I'll wire you.

Kindest Regards,
(Signed)

Lines to a Lady With an Unsplit Infinitive

Miss Margaret Mutch she raised her crutch
With a wild Bostonian cry.

"Though you went to Yale, your grammar is frail,"
She snarled as she jabbed his eye.

"Though you went to Princeton I never winced on
Such a horrible relative clause!

Though you went to Harvard no decent larva'd
Accept your syntactical flaws.

Taught not to drool at a Public School
(With a capital P and S)

You are drooling still with your shall and will
You're a very disgusting mess!"

She jabbed his eye with a savage cry.
She laughed at his anguished shrieks.

O'er the Common he fled with a hole in his head.
To heal it took Weeks and Weeks.

"O dear Miss Mutch, don't raise your crutch
To splinter my new glass eye!

There ain't no school that can teach a fool
The whom of the me and the I.

There ain't no grammar that equals a hammer
To nail down a cut-rate wit.

And the verb 'to be' as employed by me
Is often and lightly split.

A lot of my style (so-called) is vile
For I learned to write in a bar.

The marriage of thought to words was wrought
With many a strong sidecar.

A lot of my stuff is extremely rough,
For I had no maiden aunts.

O dear Miss Mutch, leave go your clutch
On Noah Webster's pants!

The grammarian will, when the poet lies still,
Instruct him in how to sing.

The rules are clean: they are right, I ween,
But where do they make the thing?

In the waxy gloam of a Funeral Home
Where the gray morticians bow?

Is it written best on a palimpsest,
Or carved on a whaleboat's prow?

Is it neatly joined with needlepoint
To the chair that was Grandma's pride?

Or smeared in blood on the shattered wood
Where the angry rebel died?

O dear Miss Mutch, put down your crutch,
and leave us to crack a bottle.

A guy like I weren't meant to die
On the grave of Aristotle.

O leave us dance on the dead romance
Of the small but clear footnote.

The infinitive with my fresh-honed shiv
I will split from heel to throat.

Roll on, roll on, thou semicolon,
ye commas crisp and brown.

The apostrophe will stretch like toffee
When we nail the full stop down.

Oh, hand in hand with the ampersand
We'll tread a measure brisk.

We'll stroll all night by the delicate light
Of a well placed asterisk.

As gay as a lark in the fragrant dark
We'll hoist and down the tipple.

With laughter light we'll greet the plight
Of a hanging participle!"

She stared him down with an icy frown.
His accidence she shivered.

His face was white with sudden fright,
And his syntax lily-livered.

"O dear Miss Mutch, leave down your crutch!"
He cried in thoughtless terror.

Short shrift she gave. Above his grave:
HERE LIES A PRINTER'S ERROR.

I SHALL BE WAITING FOR YOU

LADY SHIGENARI to KIMURA SHIGENARI
1615

In 1615, having successfully commanded an army at the Battle of Imafuku some months before, 22-year-old Japanese samurai and "peerless hero of the nation" Kimura Shigenari once again prepared to lead his men, this time at the Siege of Osaka. Despite his confidence, Shigenari's wife, Lady Shigenari, was keenly aware that his troops were heavily outnumbered and so decided not to continue without her brave husband. This letter was her goodbye. As predicted, Kimura Shigenari was killed during battle and then beheaded; by that point, his wife had already taken her own life.

I know that when two wayfarers take shelter under the same tree and slake their thirst in the same river it has all been determined by their karma from a previous life. For the past few years you and I have shared the same pillow as man and wife who had intended to live and grow old together, and I have become as attached to you as your own shadow. This is what I believed, and I think this is what you have also thought about us.

But now I have learnt about the final enterprise on which you have decided and, though I cannot be with you to share the grand moment, I rejoice in the knowledge of it. It is said that on the eve of his final battle, the Chinese general, Hsiang Yü, valiant warrior though he was, grieved deeply about leaving Lady Yü, and that (in our own country) Kiso Yoshinaka lamented his parting from Lady Matsudono. I have now abandoned all hope about our future together in this world, and, mindful of their example, I have resolved to take the ultimate step while you are still alive. I shall be waiting for you at the end of what they call the road to death.

I pray that you may never, never forget the great bounty, deep as the ocean, high as the mountains, that has been bestowed upon us for so many years by our lord, Prince Hideyori.

MY MUSE IS NOT A HORSE

NICK CAVE to MTV
October 21st, 1996

When released in 1996, Nick Cave and the Bad Seeds' ninth album, the beautifully haunting, sometimes terrifying *Murder Ballads*, attracted critical praise from far and wide and went on to reach a larger audience than any of their previous records. This heightened popularity also resulted in Nick Cave being nominated for an MTV Award in the category of Best Male Artist – a situation that left Cave feeling distinctly uncomfortable and which, in October of that year, provoked this wonderful rejection letter to the event's bemused organisers.

21 OCT 96

TO ALL THOSE AT MTV,

I WOULD LIKE TO START BY THANKING YOU ALL FOR THE SUPPORT YOU HAVE GIVEN ME OVER RECENT YEARS AND I AM BOTH GRATEFUL AND FLATTERED BY THE NOMINATIONS THAT I HAVE RECEIVED FOR BEST MALE ARTIST. THE AIR PLAY GIVEN TO BOTH THE KYLIE MINOGUE AND P. J. HARVEY DUETS FROM MY LATEST ALBUM MURDER BALLADS HAS NOT GONE UNNOTICED AND HAS BEEN GREATLY APPRECIATED. SO AGAIN MY SINCERE THANKS.

HAVING SAID THAT, I FEEL THAT IT'S NECESSARY FOR ME TO REQUEST THAT MY NOMINATION FOR BEST MALE ARTIST BE WITHDRAWN AND FURTHERMORE ANY AWARDS OR NOMINATIONS FOR SUCH AWARDS THAT MAY ARISE IN LATER YEARS BE PRESENTED TO THOSE WHO FEEL MORE COMFORTABLE WITH THE COMPETITIVE NATURE OF THESE AWARD CEREMONIES. I MYSELF, DO NOT. I HAVE ALWAYS BEEN OF THE OPINION THAT MY MUSIC IS UNIQUE AND INDIVIDUAL AND EXISTS BEYOND THE REALMS INHABITED BY THOSE WHO WOULD REDUCE THINGS TO MERE MEASURING. I AM IN COMPETITION WITH NO-ONE.

MY RELATIONSHIP WITH MY MUSE IS A DELICATE ONE AT THE BEST OF TIMES AND I FEEL THAT IT IS MY DUTY TO PROTECT HER FROM INFLUENCES THAT MAY OFFEND HER FRAGILE NATURE.

SHE COMES TO ME WITH THE GIFT OF SONG AND IN RETURN I TREAT HER WITH THE RESPECT I FEEL SHE DESERVES — IN THIS CASE THIS MEANS NOT SUBJECTING HER TO THE INDIGNITIES OF JUDGEMENT AND COMPETITION. MY MUSE IS NOT A HORSE AND I AM IN NO HORSE RACE AND IF INDEED SHE WAS, STILL I WOULD NOT HARNESS HER TO THIS TUMBREL — THIS BLOODY CART OF SEVERED HEADS AND GLITTERING PRIZES. MY MUSE MAY SPOOK! MAY BOLT! MAY ABANDON ME COMPLETELY!

SO ONCE AGAIN, TO THE PEOPLE AT MTV, I APPRECIATE THE ZEAL AND ENERGY THAT WAS PUT BEHIND MY LAST RECORD, I TRULY DO AND SAY THANK YOU AND AGAIN I SAY THANK YOU BUT NO… NO THANK YOU.

YOURS SINCERELY,

NICK CAVE

OUR FRANK

THE CONNELL FAMILY to
THE CIULLA FAMILY
1992

On the night of December
21st 1988, a bomb exploded
on board New York-bound
Pan Am Flight 103 and
ripped the aircraft apart,
its wreckage then raining
down on the sleepy Scottish
town of Lockerbie below. All
259 passengers and crew
perished, as did 11 local
residents. One of those
passengers was 45-year-old
Frank Ciulla, who had been
travelling home to his wife
and three children in New
Jersey for the Christmas
holidays; his body was
discovered on Margaret and
Hugh Connell's small farm
in Waterbeck, nearly eight
miles from the main crash
site.

Almost four years later, the
Ciulla family finally found the
strength to visit Scotland.
They went to Minsca farm
and spent time with the
Connells; they saw the quiet
spot where their father and
husband came to rest, far
away from the chaotic scenes
in Lockerbie; and they
asked all of the questions
they had been desperate to
ask since getting the news.
After the visit, the Connells
wrote a beautiful, thoughtful
letter to the Ciullas. It was
cherished and read aloud on
the seventh anniversary of
the tragedy, as the Lockerbie
Cairn was dedicated in
Arlington. The two families
remain close.

My Dears Lou, Mary Lou and family,

I can hardly believe that I am writing to you. This is something that I had longed to do since 21st December, 1988. When your dear one came to us from the night, it was so unbelievable, haunting and desperately sad. You said that your visit altered the picture for you in many ways; this is just how it was for us too. Frank was a young man with a name but connected to nobody. Now at last we can match him with a loving family. Sometimes I would stop to think as the months went past, "I wonder how his loved ones are coping now, I wonder what they are doing?"

We were told maybe some of the relatives would never come; we were afraid that you'd come and not want to get in touch. I was so thankful that you made the effort to come and ask all the questions you had always wanted to ask. You had at last found someone who could fill in those last hours, that piece that had always remained a mystery. It's the "not knowing" that can bring so much pain and bewilderment. We all have imaginations that can run riot in us, and I'm sure your dear souls must have had untold agonies wondering and worrying.

It was just wonderful to meet you face-to-face. We needed to talk to you all too. As you said, we will get to know Frank through you. He was never just "another victim" to us. For months we called him "Our Boy." Then we found out his name. He was "Our Frank." Please believe me we were deeply affected by his coming to us. We will never forget our feelings seeing him there, a whole-bodied handsome man, the life gone out of him in a twinkling. We were just past trying to grasp the whole thing.

Then to have to leave him there, but he was visited throughout the night by police and a doctor and we went back again in the morning. He was a fellow man and he had come to us in the saddest way. So now through him we have you in our hearts, and please, we want you all to know that you are welcome here whenever you come.

The Connell Family

RAY BRADBURY
AUTHOR
CHARLES ROME SMITH
DIRECTOR
JOSEPH STECK
PRODUCER
MICHAEL SHERE
SCENIC AND LIGHTING DIRECTOR
MARK S. KRAUSE
PRODUCTION STAGE MANAGER
PHIL N. LATTIN
ASSOCIATE PRODUCER
PETER LYNCH
ASSISTANT PRODUCER
DONALD C. MITCHELL
PROMOTION
JOE MUGNAINI
ART DESIGNER
ROBERT CABEEN
ART DESIGN ASSISTANT
DOUG TRUMBELL
DESIGN CONSULTANT
KAREN ARTHUR
ASSISTANT TO THE DIRECTOR
MARION CLINE
ADMINISTRATIVE ASSISTANT
TRI-ARTS INC.
GRAPHICS
SAMUEL GOLDWYN PRODUCTIONS

P.O. Box 2099
Hollywood Station
Los Angeles, CA 90028
(213) 851-2099

JUNE
10, 1974

Dear Brian Sibley:

This will have to be short. Sorry. But I am deep into my screenplay
on SOMETHING WICKED THIS WAY COMES and have no secretary, never have
had one..so must write all my own letters..200 a week!!!!

Disney was a dreamer and a doer..while the rest of us were talking
ab out the future, he built it. The things he taught us at
Disneyland about street planning, crowd movement, comfort, humanity, etc,
will influence builders, architects, urban planners for the next
century. Because of him we will humanize our cities, plan small towns
again where we can get in touch with one another again and make
democracy work creatively because we will KNOW the people we vote for.
He was so far ahead of his time it will take us the next 50 years
to catch up. You MUST come to Disneyland and eat -your words, swallow
your doubts. Most of the other architects of the ;modern world were
asses and fools who talked against Big Brother and then built
prisons to put ;us all in..our modern environments which stifle
and destroy us. Disney the so-called conservative turns out to
be Disney the great man of foresight and construction.

Enough. Come here soon. I'll toss you in the Jungle Ride River
and ride you on the train into tomorrow, yesterday, and beyond.

Good luck, and stop judging at such a great distance. You are kkkk-
simply not qualified. Disney was full of errors, paradoxes, mistakes.
He was also full of life, beauty, insight. Which speaks for all of
us, eh? We are all mysteries of light and d-ark. There are
no true ;conservatives, liberals, etc, in the world. Only people.

Best,

P.S. I can't find that issue of THE NATION, or the NEW REPUBLIC, which ever
it was, with my letter in it on Disney. Mainly I said that if Disneyland was
good enough for Captain Bligh it was good enough for me. Charles Laughton
and his wife took me to Disneyland for my very first visit and our first
ride was the Jungle Boat Ride, which Laughton immediately commandeered,
jeering at customers going by in other boats! A fantastic romp for me and
a hilarious day. What a way to start my assocation with Disneyland! R.B.

Pandemonium II Productions

P.S. Can't resist commenting on your fears of the Disney robots. Why aren't
you afraid of books, then? The fact is, of course, that people have
been afraid of books, down through history. They are extensions of people,
not people themselves. Any machine, any robot, is the sum total of the
ways we use it. Why not kknock down all robot camera devices and the means
for reproducing the stuff that goes into such devices, things called
projectors in theatres? A motion picture projector is a non-humanoid robot
which repeats truths which we inject into it. Is it inhuman? Yes. Does
it project human truths to humanize us more often than not? Yes.

The excuse could be made that we should burn all books because some books
are dreadful.

We should mash all cars because some cars get in accidents because of the
people driving them.

We should burn down all the theatres in the world because some films
are trash, drivel.

So it is finally with the robots you say you fear. Why fear something?
Why not create with it? Why not build robot teachers to help out in schools
where teaching certain subjects is a bore for EVERYONE? Why not have
Plato sitting in your Greek Class answering jolly questions about his Republic?
                    I would love to experiment with that. I am not afraid
of robots. I am afraid of people, people, people. I want them to remain
human. I can help keep them human with the wise and lovely use of books,
films, robots, and my own mind, hands, and heart.

I am afraid of Catholics killing Protestants and vice versa.

I am afraid of whites killing blacks and vice versa.

I am afraid of English killing Irish and vice versa.

I am afraid of young killing old and vice versa.

I am afraid of Communists killing Capitalists and vice versa.

But...robots? God, I love them. I will use them humanely to teach all of
the above. My vo-ice will speak out of them, and it will be a damned nice
voice.

Best, R.B.

I AM NOT AFRAID OF ROBOTS. I AM AFRAID OF PEOPLE

RAY BRADBURY to BRIAN SIBLEY
June 10th, 1974

In 1974, English author Brian Sibley wrote a letter to his favourite science fiction novelist, Ray Bradbury – the man responsible for writing, most notably, *Fahrenheit 451* – in which he spoke of his deep admiration for Bradbury's books and posed some questions related to Disney, a subject close to his heart.

"If I remember rightly," explains Sibley, "I expressed doubts about Disney's use of Audio-Animatronic creations in Disneyland. At the time, I had still to visit a Disney theme park and had probably read too many sci-fi stories about the danger of robots taking over our human world –

including, of course, some by Ray – and so saw it as a sinister rather than benign experiment. But what joy to have one's ill-formed and prejudiced views exploded by such a wordsmith. How wonderful that he bothered to take the time to ignite that explosion and how miraculous that its aftershock was a more-than-30-year friendship!"

Bradbury's letter is indeed wonderful, in both generosity and content, and comes with a postscript in which he elegantly and poetically questions Sibley's fear of robots in a way that only he could.

Dear Eva,

April 14

DO

SOL LEWITT to EVA HESSE
April 14th, 1965

In 1960, pioneering American artists Sol LeWitt and Eva Hesse met for the first time and instantly clicked, quickly forming a strong, deep bond that would last for ten years and result in countless inspirational discussions and rich exchanges of ideas. Indeed, they remained incredibly close friends until May 1970, at which point Hesse, still only 34 years of age, sadly passed away after being diagnosed with a brain tumour.

In 1965, half-way through their relationship, Hesse found herself facing a creative block during a period of self-doubt and told LeWitt of her frustrating predicament. A few weeks later, LeWitt replied with the work of art seen here – a wonderful, invaluable letter of advice, copies of which have since inspired artists the world over and which now grace the walls of art studios in all corners of the globe.

It will be almost a month since you wrote to me and you have possibly forgotten your state of mind (I doubt it though). You seem the same as always, and being you, hate every minute of it. Don't! Learn to say "Fuck You" to the world once in a while. You have every right to. Just stop thinking, worrying, looking over your shoulder, wondering, doubting, fearing, hurting, hoping for some easy way out, struggling, grasping, confusing, itching, scratching, mumbling, bumbling, grumbling, humbling, stumbling, numbling, rambling, gambling, tumbling, scumbling, scrambling, hitching, hatching, bitching, moaning, groaning, honing, boning, horse-shitting, hair-splitting, nit-picking, piss-trickling, nose sticking, ass-gouging, eyeball-poking, finger-pointing, alleyway-sneaking, long waiting, small stepping, evil-eyeing, back-scratching, searching, perching, besmirching, grinding, grinding, grinding away at yourself. Stop it and just

DO

From your description, and from what I know of your previous work and your ability; the work you are doing sounds very good "Drawing — clean — clear but crazy like machines, larger and bolder… real nonsense." That sounds fine, wonderful — real nonsense. Do more. More nonsensical, more crazy, more machines, more breasts, penises, cunts, whatever — make them abound with nonsense. Try and tickle something inside you, your "weird humor." You belong in the most secret part of you. Don't worry about cool, make your own uncool. Make your own, your own world. If you fear, make it work for you — draw & paint your fear & anxiety. And stop worrying about big, deep things such as "to decide on a purpose and way of life, a consistant approach to even some impossible end or even an imagined end." You must practice being stupid, dumb, unthinking, empty. Then you will be able to

DO

I have much confidence in you and even though you are tormenting yourself, the work you do is very good. Try to do some BAD work — the worst you can think of and see what happens but mainly relax and let everything go to hell — you are not responsible for the world — you are only responsible for your work — so DO IT.

Dear Eva,   April 14

It will be almost a month since you wrote
to me and you have possibly forgotten your
state of mind (I doubt it though.) You
seem the same as always, and being you,
hate every minute of it. Don't! Learn to
say "Fuck you" to the world once in a while.
You have every right to. Just stop thinking,
worrying, looking over your shoulder wondering, doubting, fearing, hurting, hoping for
some easy wayout, struggling, grasping,
confusing, itching, scratching, mumbling
bumbling, grumbling, humbling, stumbling
mumbling, rambling, gambling, tumbling,
scumbling, scrambling, hitching, hatching,
bitching, moaning, groaning, honing, boning
horse-shitting, hair-splitting, nit-picking,
piss-trickling, nose sticking, ass-gouging,
eyeball-poking, finger-pointing, alleyway-
sneaking, long waiting, small stepping,
evil-eyeing, back-scratching, searching,
perching, besmirching, grinding, grinding
grinding away at yourself. Stop it and just

DO

And don't think that your work has to conform to any preconceived form, idea or flavor. It can be anything you want it to be. But if life would be easier for you if you stopped working — then stop. Don't punish yourself. However, I think that it is so deeply engrained in you that it would be easier to

DO

It seems I do understand your attitude somewhat, anyway, because I go through a similar process every so often. I have an "Agonizing Reappraisal" of my work and change everything as much as possible — and hate everything I've done, and try to do something entirely different and better. Maybe that kind of process is necessary to me, pushing me on and on. The feeling that I can do better than that shit I just did. Maybe you need your agony to accomplish what you do. And maybe it goads you on to do better. But it is very painful I know. It would be better if you had the confidence just to do the stuff and not even think about it. Can't you leave the "world" and "ART" alone and also quit fondling your ego. I know that you (or anyone) can only work so much and the rest of the time you are left with your thoughts. But when you work or before your work you have to empty your mind and concentrate on what you are doing. After you do something it is done and that's that. After a while you can see some are better than others but also you can see what direction you are going. I'm sure you know all that. You also must know that you don't have to justify your work — not even to yourself. Well, you know I admire your work greatly and can't understand why you are so bothered by it. But you can see the next ones & I can't. You also must believe in your ability. I think you do. So try the most outrageous things you can — shock yourself. You have at your power the ability to do anything.

I would like to see your work and will have to be content to wait until Aug or Sept. I have seen photos of some of Tom's new things at Lucy's. They are very impressive — especially the ones with the more rigorous form; the simpler ones. I guess he'll send some more later on. Let me know how the shows are going and that kind of stuff.

My work has changed since you left and it is much better. I will be having a show May 4–29 at the Daniels Gallery 17 E 64th St (where Emmerich was), I wish you could be there. Much love to you both.

Sol

From you description, and from what ②
I know of your previous work and
you ability, the works you are doing
sounds very good "Drawings – clean – clear
out crazy like machines, large; bolder...
real nonsense." That sounds fine,
wonderful – real nonsense. Do more.
more nonsensical, more crazy, more
machines, more breasts, penises, cunts,
whatever – make Them abound with
nonsense. Try and tickle something
inside you, your "weird humor". You
belong in the most secret part of you.
Don't worry about cool, make your
own uncool. make your own, your own
world. If you fear, make it work
for you – draw & paint your fear & anxiety.
And stop worrying about big, deep Things
such as "to decide on a purpose and
way of life, a consistant approach to
even some impossible end or even an
imagened end." You must practice being
stupid, dumb, unthinking, empty. Then
you will be able to:

DO

I have much confidence in you and ③
even though you are tormenting yourself. The work you do is very good. Try
to do some BAD work – the worst you
can think of and see what happens but
mainly relax and let everything go to
hell – you are not responsible for the
world – you are only responsible for
your work – so DO IT. And don't think
that your work has to conform to any
preconceived form, idea or flavor. It
can be anything you want it to be. But
if life would be easier for you if you
stopped working – then stop. Don't punish
yourself. However, I think that it is so
deeply engrained in you that it would
be easier to

DO

It seems I do understand your attitude ④
somewhat, anyway, because I go through
a similar process every so often. I have
an "Agonizing Reappraisal" of my work and change
everything as much as possible—and hate
everything I've done, and try to do something
entirely different and better. Maybe that kind
of process is necessary to me, pushing me
on and on. The feeling that I can do better
than that shit I just did. Maybe you need
your agony to accomplish what you do.
And maybe it goads you on to do better.
But it is very painful I know. It would
be better if you had the confidence just to
do the stuff and not even think about
it. Can't you leave the "world" and "ART" alone
and also quit fondling your ego. I know
that you (or anyone) can only work so much
And the rest of the time you are left with
your thoughts. But when you work or
before you work you have to empty
your mind and concentrate on what you
are doing. After you do something it is
done and that's that. After a while you
can see some are better than others but
also you can see what direction you are

going. I'm sure you know all that. ⑤
You also must know that you don't have
to justify your work — not even to yourself.
Well you know I admire your work greatly
and can't understand why you are so bothered
by it. But you can see the next ones & I can't.
You also must believe in your ability — I think
you do. So try the most outrageous things you
can — shock yourself. You have at your power
the ability to do anything.

I would like to see your work
and will have to be content to wait until
Aug or Sept. I have seen photos of some of Tom's
new things at Lucy's. They are very
impressive — especially the ones with
the more rigorous form; the simpler
ones. I guess he'll send some more
later on. Let me know how the
shows are going and that kind of
stuff.
My work has changed since you
left and it is much better. I will
be having a show May 4-29 at the Daniels
gallery 17 E 64ᵗʰ St (where Emmerich was). I wish
you could be there. Much Love to you both
Sol

94

WHAT DID YOU SAY? I CAN'T HEAR YOU...

KATHARINE HEPBURN to
SPENCER TRACY
Circa 1985

On June 10th 1967, Spencer
Tracy, a genuine Hollywood
star who was nominated
for nine Best Actor Oscars
during his illustrious career,
two of which he won, passed
away after suffering a
heart attack at the home
he shared with his partner,
multi-Oscar-winning actress
Katharine Hepburn. Their
26-year romance was a
complicated one, not least
due to Tracy's being married
to another woman for the
duration – an uncomfortable
fact that resulted in the
situation remaining private
for much of their lives.
Approximately 18 years
after Tracy's death, Hepburn
wrote him a letter.

Dear Spence,

Who ever thought that I'd be writing you a letter. You died on the 10th of June in 1967. My golly, Spence, that's eighteen years ago. That's a long time. Are you happy finally? Is it a nice long rest you're having? Making up for all your tossing and turning in life. You know, I never believed you when you said that you just couldn't get to sleep. I thought, Oh—come on—you sleep—if you didn't sleep you'd be dead. You'd be so worn out. Then remember that night when—oh, I don't know, you felt so disturbed. And I said, Well, go on in—go to bed. And I'll lie on the floor and talk you to sleep. I'll just talk and talk and you'll be so bored, you're bound to drift off.

Well, I went in and got an old pillow and Lobo the dog. I lay there watching you and stroking Old Dog. I was talking about you and the movie we'd just finished— Guess Who's Coming to Dinner—and my studio and your new tweed coat and the garden and all the nice sleep-making topics and cooking and dull gossip, but you never stopped tossing—to the right, to the left—shove the pillows—pull the covers—on and on and on. Finally—really finally—not just then—you quieted down. I waited a while—and then I crept out.

You told me the truth, didn't you? You really could not sleep.

And I used to wonder then—why? I still wonder. You took the pills. They were quite strong. I suppose you have to say that otherwise you would never have slept at all. Living wasn't easy for you, was it?

What did you like to do? You loved sailing, especially in stormy weather. You loved polo. But then Will Rogers was killed in that airplane accident. And you never played polo again—never again. Tennis, golf, no, not really. You'd bat a few balls. Fair you were. I don't think that you ever swang a golf club. Is "swang" a word? Swimming? Well, you didn't like cold water. And walking? No, that didn't suit you. That was one of those things where you could think at the same time—of this, of that, of what, Spence? What was it? Was it some specific life thing like Johnny being deaf, or being a Catholic and you felt a bad Catholic? No comfort, no comfort. I remember Father Ciklic telling you that you concentrated on all the bad and none of the good which your religion offered. It must have been something very fundamental and very ever-present.

And the incredible fact. There you were—really the greatest movie actor. I say this because I believe it and also I have heard many people of standing in your business say it. From Olivier to Lee Strasberg to David Lean. You name it. You could do it. And you could do it with that glorious simplicity and directness: you could just do it. You couldn't enter your own life, but you could become someone else. You were a killer, a priest, a fisherman, a sportswriter, a judge, a newspaperman. You were it in an instant.

You hardly had to study. You learned the lines in no time. What a relief! You could be someone else for a while. You weren't you—you were safe. You loved to laugh, didn't you? You never missed those individual comics: Jimmy Durante, Phil Silvers, Fanny Brice, Frank McHugh, Mickey Rooney, Jack Benny, Burns and Allen, Smith and Dale, and your favorite, Bert Williams. Funny stories: you could tell them—and brilliantly. You could laugh at yourself. You enjoyed very much the friendship and admiration of people like the Kanins, Frank Sinatra, Bogie and Betty, George Cukor, Vic Flemming, Stanley Kramer, the Kennedys, Harry Truman, Lew Douglas. You were fun with them, you had fun with them, you felt safe with them.

But then back to life's trials. Oh hell, take a drink—no-yes-maybe. Then stop taking the drink. You were great at that, Spence. You could just stop. How I respected you for that. Very unusual.

Well, you said on this subject: never safe until you're seven feet underground. But why the escape hatch? Why was it always opened—to get away from the remarkable you?

What was it, Spence? I meant to ask you. Did you know what it was?

What did you say? I can't hear you...

THE AX

CHARLES M. SCHULZ to
ELIZABETH SWAIM
January 5th, 1955

On November 30th 1954,
a character by the name
of Charlotte Braun made
her debut in the much-
loved, four-year-old comic
strip *Peanuts*, and almost
immediately pushed all
the wrong buttons. Loud,
brash and opinionated,
"Good Ol' Charlotte Braun"
quickly irked *Peanuts'* loyal
readers and on February
1st 1955, after just ten
sightings in the strip, she
appeared in a storyline for
the last time. Forty-five
years later, following the
death of *Peanuts'* creator,
Charles M. Schulz, a lady
named Elizabeth Swaim
donated to the United States
Library of Congress this
fascinating letter, written to
her by Schulz in response to
a complaint she had made
about Braun just a month
before the character's
demise. In it, Schulz agrees
to kill the character off,
reminds Swaim that she
will be responsible for her
death, and then signs off
with a picture of Braun with
an axe to the head.

Dear Miss Swaim,

I am taking your suggestion regarding Charlotte Braun and will eventually discard her. If she appears anymore it will be in strips that were already completed before I got your letter or because someone writes in saying that they like her. Remember, however, that you and your friends will have the death of an innocent child on your conscience. Are you prepared to accept such responsibility?

Thanks for writing, and I hope that future releases will please you.

Sincerely,
Charles M. Schulz

Jan. 5, 1955

Dear Miss Swaim,

I am taking your suggestion
regarding Charlotte Braun, & will eventually
discard her. If she appears anymore it will
be in strips that were already completed before
I got your letter or because someone writes in
saying that they like her. Remember, however,
that you and your friends will have the death
of an innocent child on your conscience. Are
you prepared to accept such responsibility?

Thanks for writing, and I hope that
future releases will please you.

Sincerely,
Charles M. Schulz

The Ax

I LOVE MY WIFE. MY WIFE IS DEAD.

RICHARD FEYNMAN to
ARLINE FEYNMAN
October 17th, 1946

Richard Feynman was one of the best-known and most influential physicists of his generation. In the 1940s he played a part in the development of the atomic bomb; in 1984, as a key member of the Rogers Commission, he investigated the Space Shuttle *Challenger* disaster and identified its cause; in 1965 he and two colleagues were awarded the Nobel Prize "for their fundamental work in quantum electrodynamics, with deep-ploughing consequences for the physics of elementary particles". He was also an incredibly likeable character and made countless other advances in his field, the complexities of which I will never be able to understand.

In June 1945, his wife and high-school sweetheart, Arline, passed away after succumbing to tuberculosis. She was 25 years old. Sixteen months later, in October 1946, Feynman wrote his late wife a heartbreaking love letter and sealed it in an envelope. It remained unopened until after his death in 1988.

October 17, 1946

D'Arline,

I adore you, sweetheart.

I know how much you like to hear that—but I don't only write it because you like it—I write it because it makes me warm all over inside to write it to you.

It is such a terribly long time since I last wrote to you—almost two years but I know you'll excuse me because you understand how I am, stubborn and realistic; and I thought there was no sense to writing.

But now I know my darling wife that it is right to do what I have delayed in doing, and that I have done so much in the past. I want to tell you I love you. I want to love you. I always will love you.

I find it hard to understand in my mind what it means to love you after you are dead—but I still want to comfort and take care of you—and I want you to love me and care for me. I want to have problems to discuss with you—I want to do little projects with you. I never thought until just now that we can do that. What should we do. We started to learn to make clothes together—or learn Chinese—or getting a movie projector. Can't I do something now? No. I am alone without you and you were the "idea-woman" and general instigator of all our wild adventures.

When you were sick you worried because you could not give me something that you wanted to and thought I needed. You needn't have worried. Just as I told you then there was no real need because I loved you in so many ways so much. And now it is clearly even more true—you can give me nothing now yet I love you so that you stand in my way of loving anyone else—but I want you to stand there. You, dead, are so much better than anyone else alive.

I know you will assure me that I am foolish and that you want me to have full happiness and don't want to be in my way. I'll bet you are surprised that I don't even have a girlfriend (except you, sweetheart) after two years. But you can't help it, darling, nor can I—I don't understand it, for I have met many girls and very nice ones and I don't want to remain alone—but in two or three meetings they all seem ashes. You only are left to me. You are real.

My darling wife, I do adore you.

I love my wife. My wife is dead.

Rich.

PS Please excuse my not mailing this—but I don't know your new address.

YOU ARE NOT SO KIND
AS YOU USED TO BE

CLEMENTINE CHURCHILL
to WINSTON CHURCHILL
June 27th, 1940

It's difficult to imagine
the stress experienced
by Winston Churchill in
June 1940, just a couple of
months after first becoming
Prime Minister. World War
II was gathering pace and
it was during this month
that Churchill gave three
momentous and inspiring
speeches to the House of
Commons that inspired
the nation at such a tense
time. Behind the scenes,
however, the weight on his
own shoulders was noticed
and felt by all those around
him – so much so in fact
that on June 27th his wife,
Clementine, wrote him
a letter and essentially
advised him to calm down
and be kind to his staff.

Note: "On ne règne sur les
âmes que par le calme"
roughly translates as "One
can reign over hearts only by
keeping one's composure."

10 Downing Street,
Whitehall

June 27, 1940

My Darling,

I hope you will forgive me if I tell you something that I feel you ought to know.

One of the men in your entourage (a devoted friend) has been to me & told me that there is a danger of your being generally disliked by your colleagues and subordinates because of your rough sarcastic & overbearing manner — It seems your Private Secretaries have agreed to behave like school boys & 'take what's coming to them' & then escape out of your presence shrugging their shoulders — Higher up, if an idea is suggested (say at a conference) you are supposed to be so contemptuous that presently no ideas, good or bad, will be forthcoming. I was astonished & upset because in all these years I have been accustomed to all those who have worked with & under you, loving you — I said this & I was told 'No doubt it's the strain' —

My Darling Winston — I must confess that I have noticed a deterioration in your manner; & you are not so kind as you used to be.

It is for you to give the Orders & if they are bungled — except for the King, the Archbishop of Canterbury & the Speaker, you can sack anyone & everyone — Therefore with this terrific power you must combine urbanity, kindness and if possible Olympic calm. You used to quote:— 'On ne règne sur les âmes que par le calme' — I cannot bear that those who serve the Country and yourself should not love as well as admire and respect you —

Besides you won't get the best results by irascibility & rudeness. They will breed either dislike or a slave mentality — (Rebellion in War time being out of the question!)

Please forgive your loving devoted & watchful
Clemmie

I wrote this at Chequers last Sunday, tore it up, but here it is now.

YES, VIRGINIA, THERE IS A SANTA CLAUS

VIRGINIA O'HANLON to
EDITOR OF *THE SUN*
1897

In 1897, on the advice of her father, eight-year-old Virginia O'Hanlon wrote a short, inquisitive letter to the editor of New York's since-defunct newspaper *The Sun*, in which she sought confirmation of Santa Claus's existence. The paper's editor, Francis P. Church, soon replied to Virginia's letter by way of an editorial, titled *Is There a Santa Claus?*, which went on to become, and in fact remains to this day, the most reprinted English-language editorial in history, and which has since spawned numerous adaptations.

Virginia herself went on to become a teacher and as a result of her innocent question received fan mail for much of her life. She passed away in 1971, aged 81.

Dear Editor,

I am eight years old. Some of my little friends say there is no Santa Claus. Papa says "If you see it in the Sun it's so." Please tell me the truth, is there a Santa Claus?

Virginia O'Hanlon.
115 W.95th St

VIRGINIA, your little friends are wrong. They have been affected by the skepticism of a skeptical age. They do not believe except they see. They think that nothing can be which is not comprehensible by their little minds. All minds, Virginia, whether they be men's or children's, are little. In this great universe of ours man is a mere insect, an ant, in his intellect, as compared with the boundless world about him, as measured by the intelligence capable of grasping the whole of truth and knowledge.

Yes, VIRGINIA, there is a Santa Claus. He exists as certainly as love and generosity and devotion exist, and you know that they abound and give to your life its highest beauty and joy. Alas! how dreary would be the world if there were no Santa Claus. It would be as dreary as if there were no VIRGINIAS. There would be no childlike faith then, no poetry, no romance to make tolerable this existence. We should have no enjoyment, except in sense and sight. The eternal light with which childhood fills the world would be extinguished.

Not believe in Santa Claus! You might as well not believe in fairies! You might get your papa to hire men to watch in all the chimneys on Christmas Eve to catch Santa Claus, but even if they did not see Santa Claus coming down, what would that prove? Nobody sees Santa Claus, but that is no sign that there is no Santa Claus. The most real things in the world are those that neither children nor men can see. Did you ever see fairies dancing on the lawn? Of course not, but that's no proof that they are not there. Nobody can conceive or imagine all the wonders there are unseen and unseeable in the world.

You may tear apart the baby's rattle and see what makes the noise inside, but there is a veil covering the unseen world which not the strongest man, nor even the united strength of all the strongest men that ever lived, could tear apart. Only faith, fancy, poetry, love, romance, can push aside that curtain and view and picture the supernal beauty and glory beyond. Is it all real? Ah, VIRGINIA, in all this world there is nothing else real and abiding.

No Santa Claus! Thank GOD! he lives, and he lives forever. A thousand years from now, Virginia, nay, ten times ten thousand years from now, he will continue to make glad the heart of childhood.

I HAVE JUST WRITTEN
YOU A LONG LETTER

ALFRED D. WINTLE to
EDITOR OF *THE TIMES*
February 6th, 1946

Lieutenant Colonel Alfred
D. Wintle was opinionated,
brave, comical, intelligent
and, most importantly,
hugely entertaining – a
true "character". He once
attempted to escape a
hospital dressed as a
female nurse in order to
rejoin the war effort, but his
monocle gave him away; as
a prisoner of war in France
during World War II he
went on hunger strike for
a fortnight to protest his
prison guards' "slovenly"
appearance; years later,
post-war, he actually took
control of a train when
he realised there weren't
enough first-class seats,
refusing to leave the driver's
cab until the situation was
rectified. In 1958 he made
history by winning, *without
a lawyer*, a three-year legal
battle against a dishonest
solicitor that ended in the
House of Lords. The stories
are endless.

In 1946 he wrote this letter
to *The Times*. It has been
admired and preserved at
their offices ever since, and
with good reason.

From Lt. Col. A.D. Wintle.
The Royal Dragoons
Cavalry Club
127 Piccadilly W.1.

To the Editor of The Times.

Sir,

I have just written you a long letter.

On reading it over, I have thrown it into the waste paper basket.

Hoping this will meet with your approval,

I am
    Sir
Your obedient Servant

(Signed)

6 Feb '46

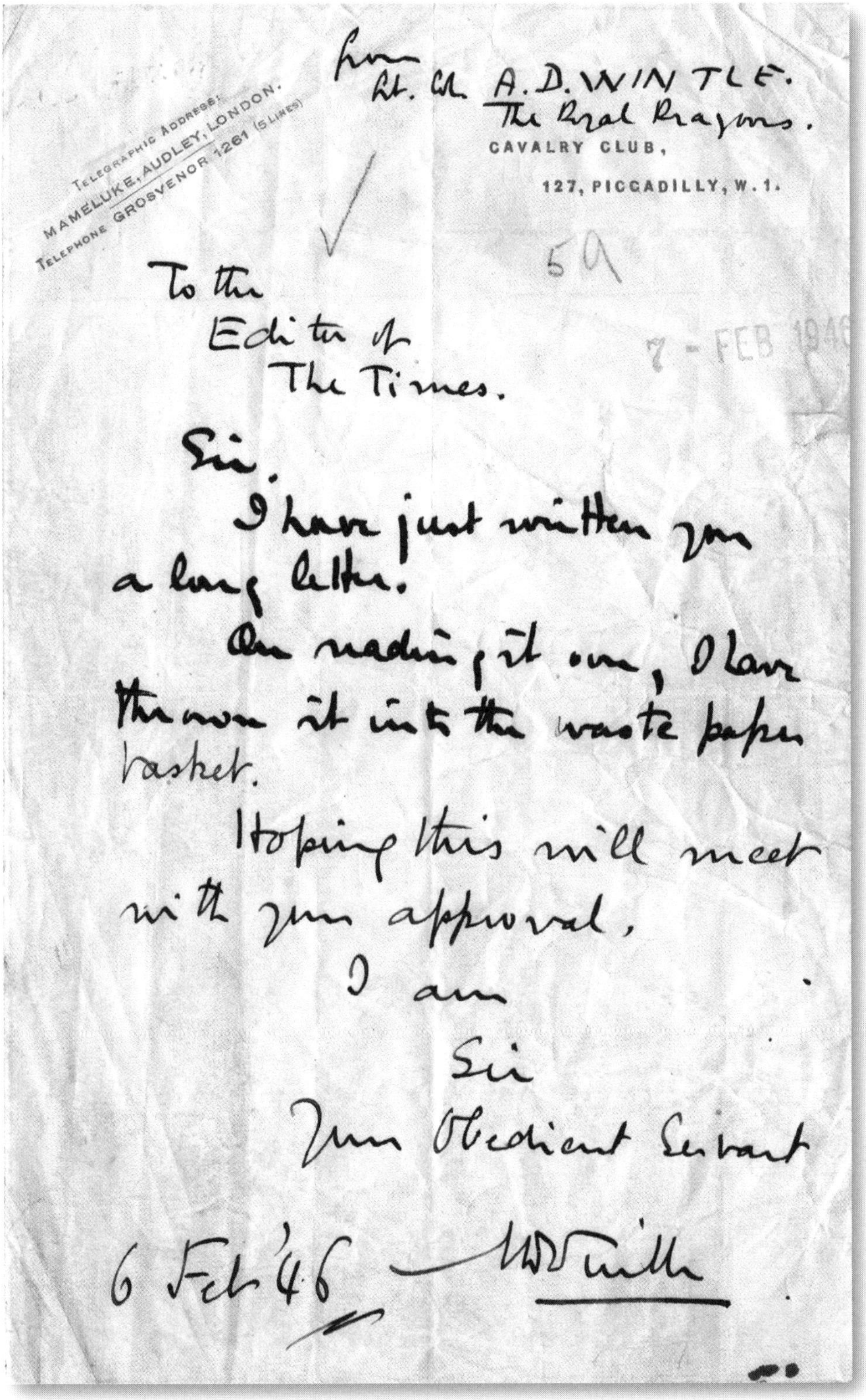

59

7 - FEB 1946

To the
Editor of
The Times.

Sir,

I have just written you a long letter.

On reading it over, I have thrown it into the waste paper basket.

Hoping this will meet with your approval,

I am

Sir

Your Obedient Servant

6 Feb '46   A.D. Wintle

SWEETHEART COME

EMMA HAUCK to MARK
HAUCK
1909

On February 7th 1909, a
30-year-old mother of two by
the name of Emma Hauck was
admitted to the psychiatric
hospital at the University of
Heidelberg in Germany, having
recently been diagnosed
with dementia praecox – a
mental disorder now known
as schizophrenia. The outlook
improved briefly and a month
later she was discharged, only
to be readmitted within weeks
as her condition deteriorated
further. Sadly, the downturn
continued and in August of that
year, with her illness deemed
"terminal" and rehabilitation
no longer an option, Hauck
was transferred to Wiesloch
Asylum, the facility in which
she would pass away 11 years
later.

It was around this time that
a harrowing collection of
letters were discovered
in the archives of the
Heidelberg hospital, all written
obsessively in Emma's hand
during her second stay at
the clinic in 1909, at a time
when reports indicate she
was relentlessly speaking of
her family. Each desperate
letter is directed to her absent
husband, Mark, and every
page is thick with overlapping
text. Some are so condensed
as to be illegible; some read
"Herzensschatzi komm"
("Sweetheart come") over and
over; others simply repeat
the plea, "komm komm
komm," ("come come come")
thousands of times.

None were sent.

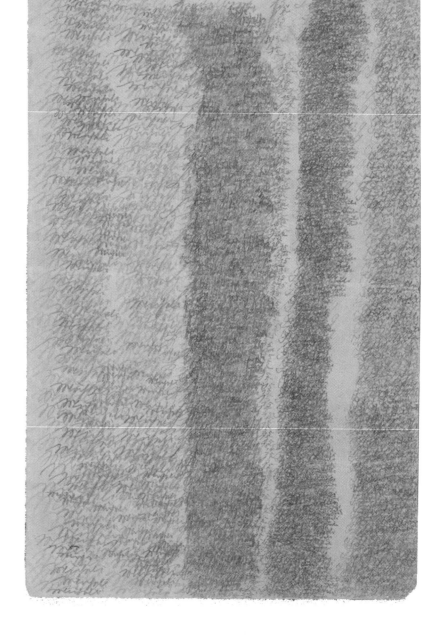

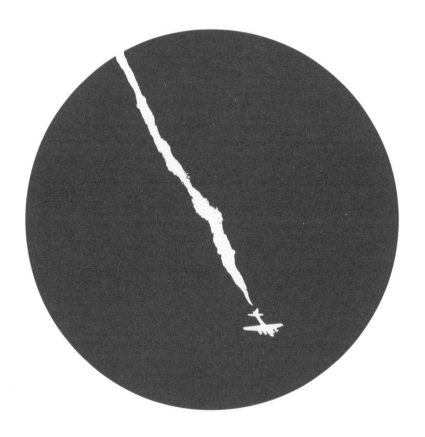

AVENGE MY DEATH

MASANOBU KUNO to HIS
CHILDREN
May 23rd, 1945

On the evening of May
23rd 1945, in the Japanese
town of Chiran, Masanobu
Kuno sat down and hand-
wrote this farewell letter
to his five-year-old son,
Masanori, and two-year-old
daughter, Kiyoko; the next
day he proudly boarded his
explosive-laden aircraft,
took to the skies, and
deliberately flew his plane
into an Allied warship
as part of the Battle of
Okinawa. Captain Kuno's
suicidal tactics weren't
unique in the 1940s – he was
just one of approximately
4,000 *kamikaze* pilots who
chose to sacrifice their
lives in such a way during
World War II on behalf of
the Japanese population,
and it certainly was an
effective form of attack:
kamikazes were responsible
for the deaths of thousands
of Allied troops during the
war and the destruction of
dozens of warships.

Dear Masanori and Kiyoko,

Even though you can't see me, I'll always be watching you. When you grow up,
follow the path you like and become a fine Japanese man and woman. Do not envy
the fathers of others. Your father will become a god and watch you two closely.
Both of you, study hard and help out your mother with work. I can't be your
horse to ride, but you two be good friends. I am a cheerful person who flew a large
bomber and finished off all the enemy. Please be an unbeatable person like your
father and avenge my death.

From Father

DON'T TOUCH HIS
HAIR

THREE ELVIS PRESLEY
FANS to US PRESIDENT
DWIGHT D. EISENHOWER
1958

On March 24th 1958, on
what was named "Black
Monday" by many of his
distraught followers,
22-year-old Elvis Presley
– King of Rock 'n' Roll and
still to this day one of the
most famous entertainers
on earth – was inducted into
the US Army. Worse still, he
was to be stationed many
miles away, in Germany,
where he would stay until
being discharged two years
later. Naturally, Presley's
fans became consumed
with panic and spent much
of their time speculating
about his future, some
even aiming for the top by
sending urgent mail to the
White House in an effort to
keep him away from harm.
This letter is just one of
thousands sent to President
Eisenhower in 1958 by three
female fans seemingly
resigned to their idol's US
Army induction, but not to
suspected changes to his
physical appearance.

Box 755
Noxon, Mont

Dear President Eisenhower,

My girlfriend's and I are writting all the way from Montana, We think its bad enough to send Elvis Presley in the Army, but if you cut his side burns off we will just die! You don't no how we fell about him, I really don't see why you have to send him in the Army at all, but we beg you please please don't give him a G.I. hair cut, oh please please don't! If you do we will just about die!

Elvis Presley Lovers

Linda Kelly
Sherry Bane
Mickie Mattson

Presley
Presley
IS OUR CRY
P-R-E-S-L-E-Y

Box 755
Noxon, Mont.

Dear President Eisenhower,

My girlfriends and I are writting all the way from Montana. We think its bad enough to send Elvis Presley in the Army, but if you cut his side burns off we will just die! You don't no how we fell about him. I really don't see why you have to send him in the Army at all, but we beg you please please don't give him a G.I. hair cut, oh please please don't! If you do we will just about die!

Presley
Presley
IS OUR CRY
P-R-E-S-L-E-Y

E. P.
lover

Elvis Presley
Lovers

Linda Kelly
Sherry Bare
Micke Mattson

TO: MY WIDOW

ROBERT SCOTT to
KATHLEEN SCOTT
1912

On January 17th 1912,
following years of
preparation, British explorer
Robert Falcon Scott and
his four team members
reached the South Pole
– an incredible feat that
was quickly overshadowed
upon arrival by the news
that the race had already
been won four weeks
earlier by a Norwegian
expedition led by Roald
Amundsen. Understandably
demoralised and tired, Scott
and his team soon began
their 800-mile journey
home. A month later, with
just over half of the return
journey still to go, one of the
men, Edgar Evans, passed
away; a month after his
death, another man died.
The rest soon followed. The
bodies and possessions
of Scott and his men were
discovered on November
12th 1912. It is believed
that the final three, Scott
included, perished on March
29th.

Over the course of his
final days, Scott, fearing
the worst, wrote this
heartbreaking letter to his
"widow" and two-year-old
son.

To: My widow

Dearest darling — we are in a very tight corner and I have doubts of pulling through — In our short lunch hours I take advantage of a very small measure of warmth to write letters preparatory to a possible end — the first is naturally to you on whom my thoughts mostly dwell waking or sleeping — If anything happens to me I shall like you to know how much you have meant to me and that pleasant recollections are with me as I depart —

I should like you to take what comfort you can from these facts also — I shall not have suffered any pain but leave the world fresh from harness and full of good health and vigour — this is dictated already, when provisions come to an end we simply stop where we are within easy distance of another depot. Therefore you must not imagine a great tragedy — we are very anxious of course and have been for weeks but on splendid physical condition and our appetites compensate for all discomfort. The cold is biting and sometimes angering but here again the hot food which drives it forth is so wonderfully enjoyable that we would scarcely be without it.

We have gone down hill a good deal since I wrote the above. Poor Titus Oates has gone — he was in a bad state — the rest of us keep going and imagine we have a chance to get through but the cold weather doesn't let up at all — we are now only 20 miles from a depot but we have very little food or fuel.

Well dear heart I want you to take the whole thing very sensibly as I am sure you will — the boy will be your comfort I had looked forward to helping you to bring him up but it is a satisfaction to feel that he is safe with you. I think both he and you ought to be specially looked after by the country for which after all we have given our lives with something of spirit which makes for example — I am writing letters on this point in the end of this book after this. Will you send them to their various destinations?

I must write a little letter for the boy if time can be found to be read when he grows up — dearest that you know cherish no sentimental rubbish about remarriage — when the right man comes to help you in life you ought to be your happy self again — I hope I shall be a good memory certainly the end is nothing for you to be ashamed of and I like to think that the boy will have a good start in parentage of which he may be proud.

Dear it is not easy to write because of the cold — 70 degrees below zero and nothing but the shelter of our tent — you know I have loved you, you know my thoughts must have constantly dwelt on you and oh dear me you must know that quite the worst aspect of this situation is the thought that I shall not see you again — The inevitable must be faced — you urged me to be leader of this party and I know you felt it would be dangerous — I've taken my place throughout, haven't I? God bless you my own darling I shall try and write more later — I go on across the back pages.

Since writing the above we have got to within 11 miles of our depot with one hot meal and two days cold food and we should have got through but have been held for four days by a frightful storm — I think the best chance has gone we have decided not to kill ourselves but to fight it to the last for that depot but in the fighting there is a painless end so don't worry. I have written letters on odd pages of this book — will you manage to get them sent? You see I am anxious for you and the boy's future — make the boy interested in natural history if you can, it is better than games — they encourage it at some schools — I know you will keep him out in the open air — try and make him believe in a God, it is comforting. Oh my dear my dear what dreams I have had of his future and yet oh my girl I know you will face it stoically — your portrait and the boy's will be found in my breast and the one in the little red Morocco case given by Lady Baxter — There is a piece of the Union flag I put up at the South Pole in my private kit bag together with Amundsen's black flag and other trifles — give a small piece of the Union flag to the King and a small piece to Queen Alexandra and keep the rest a poor trophy for you! — What lots and lots I could tell you of this journey. How much better it has been than lounging in comfort at home — what tales you would have for the boy but oh what a price to pay — to forfeit the sight of your dear dear face — Dear you will be good to the old mother. I write her a little line in this book. Also keep in with Ettie and the others— oh but you'll put on a strong face for the world — only don't be too proud to accept help for the boys sake — he ought to have a fine career and do something in the world. I haven't time to write to Sir Clements — tell him I thought much of him and never regretted him putting me in command of the Discovery Discovery – Give messages of farewell to Lady Baxter and Lady Sandhurst keep friends with them for both are dear women & to also both the Reginald Smiths

To My Widow

Dearest darling — We are in a very tight corner and I have doubts of pulling through — In one short lucid hour I take advantage of a very small measure of warmth to write letters preparatory to a possible end — The first is naturally to you on whom my thoughts mostly dwell waking or sleeping — If anything happens to me I shall like you to know how much you have meant to me and what pleasant recollections are with me as I depart —

I should like you to take what comfort you can from these facts also — I shall not have suffered any pain but leave the world fresh from harness & full of good health & vigour — this is decided already when provisions come to an end we simply stop unless we are within easy distance of another depôt. Therefore you must not imagine a great tragedy — we are very anxious of course & have been for weeks but our splendid physical condition and our appetites compensate for all discomfort. The cold is biting & sometimes angering but here again the

hot food which turns it forth in
so wonderfully enjoyable that one
would scarcely be without it.
We have gone down hill a good
deal since I wrote the above.
Poor Titus Oates has gone - he was
in a bad state. The rest of us
keep going and imagine we have
a chance to get through but the
cold weather doesn't let up at
all - We are now only 20 miles
from a depot but we have very little
food & fuel.

Well dear heart - I want you to take
the whole thing very sensibly as
I'm sure you will - The boy will
be your comfort - I had looked
forward to helping you to bring him
up but - & it is a satisfaction
to feel that he is safe with you
I think both he and you ought
to be specially looked after by the
country for which after all we
have given our lives with
something of spirit which makes
for example — I am writing

letter on this point in the end
of the book, will you read them
to their solemn declaration

- I must write a little letter for
the boy if time can be found
to be read when he grows up
the inherited vice from my side
of the family is indolence —
above all he must guard & you
most guard him against - that -
make him a strenuous man
I had to force myself into being
strenuous as you know - I had
always an inclination to be idle
My father was idle and it
brought much trouble

— Dearest, honour you know !
Cheerily no sentiment to get at it
about re marriage — When the
right man comes to help you in
life you ought to be quite
happy with again ———— I want
a very good man and - I
hope I shall be a good anyhow
Certainly the idea is nothing
for you to be ashamed of —

and I like to think that the boy will have a good start in his parentage of which he may be proud

Dear it is not easy to write because of the cold – 40° below zero and nothing but the shelter of our tent – You know I have loved you, you know my thoughts must have constantly dwelt on you and oh dear me you must know that quite the worst aspect of this situation is the thought that I shall not see you again – The inevitable must be faced – You urged me to be leader of this party and I know you felt it would be dangerous – I've taken my place throughout haven't I? God bless you my own darling I shall try & write more later – I go on across the back pages

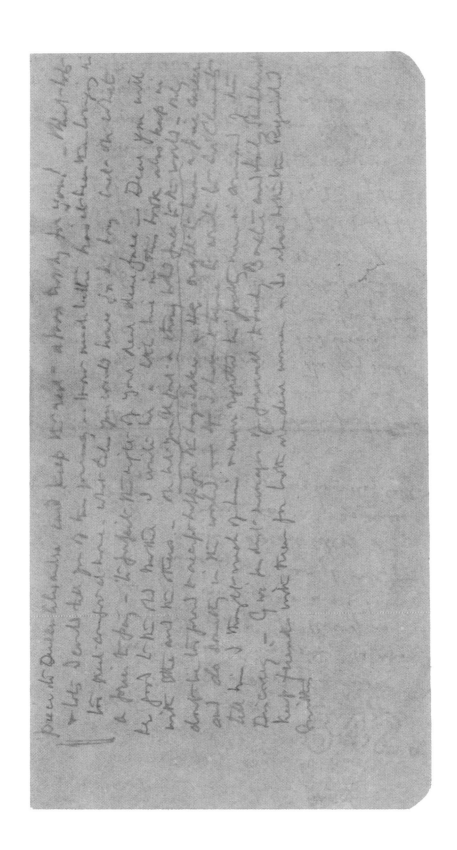

Jack Kerouac
1418½ Clouser St
Orlando, Fla

Dear Marlon

I'm praying that you'll buy ON THE ROAD and make a movie of it. Dont worry about structure, I know how to compress and re-arrange the plot a bit to give perfectly acceptable movie-type structure: making it into one all-inclusive trip instead of the several voyages coast-to-coast in the book, one vast round trip from New York to Denver to Frisco to Mexico to New Orleans to New York again. I visualize the beautiful shots could be made with the camera on the front seat of the car showing the road (day and night) unwinding into the windshield, as Sal and Dean yak. I wanted you to play the part because Dean (as you know) is no dopey hotrodder but a real intelligent (in fact Jesuit) Irishman. You play Dean and I'll play Sal (Warner Bros. mentioned I play Sal) and I'll show you how Dean acts in real life, you couldnt possibly imagine it without seeing a good imitation. Fact, we can go visit him in Frisco, or have him come down to L.A. still a real frantic cat but nowadays settled down with his final wife saying the Lord's Prayer with his kiddies at night...as you'll seen when you read the play BEAT GENERATION. All I want out of this is to be able to establish myself and my mother a trust fund for life, so I can really go roaming around the world writing about Japan, India, France etc. ...I want to be free to write what comes out of my head & free to feed my buddies when they're hungry & not worry about my mother.

Incidentally, my next novel is THE SUBTERRANEANS coming out in N.Y. next March and is about a love affair between a white guy and a colored girl and very hep story. Some of the characters in it you knew in the Village (Stanley Gould? etc.) It easily could be turned into a play, easier than ON THE ROAD.

What I wanta do is re-do the theater and the cinema in America, give it a spontaneous dash, remove pre-conceptions of "situation" and let people rave on as they do in real life. That's what the play is: no plot in particular, no "meaning" in particular, just the way people are. Everything I write I do in the spirit where I imagine myself an Angel returned to the earth seeing it with sad eyes as it is. I know you approve of these ideas, & incidentally the new Frank Sinatra show is based on "spontaneous" too, which is the only way to come on anyway, whether in show business or life. The French movies of the 30's are still far superior to ours because the French really let their actors come on and the writers didnt quibble with some preconceived notion of how intelligent the movie audience is, the talked soul from soul and everybody understood at once. I want to make great French Movies in America, finally, when I'm rich ...American Theater & Cinema at present is an outmoded Dinosaur that aint mutated along with the best in American Literature.

If you really want to go ahead, make arrangements to see me in New York when next you come, or if you're going to Florida here I am, but what we should do is talk about this because I prophesy that it's going to be the beginning of something real great. I'm bored nowadays and I'm looking around for something to do in the void, anyway——writing novels is getting too easy, same with plays, I wrote the play in 24 hours.

Come on now, Marlon, put up your dukes and write!

Sincerely, later, *Jack Kerouac*

PUT UP YOUR DUKES AND WRITE!

JACK KEROUAC to MARLON BRANDO
Circa 1957

Late 1957, with his recently published novel attracting near-universal praise from critics, *Beat Generation* author Jack Kerouac aimed for the sky and wrote a passionate letter to Hollywood heavyweight Marlon Brando in an effort to bring his work to the big screen. The book in question was *On the Road*, a sprawling, autobiographical road novel that chronicles the travels and friendship of Sal Paradise and Dean Moriarty, the alter-egos of Kerouac and fellow writer Neal Cassady, respectively. Desperate to see it filmed, Kerouac wanted Brando to first buy the rights to the movie adaptation and then play the part of Moriarty opposite Kerouac's Sal. Sadly for him, Brando never responded. Jack Kerouac passed away 12 years later. *On the Road* was finally released in cinemas in 2012.

```
                                              Noank
                                              Connecticut

                      The Square House
                      Church Street


        Dear GPP

                There are some things which should be writ before
        we are married -- things we have talked over before -- most of
        them.

                You must know again my reluctance to marry, my
        feeling that I shatter thereby chances in work which means most
        to me.  I feel the move just now as foolish as anything I
        could do.   I know there may be compensations but have no heart
        to look ahead.

                On our  life together I want you to understand I
        shall not hold you to any midaevil code of faithfulness to me
        nor shall I consider myself bound to you similarly.   If we can
        be honest I think the difficulties which arise may best be avoided
        should you or I become interested deeply (or inpassing) in anyone
        else.

                Please let us not interfere with the others' work or
        play, nor let the world see our private joys or disagreements.
        In this connection I may have to keep some place where I can go to
        be myself, now and then, for I cannot guarantee to endure at all
        times the confinement of even an attractive cage.

                I must exact a cruel promise and that is you will let
        me go in a year if we find no happiness together.

                I will try to do my best in every way and give you that
        part  of me you know and seem to want.

                                              A.E.
```

YOU MUST KNOW AGAIN MY RELUCTANCE TO MARRY

AMELIA EARHART to GEORGE PUTNAM
February 7th, 1931

In May 1932, 34-year-old pioneering aviatrix Amelia Earhart became the first woman to fly solo across the Atlantic Ocean following a 14-hour, 56-minute flight from Newfoundland to Northern Ireland in her single-engine Lockheed Vega 5B – just one of many aviation records that she broke during a lifetime fuelled by ambition. Earhart was fiercely independent and wanted nothing to block her life's path, marriage included. A year before that historic flight, on the morning of their wedding, she wrote a letter to her publicist and fiancé, George Putnam – whom she loved dearly – and reiterated her "reluctance to marry".

The marriage was a happy one, but brief. Tragically, in 1937, Earhart disappeared over the Pacific Ocean during an attempt to circumnavigate the globe. Her body has never been found.

I'D LIKE TO CONTINUE TO BE A GOOD SOLDIER

EDDIE SLOVIK to GENERAL
DWIGHT D. EISENHOWER
December 9th, 1944

In October 1944, while
stationed in France during
World War II, 24-year-old
Pvt. Eddie Slovik became
one of over 20,000 soldiers
to desert the US Army after
finding himself frozen with
fear whilst under attack,
unable to serve on the
front line. A request to be
reassigned had also been
denied. Three months later,
shortly after 10 a.m. on
January 31st 1945, Slovik
was killed by firing squad
for desertion – the only
US soldier to be executed
for such a crime since the
1860s. Two months before
his death, fearing the worst,
Slovik wrote a desperate
letter to General Dwight
D. Eisenhower and begged
for forgiveness. His plea
fell on deaf ears, however,
and future US President
Eisenhower soon ordered
his execution.

Dear General Eisenhowser:

I, Private Eddie D. Slovik, ASN 36896415, was convicted on the 11th day of November year 1944 Armistice Day by General Court Martial to be shot to death for desertion of the United States Army.

The time of my conviction or before my conviction I had no intentions of deserting the army whatsoever. For if I intended too I wouldnt have given or surrendered myself as I did. I have nothing against the United States army whatsoever, I merely wanted a transfer from the line. I asked my CO when I came back if their was a possible chance of my being transferred cause I feared hazardars duty to myself, and because of my nerves. I'll admit I have some awfull bad nerves, which no doubt in my mind we all have. I was refused this transfer.

I must tell you more about my past. I assume you have my records of my past criminal life in my younger stage of life. After being released from jail I was put on a two year parole after spending five years in jail. In them two years I was on parole I got myself a good job cause I was in class 4-F, the army didn't want anything to do with me at the time. So after five months out of jail I decided to get married which I did. I have a swell wife now and a good home. After being married almost a year and a half I learned to stay away from bad company which was the cause of my being in jail. Then the draft came. I didn't have to come to the army when they called me. I could of went back to jail. But I was sick of being locked up all my life so I came to the army. When I went down to the draft board, I was told that the only reason they were taking a chance on me in the army was cause I got married and had a good record after being out of jail almost two years. To my knowledge sir I have a good record in the past two years. I also have a good record as a soldier up to the time I got in this trouble. I tried my best to do what the army wanted me to do till I first ran away or should I say left the company.

I don't believe I ran away the first time as I stated in my first confession. I came over to France as a replacement, and when the enemy started to shelling us I got scared and nerves that I couldn't move out of my fox hole. I guess I never did give myself the chance to get over my first fear of shelling. The next day their wasn't any American troops around so I turned myself over to the Canadian MPs. They in turn were trying to get in touch with my outfit about me. I guess it must have taken them six weeks to catch up with the American troops. Well sir when I was turned over to my outfit I tried to explain to my CO just what took place, and what had happened to me. Then I asked for a transfer. Which was refused. Then I wrote my confession. I was then told that if I would go back to the line they would distroy my confession, however if I refused to go back on the line they would half to hold it against me which they did.

How can I tell you how humbley sorry I am for the sins I've committed. I didn't realize at the time what I was doing, or what the word desertion meant. What it is like to be condemned to die. I beg of you deeply and sincerely for the sake of my dear wife and mother back home to have mercy on me. To my knowledge I have a good record since my marriage and as a soldier. I'd like to continue to be a good soldier.

Anxiously awaiting your reply, which I earnestly pray is favorable, God bless you and in your Work for victory:

I Remain Yours for Victory,

Pvt. Eddie D. Slovik

THE GALILEAN MOONS

GALILEO GALILEI to
LEONARDO DONATO
1610

According to the great Stephen Hawking, Italian physicist and astronomer Galileo Galilei was, more than any other person, "responsible for the birth of modern science". In 1609, having seen details of a very early telescope that had been constructed in the Netherlands, Galileo designed and built his own superior version that boasted far better magnification and which he subsequently used to make countless discoveries in the skies. In January 1610 he wrote a letter, the draft of which is shown here, to Leonardo Donato, Doge of Venice; in it he describes the instrument itself and then for the first time illustrates Jupiter's four largest moons, all of which he had just discovered.

Most Serene Prince.

Galileo Galilei most humbly prostrates himself before Your Highness, watching carefully, and with all spirit of willingness, not only to satisfy what concerns the reading of mathematics in the study of Padua, but to write of having decided to present to Your Highness a telescope ("Occhiale") that will be a great help in maritime and land enterprises. I assure you I shall keep this new invention a great secret and show it only to Your Highness. The telescope was made for the most accurate study of distances. This telescope has the advantage of discovering the ships of the enemy two hours before they can be seen with the natural vision and to distinguish the number and quality of the ships and to judge their strength and be ready to chase them, to fight them, or to flee from them; or, in the open country to see all details and to distinguish every movement and preparation.

Ser.mo Prncipe.

Galileo Galilei Humiliss.o Seruo della Ser:a V.a inuigilando assiduam.te, et co ogni spirito p potere nõ solam.te satisfare al carico che tiene della lettura di Matematica nello Studio di Padoua,

Si riuere dauere determinato di presentare al Ser.mo Prncipe l'Occhiale et A p essere di giouamento inestimabile p ogni negozio et impresa marittima o terrestre stima di tenere questo nuouo artifizio nel maggior segreto et solam.te a dispositione di S. Ser:a L'Occhiale conato dalle più recodite speculazioni di prospettiua hà il uantaggio di scoprire Legni et Vele dell'inimico p due hore et più di tempo prima ch' egli scuopra noi et distinguendo Il numero et la qualità dei Vasselli giudicare le sue forze ballestirsi alla caccia al combattimento o alla fuga, ò pure anco nella campagna aperta uedere et particularm.te distinguere ogni suo moto et preparamento.

Adi 7. di Genaio

Gioue si uedde così * * occi:

Adi 8 così ori: * * * *

era dig diretto et nõ retrogrado occi:

Adi 12. si uedde in tale costitutione * * *

Il 13 si ueddono uiciniss.e à Gioue 4 stelle * * * * ò meglio così

Adi 14 è nugolo

Il 15 * * * * * la pross.a à 4 era la minore la 4.a era distante dalla 3.a il doppio circa

Lo spatio delle 3 ocedetali nõ era maggiore del diametro di 4 et erano in linea retta.

4 long. 71·38 Lat. 1·13

THE BIRCH BARK LETTERS

GAVRILA POSENYA to
VARIOUS
Circa 1350

On July 26th 1951, in the historic Russian city of Novgorod, an archaeologist named Nina Fedorovna Akulova unearthed something incredible: a layer of birch bark onto which a personal letter had been carved, written in a largely unstudied form of an Old East Slavic language to be later named "Old Novgorodian". That particular note was determined to have been written *c.*1400 and is just one of over a thousand birch bark letters since discovered in the region by archaeologist Artemiy Artsikhovsky. Although many are personal letters and unremarkable in terms of subject matter, combined they offer a fascinating insight into the lives and language of East Slavs in centuries past and a better understanding of the Russian Middle Ages.

This particular letter was found in 1972 and has been dated to the mid-1300s.

поколоно ѿ гаврили ѿ посени ко зати моемоу ко горигори жи коумоу ко сестори моеи ко оулите чо би есте поихали во городо ко радости моеи а нашего солова не ѡставили да бого вамо радосте ми вашего солова вохи не ѡсотавимо

Translation:

Greeting from Gavrila Posenya to my brother-in-law, godfather Grigory and my sister Ulita. Would you not like to give me the pleasure of riding into the city, not leaving our word? God give you happiness. We all do not leave your word.

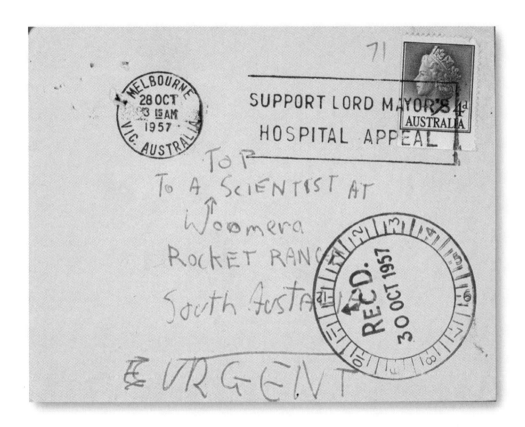

TO A TOP SCIENTIST

DENIS COX to A TOP
SCIENTIST
October 28th, 1957

In 1957, following the announcement
that the Soviets had trumped the US
with the successful launch of *Sputnik 1*,
Australian schoolboy Denis Cox sent this
urgent letter to the Royal Australian Air
Force's Rocket Range at Woomera, in an
attempt to enter Australia into the Space
Race. Much to Denis's dismay, his letter,
addressed "TO A TOP SCIENTIST" and
consisting of a basic rocket ship design

accompanied by instructions for engineers
to "put in other details", fell on deaf ears
until, 52 long years later, in 2009, Denis's
original letter and rocket ship made the
news after being featured on the website
of the National Archives of Australia. As
a result of the coverage, he finally got
a wonderful reply from the Australian
Department of Defence.

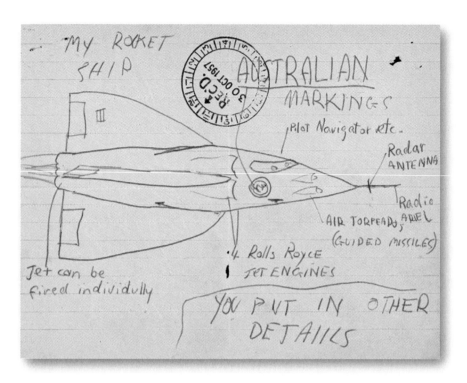

MY ROCKET
SHIP

AUSTRALIAN
MARKINGS

Pilot Navigator etc.

Radar
ANTENNA

Radio
ARIEL

AIR TORPEADO;
(GUIDED MISSILES)

4 Rolls Royce
JET ENGINES

Jet can be
fired individully

YOU PUT IN OTHER
DETAILS

PLEASE WRITE
ME A LETTER
BACK

HERE IS
A ROCKET
SHIP DESIGNED
BY
DENIS COX
26 CHUTE ST.
MORIALLOC
VICTORIA.

56/486. 26.
70.

Australian Government
Department of Defence
Defence Science and
Technology Organisation

Mr Denis Cox

28/8/09

Dear Mr Cox,

I would like to thank you for your letter we received on 20th Oct. 1957 regarding the design of your rocketship. I apologise for the late response to your letters. You will appreciate, that as you requested "A Top Scientist" that uses the "WOOMERA ROCKET RANGE" it took a little while for your letter to get to me and in addition, it took some time to provide due consideration to your ideas.

In any case, I have included a picture of our latest flight of a hypersonic vehicle under the HIFiRE Program, so that you may see that many of your designs have merit. The fins are a little smaller, and on our work, we haven't advanced sufficiently to put people on board, as you clearly indicated we should. Curiously enough though, people are still toying with the idea of combining rocket engines with turbines as suggested in your letter. These engines are now called Rocket Based Combined Cycle Engines and seem to work about as well as they did back in 1957! I am also quite interested in the shape of the fuselage, it actually shows a lot of merit!

I think that the most interesting statement you made in your letter was "YOU PUT IN OTHER DETAILS". You were clearly going to be an excellent Program Manager, by providing those that know best the freedom in the matter to get it right. Furthermore, you did have your priorities right as "AUSTRALIAN MARKINGS" are the most prominent feature of the design.

I remember as a boy designing rocket ships and planes at about the same time that you wrote your letter. I don't know why or how, but somehow I was lucky enough to get to a position where I now head a team that designs planes and engines that will soon fly at Mach 8, or around 9000km/hr. I am proud to tell you that these planes will have an "AUSTRALIAN MARKING" on them as you indicated they should have. My one hope is that we do a sufficiently good job that is worthy of the inspiration, dreams and hopes that you provided in your letter those many years ago.

Once again, thank you for your letter.

(Signed)

Allan Paul BSc PhD MEngSc
Research Leader Applied Hypersonics
Air Vehicles Division
DSTO-Brisbane

DEEP SICKNESS
SEIZED ME

LUCY THURSTON to MARY
THURSTON
October 29th, 1855

In October 1819, 23-year-
old schoolteacher Lucy
Thurston and her husband,
Asa, left their home in
Massachusetts to become
members of the first
expedition of Christian
missionaries to the Hawaiian
Islands. Their efforts were
welcomed and for the rest
of their lives they educated
the locals, helped build
schools and churches and
even translated the Bible.
In 1855, 36 years after
arriving, and by which time
they had five children,
Thurston developed cancer
and had no option but to
undergo a mastectomy to
remove her left breast,
an already distressing
procedure further worsened
by the fact that she was to
endure the operation wide-
awake, without any form of
anaesthetic. A month later
she wrote a letter to her
daughter and described the
unimaginably harrowing
experience. Thankfully, the
procedure was a success:
Thurston lived for another
21 years.

October 29, 1855

My Dear Daughter Mary:

I have hitherto forborne to write respecting the surgical operation I experienced
in September, from an expectation that you would be with us so soon. That is now
given up; so I proceed to give a circumstantial account of those days of peculiar
discipline. At the end of the General Meeting in June your father returned to
Kailua, leaving me at Honolulu, in Mr. Taylor's family, under Dr. Ford's care. Dr.
Hillebrand was called in counsel. During the latter part of August they decided
on the use of the knife. Mr. Thurston was sent for to come down according to
agreement should such be the result. I requested him to bring certain things
which I wished, in case I no more returned to Kailua. Tremendous gales of wind
were now experienced. One vessel was wrecked within sight of Kailua. Another,
on her way there, nearly foundered, and returned only to be condemned. In vain
we looked for another conveyance. Meantime, the tumor was rapidly altering. It
had nearly approached the surface, exhibiting a dark spot. Should it become an
open ulcer, the whole system would become vitiated with its malignity. Asa said
he should take no responsibility of waiting the arrival of his father. Persis felt the
same. Saturday P.M., the doctors met in consultation, and advised an immediate
operation. The next Thursday (12th of September), ten o'clock A.M., was the
hour fixed upon. In classifying, the Dr. placed this among "capital operations."
Both doctors advised not to take chloroform because of my having had the
paralysis. I was glad they allowed me the use of my senses. Persis offered me her
parlor, and Asa his own new bridal room for the occasion. But I preferred the
retirement and quietude of the grass-thatched cottage. Thomas, with all his effects
moved out of it into a room a few steps off. The house was thoroughly cleaned
and prettily fitted up. One lady said it seemed as though it had been got up by
magic. Monday, just at night, Dr. Ford called to see that all was in readiness. There
were two lounges trimmed, one with white, the other with rose-colored mosquito
netting. There was a reclining Chinese chair, a table for the instruments, a wash-
stand with wash bowls, sponges, and pails of water. There was a frame with two
dozen towels, and a table of choice stimulants and restoratives. One more table with
the Bible and hymn book.

That night I spent in the house alone for the first time. The family had all retired
for the night. In the still hour of darkness, I long walked back and forth in the
capacious door-yard. Depraved, diseased, helpless, I yielded myself up entirely
to the will, the wisdom, and the strength of the Holy One. At peace with myself,
with earth, and with heaven, I calmly laid my head upon my pillow and slept
refreshingly. A bright day opened upon us. My feelings were natural, cheerful,
elevated. I took the Lord at his own word: "As the day is, so shall thy strength
be." There with an unwavering heart, I leaned for strength and support. Before
dressing for the occasion, I took care to call on Ellen, who had then an infant a
week old by her side. It was a cheerful call, made in a common manner, she not
being acquainted with the movements of the day. I then prepared myself for the
professional call. Dr. Judd was early on the ground. I went with him to Asa's room,

where with Asa and Sarah we sat and conversed till other medical men rode up. Dr. Judd rose to go out. I did the same. Asa said: "You had better not go, you are not wanted yet." I replied: "I wish to be among the first on the ground, to prevent its coming butt end first." On reaching my room. Dr. Ford was there. He introduced me to Dr. Hoffman of Honolulu, and to Dr. Brayton of an American Naval ship, then in port. The instruments were then laid out upon the table. Strings were prepared for tying arteries. Needles threaded for sewing up the wound. Adhesive plasters were cut into strips, bandages produced, and the Chinese chair placed by them in the front double door. Everything was now in readiness, save the arrival of one physician. All stood around the house or in the piazza. Dr. Ford, on whom devolved the responsibility, paced the door-yard. I stood in the house with others, making remarks on passing occurrences. At length I was invited to sit. I replied: "As I shall be called to lie a good while, I had rather now stand." Dr. Brayton, as he afterwards said, to his *utter astonishment* found that the lady to be operated on was standing in their midst.

Dr. Hillebrand arrived. It was a signal for action. Persis and I stepped behind a curtain. I threw off my cap and dressing gown, and appeared with a white flowing skirt, with the white bordered shawl purchased in 1818, thrown over my shoulders. I took my seat in the chair. Persis and Asa stood at my right side; Persis to hand me restoratives; Asa to use his strength, if self-control were wanting. Dr. Judd stood at my left elbow for the same reason; my shawl was thrown off, exhibiting my left arm, breast and side, perfectly bare. Dr. Ford showed me how I must hold back my left arm to the greatest possible extent, with my hand taking a firm hold of the arm of my chair: with my right hand, I took hold of the right arm, with my feet I pressed against the foot of the chair. Thus instructed, and everything in readiness. Dr. Ford looked me full in the face, and with great firmness asked: "Have you made up your mind to have it cut out?" "Yes, sir." "Are you ready now?" "Yes, sir; but let me know when you begin, that I may be able to bear it. Have you your knife in that hand now?" He opened his hand that I might see it, saying, "I am going to begin now." Then came a gash long and deep, first on one side of my breast, then on the other. Deep sickness seized me, and deprived me of my breakfast. This was followed by extreme faintness. My sufferings were no longer local. There was a general feeling of agony throughout the whole system. I felt, every inch of me, as though flesh was failing. During the whole operation, I was enabled to have entire self control over my person, and over my voice. Persis and Asa were devotedly employed in sustaining me with the use of cordials, ammonia, bathing my temples, etc. I myself fully intended to have seen the thing done. But on recollection, every glimpse I happened to have, was the doctor's right hand completely covered with blood, up to the very wrist. He afterwards told me, that at one time the blood from an artery flew into his eyes, so that he could not see. It was nearly an hour and a half that I was beneath his hand, in cutting out the entire breast, in cutting out the glands beneath the arm, in tying the arteries, in absorbing the blood, in sewing up the wound, in putting on the adhesive plasters, and in applying the bandage.

The views and feelings of that hour are now vivid to my recollection. It was during the cutting process that I began to talk. The feeling that I had reached a different point from those by whom I was surrounded, inspired me with freedom. It was thus that I expressed myself. "It has been a great trial to my feelings that Mr. Thurston is not here. But it is not necessary. So many friends, and Jesus Christ besides. His left hand is underneath my head, His right hand sustains and embraces me. I am willing to suffer. I am willing to die. I am not afraid of death. I am not afraid of hell. I anticipate a blessed immortality. Tell Mr. Thurston my peace flows like a river.

"Upward I lift mine eyes.
From God is all my aid:
The God that built the skies,
And earth and nature made.
God is the tower
To which I fly;
His grace is nigh
In every hour."

God disciplines me, but He does it with a gentle hand. At one time I said, "I know you will bear with me." Asa replied, "I think it is you that have to bear from us."

The doctor, after removing the entire breast, said to me, "I want to cut yet more, round under your arm." I replied, "Do just what you want to do, only tell me when, so that I can bear it." One said the wound had the appearance of being more than a foot long. Eleven arteries were taken up. After a beginning had been made in sewing it up, Persis said: "Mother, the doctor makes as nice a seam as you ever made in your life." "Tell me, Persis, when he is going to put in the needle, so that I can bear it." "Now—now—now," etc. "Yes, tell me. That is a good girl." Ten stitches were taken, two punctures at every stitch, one on either side. When the whole work was done, Dr. Ford and Asa removed my chair to the back side of the room, and laid me on the lounge. Dr. Brayton came to my side, and taking me by the hand said: "There is not one in a thousand who would have borne it as you have done."

Up to this time, everything is fresh to my recollection. Of that afternoon and night, I only remember that the pain in the wound was intense and unremitting, and that I felt willing to be just in the circumstances in which I was placed. I am told that Dr. Ford visited me once in the afternoon, and once in the night, that Persis and Asa took care of me, that it seemed as if I suffered nearly as much as during the operation, and that my wound was constantly wet with cold water. I have since told Persis, that "I thought they kept me well drugged with paregoric." He replied, "We did not give you a drop." "Why then do I not remember what took place?" "Because you had so little life about you." By morning light the pain had ceased. Surgeons would understand the expression, that the wound healed by a "union of the first intention."

The morning again brought to my mind a recollection of events. I was lying on my lounge, feeble and helpless. I opened my eyes and saw the light of day. Asa was crossing the room bearing a Bible before him. He sat down near my couch, read a portion, and then prayed.

For several days, I had long sinking turns of several hours. Thursday night, the third of suffering, Thomas rode nearly two miles to the village for the Dr., once in the fore part of the evening, again at eleven. At both times he came. At two o'clock he unexpectedly made his third call that night. It was at his second call that he said to Persis: "In the morning make your mother some chicken soup. She has starved long enough." (They had been afraid of fever.) Persis immediately aroused Thomas, had a chicken caught, a fire made, and a soup under way that same midnight hour. The next day, Friday, I was somewhat revived by the use of wine and soup. In the afternoon, your father arrived. It was the first time since the operation, that I felt as if I had life enough to endure the emotion of seeing him. He left Kailua the same day the operation was performed. A vessel was passing in sight of Kailua. He rowed out in a canoe and was received on board. Hitherto, Persis, Asa and Thomas, had been my only nurses both by day and by night. The doctor gave directions that no one enter the room, but those that took care of me.

For weeks my debility was so great, that I was fed with a teaspoon, like an infant. Many dangers were apprehended. During one day, I saw a duplicate of every person and every thing that my eye beheld. Thus it was, sixteen years before, when I had the paralysis. Three weeks after the operation, your father for the first time, very slowly raised me to the angle of 45 degrees. It seemed as if it would have taken away my sense. It was about this time that I perceptibly improved from day to day, so much so, that in four weeks from my confinement, I was lifted into a carriage. Then I rode with your father almost every day. As he was away from his field of labor, and without any family responsibilities, he was entirely devoted to me. It was of great importance to me, that he was at liberty and in readiness ever to read simple interesting matter to me, to enliven and to cheer, so that time never passed heavily. After remaining with me six weeks, he returned to Kailua, leaving me with the physician and with our children.

In a few weeks, Mother, Mr. Taylor, Persis, Thomas, Lucy, Mary, and George bade farewell to Asa and Sarah, and to little Robert, their black-eyed baby boy. Together we passed over the rough channels up to the old homestead. Then, your father instead of eating his solitary meals, had his family board enlarged for the accommodation of three generations.

And here is again your mother, engaged in life's duties, and life's warfare. Fare thee well. Be one with us in knowledge, sympathy, and love, though we see thee not, and when sickness prostrates, we feel not thy hand upon our brow.

Your loving Mother.

HE'S HERE, LIVING AND VIVID AND UNFORGETTABLE FOREVER

STEWART STERN to THE WINSLOWS
October 12th, 1955

On September 30th 1955, less than a month before audiences were wowed by his iconic performance as Jim Stark in *Rebel Without a Cause*, 24-year-old James Dean passed away shortly after his Porsche collided with another car at high speed. Nine days later his funeral took place in Fairmount, not far from the farm on which he was raised by his aunt and uncle, Ortense and Marcus Winslow. Thousands attended the service. A few days later, as millions continued to mourn his untimely death, this stunning letter of condolence was sent to the Winslows by Stewart Stern, a friend of Dean's and the man who wrote the screenplay for *Rebel Without a Cause*.

Hollywood 46, California
1372 Miller Drive
12 October, 1955

Dear Marcus and Mrs. Winslow:

I shall never forget that silent town on that particular sunny day. And I shall never forget the care with which people set their feet down — so carefully on the pavements — as if the sound of a suddenly scraped heel might disturb the sleep of a boy who slept soundly. And the whispering. Do you remember one voice raised beyond a whisper in all those reverential hours of goodbye? I don't. A whole town struck silent, a whole town with love filling its throat, a whole town wondering why there had been so little time in which to give the love away.

Gandhi once said that if all those doomed people at Hiroshima had lifted their faces to the plane that hovered over them and if they had sent up a single sigh of spiritual protest, the pilot would not have dropped his bomb. That may or may not be. But I am sure, I am certain, I know — that the great wave of warmth and affection that swept upward from Fairmount has wrapped itself around that irresistible phantom securely and forever.

Nor shall I forget the land he grew on or the stream he fished, or the straight, strong, gentle people whom he loved to talk about into the nights when he was away from them. His great-grandma whose eyes have seen half of America's history, his grandparents, his father, his treasured three of you — four generations for the coiling of a spring — nine decades of living evidence of seed and turning earth and opening kernel. It was a solid background and one to be envied. The spring, released, flung him into our lives and out again. He burned an unforgettable mark in the history of his art and changed it as surely as Duse, in her time, changed it.

A star goes wild in the places beyond air — a dark star born of coldness and invisible. It hits the upper edges of our atmosphere and look! It is seen! It flames and arcs and dazzles. It goes out in ash and memory. But its after-image remains in our eyes to be looked at again and again. For it was rare. And it was beautiful. And we thank God and nature for sending it in front of our eyes.

So few things blaze. So little is beautiful. Our world doesn't seem equipped to contain its brilliance too long. Ecstasy is only recognizable when one has experienced pain. Beauty only exists when set against ugliness. Peace is not appreciated without war ahead of it. How we wish that life could support only the good. But it vanishes when its opposite no longer exists as a setting. It is a white marble on unmelting snow. And Jimmy stands clear and unique in a world where much is synthetic and dishonest and drab. He came and rearranged our molecules.

I have nothing of Jim's — nothing to touch or look at except the dried mud that clung to my shoes — mud from the farm that grew him — and a single kernel of seed corn from your barn. I have nothing more than this and I want nothing more. There is no need to touch something he touched when I can still feel his hand on me. He gave me his faith, unquestioningly and trustfully — once when he said he would play in REBEL because he knew I wanted him to, and once when he tried to get LIFE to let me write his biography. He told me he felt I understood him and if LIFE refused to let me do the text for the pictures Dennis took, he would refuse to let the magazine do a spread on him at all. I managed to talk him out of that, knowing that LIFE had to use its own staff writers, but will never forget how I felt when he entrusted his life to me. And he gave me, finally, the gift of his art. He spoke my words and played my scenes better than any other actor of our time or of our memory could have done. I feel that there are other gifts to come from him — gifts for all of us. His influence did not stop with his breathing. It walks with us and will profoundly affect the way we look at things. From Jimmy I have already learned the value of a minute. He loved his minutes and I shall now love mine.

These words aren't clear. But they are clearer than what I could have said to you last week.

I write from the depths of my appreciation — to Jimmy for having touched my life and opened my eyes — to you for having grown him all those young years and for having given him your love — to you for being big enough and humane enough to let me come into your grief as a stranger and go away a friend.

When I drove away the sky at the horizon was yellowing with twilight and the trees stood clean against it. The banks of flowers covering the grave were muted and grayed by the coming of evening and had yielded up their color to the sunset. I thought — here's where he belongs — with this big darkening sky and this air that is thirst-quenching as mountain water and this century of family around him and the cornfield crowding the meadow where his presence will be marked. But he's not in the meadow. He's out there in the corn. He's hunting the winter's rabbit and the summer's catfish. He has a hand on little Mark's shoulder and a sudden kiss for you. And he has my laughter echoing his own at the great big jokes he saw and showed to me — and he's here, living and vivid and unforgettable forever, far too mischievous to lie down long.

My love and gratitude, to you and young Mark,

(Signed)

I MISS MY BIGGEST HEART

11 June 1852

EMILY DICKINSON to
SUSAN GILBERT
June 11th, 1852

It wasn't until her death, in 1886, that the true scale of Emily Dickinson's profound poetry was both discovered and appreciated by family and friends, many of whom had only glimpsed her talents in the numerous poem-filled letters that she wrote. She found an even wider audience in 1890 with the posthumous publication of a volume of her work; a collection of her letters followed in 1894. Her most frequent correspondent, and a person now thought to have been the inspiration for much of her passionate material, was close friend (and, from 1856 onwards, sister-in-law) Susan Huntington Gilbert, a lady who provoked some undeniably intimate and romantic letters from the poet, the intensity of which to this day generate speculation about their relationship.

I have but one thought, Susie, this afternoon of June, and *that* of you, and I have one prayer, only; dear Susie, *that* is *for* you. That you and I in *hand* as we e'en *do* in heart, might ramble away as children, among the woods and fields, and forget these many years, and these sorrowing cares, and each become a child again — I would it were so, Susie, and when I look around me and find myself alone, I sigh for you again; little sigh, and vain sigh, which will not bring you home.

I need you more and more, and the great world grows wider, and dear ones fewer and fewer, every day that you stay away — I miss my biggest heart; my own goes wandering round, and calls for Susie — Friends are too dear to sunder, Oh they are far too few, and how soon they will go away where you and I cannot find them, *dont* let us forget these things, for their remembrance *now* will save us many an anguish when it is *too late* to love them! Susie, forgive me Darling, for every word I say — my heart is full of you, none other than you in my thoughts, yet when I seek to say to you something not for the world, words fail me. If you were here — and Oh that you were, my Susie, we need not talk at all, our eyes would whisper for us, and your hand fast in mine, we would not ask for language — I try to bring you nearer, I chase the weeks away till they are quite departed, and fancy you have come, and I am on my way through the green lane to meet you, and my heart goes scampering so, that I have much ado to bring it back again, and learn it to be patient, till that dear Susie comes. Three weeks — they cant last always, for surely they must go with their little brothers and sisters to their long home in the west!

I shall grow more and more impatient until that dear day comes, for till now, I have only *mourned* for you; now I begin to *hope* for you.

Dear Susie, I have tried hard to think what you would love, of something I might send you — I at last saw my little Violets, they begged me to let *them* go, so here they are — and with them as Instructor, a bit of knightly grass, who also begged the favor to accompany them — they are but small, Susie, and I fear not fragrant now, but they will speak to you of warm hearts at home, and of the something faithful which "never slumbers nor sleeps" — Keep them 'neath your pillow, Susie, they will make you dream of blue-skies, and home, and the "blessed contrie"! You and I will have an hour with "Edward" and "Ellen Middleton", sometime when you get home — we must find out if some things contained therein are true, and if they are, what you and me are coming to!

Now, farewell, Susie, and Vinnie sends her love, and mother her's, and I add a kiss, shyly, lest there is somebody there! Dont let them see, *will* you Susie?

Emilie —

Why cant *I* be the delegate to the great Whig Convention? — dont I know all about Daniel Webster, and the Tariff, and the Law? Then, Susie I could see you, during a pause in the session — but I dont like this country at all, and I shant stay here any longer! "Delenda est" America, Massachusetts and all!

open me carefully

I MISS MY BIGGEST HEART

YOUR END IS APPROACHING

UNKNOWN to MARTIN
LUTHER KING, JR
November, 1964

In November 1964, fearful of his connection to the Communist Party through his friend and political advisor, Stanley Levison, the FBI anonymously sent Martin Luther King this alarmingly threatening letter, along with a cassette on which was recorded allegedly incriminating audio recordings of King with women in various hotel rooms – the fruits of a nine-month surveillance project headed by FBI agent William C. Sullivan. Unsurprisingly, King saw the strongly worded letter as an invitation for him to take his own life, as did an official investigation in 1976, named the Report of the Select Committee on Assassinations of the US House of Representatives, which concluded that the letter "clearly implied that suicide would be a suitable course of action for Dr. King".

<u>KING,</u>

In view of your low grade [...] I will not dignify your name with either a Mr. or a Reverend or a Dr. And, your last name calls to mind only the type of King such as King Henry the VIII [...]

King, look into your heart. You know you are a complete fraud and a great liability to all of us Negroes. White people in this country have enough frauds of their own but I am sure they don't have one at this time anywhere near your equal. You are no clergyman and you know it. I repeat you are a colossal fraud and an evil, vicious one at that. You could not believe in God [...] Clearly you don't believe in any personal moral principles.

King, like all frauds your end is approaching. You could have been our greatest leader. You, even at an early age have turned out to be not a leader but a dissolute, abnormal moral imbecile. We will now have to depend on our older leaders like Wilkins, a man of character and thank God we have others like him. But you are done. Your "honorary" degrees, your Nobel Prize (what a grim farce) and other awards will not save you. King, I repeat you are done.

No person can overcome facts, not even a fraud like yourself [...] I repeat — no person can argue successfully against facts. You are finished [...] And some of them to pretend to be ministers of the Gospel. Satan could not do more. What incredible evilness [...] King you are done.

The American public, the church organizations that have been helping — Protestant, Catholic and Jews will know you for what you are — an evil, abnormal beast. So will others who have backed you. You are done.

King, there is only one thing left for you to do. You know what it is. You have just 34 days in which to do (this exact number has been selected for a specific reason, it has definite practical significant. You are done. There is but one way out for you. You better take it before your filthy, abnormal fraudulent self is bared to the nation.

KING,

King, look into your heart. You know you are a complete
fraud and a great liability to all of us Negroes. White
people in this country have enough frauds of their own but I
am sure they don't have one at this time that is any where near
your equal. You are no clergyman and you know it. I repeat you
are a colossal fraud and an evil, vicious one at that.

King, like all frauds your end is approaching. You could
have been our greatest leader.

But you are done. Your "honorary" degrees, your Nobel
Prize (what a grim farce) and other awards will not save you.
King, I repeat you are done.

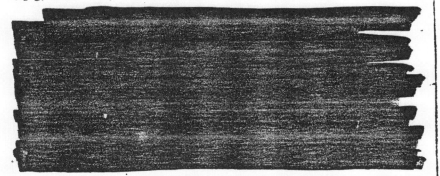

The American public, the church organizations that have been
helping - Protestant, Catholic and Jews will know you for what
you are - an evil, abnormal beast. So will others who have backed
you. You are done. #2

King, there is only one thing left for you to do. You know
what it is. You have just 34 days in which to do (this exact
number has been selected for a specific reason, it has definite

19 Portugal Place
Cambridge

A MOST IMPORTANT DISCOVERY

FRANCIS CRICK to MICHAEL CRICK
March 19th, 1953

On March 19th 1953, weeks before it was announced to the public, scientist Francis Crick excitedly wrote a letter to his son and told him of one of the most important scientific developments of modern times: his co-discovery of the "beautiful" structure of DNA, the molecule responsible for carrying the genetic instructions of living organisms; or, as Crick explained it to 12-year-old Michael, "the basic copying mechanism by which life comes from life". Although DNA was isolated back in the 1860s by Friedrich Miescher, its now famous double helix structure wasn't correctly modelled until the early 1950s by Crick and his colleague, James Watson, thanks in no small part to work already done by Maurice Wilkins, Rosalind Franklin and Raymond Gosling. In 1962, Crick, Watson and Wilkins were awarded the Nobel Prize for their efforts.

In April 2013, this letter became the most expensive in history after being sold at auction for $5.3million.

19 March '53

My Dear Michael,

Jim Watson and I have probably made a most important discovery. We have built a model for the structure of dex-oxi-ribose-nucleic-acid (read it carefully) called D.N.A. for short. You may remember that the genes of the chromosomes — which carry the hereditary factors — are made up of protein and D.N.A.

Our structure is very beautiful. D.N.A. can be thought of roughly as a very long chain with flat bits sticking out. The flat bits are called the "bases". The formula is rather like this.

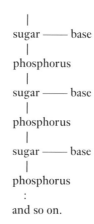

and so on.

Now we have two of these chains winding round each other — each one is a helix — and the chain, made up sugar and phosphorus, is on the <u>outside</u>, and the bases are all on the <u>inside</u>. I can't draw it very well, but it looks like this.

[diagram of the double helix]

The model looks <u>much</u> nicer than this.

Now the exciting thing is that while there are 4 <u>different</u> bases, we find we can only put certain pairs of them together. The bases have names. They are Adenine, Guanine, Thymine & Cytosine. I will call them A, G, T and C. Now we find that the pairs we can make — which have one base from one chain joined to one base from another — are only

A with T
and   G with C.

Now on one chain, as far as we can see, one can have the bases in any order, but if their order is <u>fixed</u>, then the order on the other chain is also fixed. For example, suppose the first chain goes ↓ then the second <u>must</u> go

A — — — — T
T — — — — A
C — — — — G

```
A — — — — — T
G — — — — — C
T — — — — — A
T — — — — — A
```

It is like a code. If you are given one set of letters you can write down the orders.

Now we believe that the D.N.A. is a code. That is, the order of the bases (the letters) makes one gene different from another gene (just as one page of print is different from another). You can now see how Nature makes copies of the genes. Because if the two chains unwind into two separate chains, and if each chain then makes another chain come together on it, then because A always goes with T, and G with C, we shall get two copies where we had one before.

For example

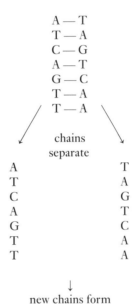

In others words we think we have found the basic copying mechanism by which life comes from life. The beauty of our model is that the shape of it is such that only these pairs can go together, though they could pair up in other ways if they were floating about freely. You can understand that we are very excited. We have to have a letter off to Nature in a day or so.

Read this carefully so that you understand it. When you come home we will show you the model.

Lots of love,
Daddy

19 Portugal Place
Cambridge.

19 March '53

My Dear Michael,

Jim Watson and I have probably made a
most important discovery. We have built a model for
the structure of des-oxy-ribose-nucleic-acid (read it
carefully) called D.N.A. for short. You may remember
that the genes of the chromosomes — which carry the
hereditary factors — are made up of protein and
D.N.A.

Our structure is very beautiful. D.N.A.
can be thought of roughly as a very long chain
with flat bits sticking out. The flat
bits are called the "bases": The formula is rather

like this

$$\begin{array}{c} \vdots \\ Sugar \underline{\hspace{1cm}} base \\ | \\ phosphorus \\ | \\ sugar \underline{\hspace{1cm}} base \\ \\ phosphorus \\ | \\ sugar \underline{\hspace{1cm}} base \\ | \\ phosphorus \\ | \\ Sugar \underline{\hspace{1cm}} base \\ \vdots \\ and\ so\ on. \end{array}$$

Now we have two ~~the~~ of these chains winding

round each other — each one is a helix — and

the chain, made up of sugar and phosphorus, is

on the outside, and the bases are all on the

inside. I can't draw it very well, but it looks

like this

The model looks much nicer than this.

Now the exciting thing is that while these are 4 different bases, we find we can only put ~~them~~ certain pairs of them together. The bases have names. They are Adenine, Guanine, Thymine & Cytosine. I will call them A, G, T and C. Now we find that the ~~two~~ pairs we can make — which have one base from one chain joined to one base from another — are only A with T

and G with C.

Now on one chain, as far as we can see, one can have the bases in any order, but if their order is <u>fixed</u>, then the order on the other chain is also fixed. For example, suppose the first chain goes ↓ then the second must go

A	T
T	A
C	G
A	T
G	C
T	A
T	A

It is like a code. If you ~~are~~ are given one set of letters you can write down the others.

Now we believe that the D.N.A. <u>is</u> a code.

That is, the order of the bases (the letters) makes one gene different from another gene (just as one page of print is different from another).

You can now see how Nature <u>makes copies of the genes</u>. Because if the two chains unwind into two separate chains, and if each chain then makes another chain ~~to~~ come together on it, then ~~because~~ A always goes with T, and G with C, we shall ~~↓~~ get two ~~or~~ copies where we had one before.

For example

```
A — T
T — A
C — G
A — T
G — C
T — A
T — A
```

↙ chains ↘
separate

```
A            T
T            A
C            G
A            T
G            C
T            T
T            A
                A
```

A T C A G T T

T A G T C A A

↓ new chains form

```
A — T        T — A
T — A        A — T
C — G        G — C
A — T        T — A
G — C        C — G
T — A        A — T
T — A        A — T
```

In other words & we think we have found the basic copying mechanism by which life comes from life. The beauty of our model is that the shape of it is such that only these pairs can go together, though they could pair up in other ways if they were floating about freely. You can understand that we are very excited. We have to have a letter off to Nature in a day or so.

Read Read this carefully so that you understand it. When you come home we will show you the model.

Lots of love,

Daddy.

THE SKILLS OF
LEONARDO DA VINCI

LEONARDO DA VINCI to
LUDOVICO SFORZA
Circa 1483

In the early 1480s, many years before he painted the world-famous pieces for which he is now best known – the *Mona Lisa* being just one – Italian polymath Leonardo da Vinci sought a job at the court of Ludovico Sforza, the then de facto ruler of Milan. Fully aware that Sforza was looking to employ military engineers, da Vinci drafted an application letter that put his seemingly endless engineering talents front and centre by way of a ten-point list of his abilities; interestingly, his artistic genius is merely hinted at towards the very end. It is believed that the final document, seen here, was penned not in da Vinci's hand, but by a professional writer. The effort paid off and he was eventually employed. A decade later it was Sforza who commissioned him to paint *The Last Supper*.

My Most Illustrious Lord,

Having now sufficiently seen and considered the achievements of all those who count themselves masters and artificers of instruments of war, and having noted that the invention and performance of the said instruments is in no way different from that in common usage, I shall endeavour, while intending no discredit to anyone else, to make myself understood to Your Excellency for the purpose of unfolding to you my secrets, and thereafter offering them at your complete disposal, and when the time is right bringing into effective operation all those things which are in part briefly listed below:

1. I have plans for very light, strong and easily portable bridges with which to pursue and, on some occasions, flee the enemy, and others, sturdy and indestructible either by fire or in battle, easy and convenient to lift and place in position. Also means of burning and destroying those of the enemy.

2. I know how, in the course of the siege of a terrain, to remove water from the moats and how to make an infinite number of bridges, mantlets and scaling ladders and other instruments necessary to such an enterprise.

3. Also, if one cannot, when besieging a terrain, proceed by bombardment either because of the height of the glacis or the strength of its situation and location, I have methods for destroying every fortress or other stranglehold unless it has been founded upon a rock or so forth.

4. I have also types of cannon, most convenient and easily portable, with which to hurl small stones almost like a hail-storm; and the smoke from the cannon will instil a great fear in the enemy on account of the grave damage and confusion.

5. Also, I have means of arriving at a designated spot through mines and secret winding passages constructed completely without noise, even if it should be necessary to pass underneath moats or any river.

6. Also, I will make covered vehicles, safe and unassailable, which will penetrate the enemy and their artillery, and there is no host of armed men so great that they would not break through it. And behind these the infantry will be able to follow, quite uninjured and unimpeded.

7. Also, should the need arise, I will make cannon, mortar and light ordnance of very beautiful and functional design that are quite out of the ordinary.

8. Where the use of cannon is impracticable, I will assemble catapults, mangonels, trebuchets and other instruments of wonderful efficiency not in general use. In short, as the variety of circumstances dictate, I will make an infinite number of items for attack and defence.

Hauedo ɛ̃ mio sig. uisto et consideraci horamay ad sufficiena le proue di tutti quelli chi si
repucono maestri et compositori de instrumti bellici: et chi le inuētione et operationi di dicti
instrumti nõ sono niente alieni dal cõe uso: mi exforzzo nõ derogando a nessuno alt
farmi intende da v. exɛ: aprēdo a ella li secreti mei: et apresso offerendoli ad ō̃ suo piacimto
i tempi oportuni oporē et effecto circa tutte q̃lle cose ch sub breuita saranno q̃ disotto
notate ɛ ancora i molte piu secōdo le occurrētie de diuersi casi ɛ

§ Io modi de ponti leggerissimi et forti et atti ad portare facilissimamt: et cũ q̃lli seguire
et alcuna uolta fugg̃ le occurrētie fuggire li inimici et alcri secur̃ et inoffensibili da foco
et battaglia: facili et cōmodi da leuare et ponere. Et modi de ard̃ et disfare q̃lli de lininim

§ I la obsidione de una terra toglie uia laqua de fossi: et fare īfiniti pōti ghatti et scale
et altj istrumti pertinēti ad dicta expedicione

§ Itē se p alcezza de argine o p forterzza de loco et di sito nõ si potesse ī la obsidione de
una terra usare lofficio de le bombarde: ho modi di ruinare ōmi forte o altra forcezza
se g̃ia nõ fusse fondata ī su el sazzo ɛ

§ Ho ancora modi de bombarde cōmodissime et facili ad portare: Et cũ q̃lle buttare minuta
adi similitudine quasi di tempesta: ɛ cũ el fumo di q̃lla dando grāde spauēto al inimico
cũ graue suo danno et confusione ɛ

§ Et quādo accadesse essere ī mare ho modi de molti istrumti actissimi da offend̃ et defend̃
et nauili ch faranno resistencia al trarre de ōmi grossissima bōbarda: et poluere et fumi

§ ... caue et uie secrete et distorte facte senza alcuno strepito peruenire ad ...
... passare sotto fossi o alcuno fiume

§ ... cũ inuulo sera un liniminca da fra artiglieria: nõ ...
... come compassino Et dietro a questi potranno seguire faterie assa ...

§ Ho ancora di ī fct̃ fare bōbarde mortari et passauolanti di bellissime et utile forme fori del cõe uso

§ Doue mācass lioperare de le bōbarde conporrò briccole mangani trabuchi et altri istrumti di miracolo
... et tora del uso: Et īsōma sec̃do la uarieta de casi conporrò uarie et īfinite cose da offend̃ et

§ In tpo di pace credo satisfare benissime ad paragone de ō̃ altro ī architectura ī compositione di edificij ɛ...
et... conducre aqua daluno loco ad uno altro actto ad p̃fecta difende

§ Itē cōduro ī sculptura di marmore di bronzo et di terra: similīte ī pictura ciò chi si possa fare
ad paragone de ō̃ altro et sia chi uole.

§ ancora si potra dare opera al cauallo di bronzo chi sera gloria īmortale et etterno honore de la
felice memoria del S. vostro padre et de la īclyta casa sforzesca

§ Et se alcuna de le sopradicte cose a alcuno paressino īpossibile et īfactibile mi offero
paratissimo ad farne experimēto ī el parcho uostro o ī q̃l loco piacera a ṽs. exɛ. al
quale ūmilmt̃ quanto piu posso me recomando ɛ

9. And should a sea battle be occasioned, I have examples of many instruments which are highly suitable either in attack or defence, and craft which will resist the fire of all the heaviest cannon and powder and smoke.

10. In time of peace I believe I can give as complete satisfaction as any other in the field of architecture, and the construction of both public and private buildings, and in conducting water from one place to another.

Also I can execute sculpture in marble, bronze and clay. Likewise in painting, I can do everything possible as well as any other, whosoever he may be.

Moreover, work could be undertaken on the bronze horse which will be to the immortal glory and eternal honour of the auspicious memory of His Lordship your father, and of the illustrious house of Sforza.

And if any of the above-mentioned things seem impossible or impracticable to anyone, I am most readily disposed to demonstrate them in your park or in whatsoever place shall please Your Excellency, to whom I commend myself with all possible humility.

I AM IN A STATE OF SHOCK

FLANNERY O'CONNOR to A
PROFESSOR OF ENGLISH
March 28th, 1961

In 1961, a professor of English wrote
to author Flannery O'Connor and
asked her, on behalf of his students, to
explain *A Good Man is Hard to Find* – a
short story of O'Connor's that his class
had recently been studying, and for
which they were struggling to find an
acceptable interpretation.

"We have debated at length several
possible interpretations," he explained
in his letter, "none of which fully
satisfies us. In general we believe
that the appearance of the Misfit is
not 'real' in the same sense that the
incidents of the first half of the story
are real. Bailey, we believe, imagines
the appearance of the Misfit, whose
activities have been called to his
attention on the night before the trip
and again during the stopover at the
roadside restaurant. Bailey, we further
believe, identifies himself with the
Misfit and so plays two roles in the
imaginary last half of the story. But we
cannot, after great effort, determine
the point at which reality fades into
illusion or reverie. Does the accident
literally occur, or is it part of Bailey's
dream? Please believe me when I say
we are not seeking an easy way out
of our difficulty. We admire your story
and have examined it with great care,
but we are not convinced that we are
missing something important which
you intended us to grasp. We will all
be very grateful if you comment on the
interpretation which I have outlined
above and if you will give us further
comments about your intention in
writing 'A Good Man is Hard to Find.'"

Judging by the letter with which
O'Connor responded, she was
unimpressed to say the least.

28 March 61

The interpretation of your ninety students and three teachers is fantastic
and about as far from my intentions as it could get to be. If it were a
legitimate interpretation, the story would be little more than a trick and
its interest would be simply for abnormal psychology. I am not interested
in abnormal psychology.

There is a change of tension from the first part of the story to the second
where the Misfit enters, but this is no lessening of reality. This story
is, of course, not meant to be realistic in the sense that it portrays the
everyday doings of people in Georgia. It is stylized and its conventions
are comic even though its meaning is serious.

Bailey's only importance is as the Grandmother's boy and the driver of
the car. It is the Grandmother who first recognized the Misfit and who
is most concerned with him throughout. The story is a duel of sorts
between the Grandmother and her superficial beliefs and the Misfit's
more profoundly felt involvement with Christ's action which set the
world off balance for him.

The meaning of a story should go on expanding for the reader the more
he thinks about it, but meaning cannot be captured in an interpretation.
If teachers are in the habit of approaching a story as if it were a research
problem for which any answer is believable so long as it is not obvious,
then I think students will never learn to enjoy fiction. Too much
interpretation is certainly worse than too little, and where feeling for a
story is absent, theory will not supply it.

My tone is not meant to be obnoxious. I am in a state of shock.

Flannery O'Connor

FEDERAL AGENT AT LARGE

ELVIS PRESLEY to US PRESIDENT RICHARD NIXON
December 21st, 1970

Elvis Presley was an avid collector of police badges and the owner of dozens from departments and agencies the length and breadth of the United States. But there was one badge in particular that he was desperate to get his hands on; one which had, for a long time, proven elusive: a badge from the Bureau of Narcotics and Dangerous Drugs. In fact, the King of Rock 'n' Roll was *so* keen to obtain one that in December 1970 he took a flight to the White House in order to hand-deliver this letter, written mid-flight, in which he cunningly offered his services in the war on drugs – as a "Federal Agent at Large". His arrival at the White House gates proved effective. A few hours later he had a meeting with President Nixon, gifted him with a Colt .45 pistol after a quick photocall, and asked for the badge he so wanted to own. Nixon obliged, they had their photograph taken, and the next day Elvis returned to Graceland.

All in all, an incredible and bizarre event, the official photos of which have since become the most requested in the history of the National Archives.

AmericanAirlines

Dear Mr. President:

First, I would like to introduce myself. I am Elvis Presley and admire you and have great respect for your office. I talked to Vice President Agnew in Palm Springs three weeks ago and expressed my concerns for our country. The drug culture, the hippie elements, the SDS, Black Panthers, etc. do not consider me as their enemy or as they call it, the establishment. I call it America and I love it. Sir, I can and will be of any service that I can to help the country out. I have no concerns or motives other than helping the country out. So, I wish not to be given a title or an appointed position. I can and will do more good if I were made a Federal Agent at Large and I will help out by doing it my way through communications with people of all ages. First and foremost, I am an entertainer, but all I need is the Federal credentials. I am on the plane with Senator George Murphy and we have been discussing the problems that our country is faced with.

Sir, I am staying at the Washington Hotel, Room 505-506-507. I have two men who work with me by the name of Jerry Schilling and Sonny West. I am registered under the name of Jon Burrows. I will be here for as long as it takes to get the credentials of a Federal Agent. I have done an in-depth study of drug abuse and Communist brainwashing techniques and I am right in the middle of the whole thing I can and will do the most good.

I am glad to help just so long as it is kept very private. You can have your staff or whomever call me anytime today, tonight or tomorrow. I was nominated this coming year one of America's Ten Most Outstanding Young Man. That will be in January 18 in my home town of Memphis, Tennessee. I am sending you a short autobiography about myself so you can better understand this approach. I would love to meet you just to say hello if you're not too busy.

Respectfully,
Elvis Presley

P.S. I believe that you, Sir, were one of the Top Ten Outstanding Men of America Also.

I have a personal gift for you which I would like to present to you and you can accept it or I will keep it for you until you can take it.

AmericanAirlines

In Flight…

Altitude;

Location; ①

Dear Mr. President,

First I would like to introduce myself.
I am Elvis Presley and admire you
and Have Great Respect for your
office. I talked to Vice President
agnew in Palm Springs 3 weeks and
expressed my concern for our country.
The Drug Culture, The Hippie Elements,
The SDS, Black Panther, etc do _not_
consider me as their enemy or as they
call it the Establishment. I call it america and

I Love it. Sir I can and Will
be of any Service that I can to help
the country out. I have no concern
or Motives other than helping the
country out. So I wish not to be
given a title or an appointed position, I can
and will do more good if I were
made a Federal agent at Large, and
I will help start by doing it my
way through my communications with people
of all ages. First and Foremost I am an
entertainer but All I need is the Federal
Credentials. I am on the Plane with

Sen. George Murphy and We
have been discussing the problems
that our Country is faced with.
So I am Staying at the Washington
hotel Room 505-506-507 - I have
2 men who work with me by the
name of Jerry Schilling and Sonny
West. I am registered under the name
of Jon Burrows. I will be here
for as long as it takes To get
the credentials of a Federal agent.
I have done an in depth study of
Drug abuse and Communist Brainwashing

Techniques and I am right in the
middle of the whole thing, where
I can and will do the most good
I am Glad to help; just so long
as it is kept very Private. You can
have your staff or whomever call
me anytime today, tonight or Tomorrow
I was nominated the coming year
one of America's Ten most outstanding
young men. That will be in January
18 in my Home Town of Memphis Tenn.
I am sending you the short autobiography
about myself so you can better understand This

~~approach~~

approach. I would love to meet you just to say hello if you're not to Busy.

Respectfully

Elvis Presley

P.S. I believe that you Sir were one of the Top Ten Outstanding Men of America also.

I have a personal gift for you also which I would like to present to you and you can accept it or I will keep it for you until you can take it .

DO NOT GRIEVE FOR ME

FYODOR DOSTOEVSKY to
MIKHAIL DOSTOEVSKY
December 22nd, 1849

In April 1849, influential Russian novelist Fyodor Dostoevsky was arrested along with numerous other members of the Petrashevsky Circle, a secret society of intellectuals who regularly gathered to discuss literature banned by Nicholas I, the Emperor of Russia. Eight months later, on December 22nd, they were led to Semyonov Place in St Petersburg where three were tied to posts, hooded. A firing squad raised their rifles and took aim. Silence filled the air. That silence was soon punctured, not by the sound of triggers being pulled, but by an order for the gunmen to stand down. At the very last second, the executions had been called off, and instead the Circle's distraught members were sent to prison.

Later that day, Dostoevsky wrote a letter to his brother, Mikhail. In it he described the day's unimaginably distressing events, asked him not to worry about his wellbeing while imprisoned, and spoke of being "reborn" as a result of the experience. Dostoevsky was released five years later and went on to write such classics as *Crime and Punishment* and *The Brothers Karamazov*.

The Peter and Paul Fortress,
December 22, 1849.

MIHAIL MIHAILOVICH DOSTOEVSKY,
Nevsky Prospect, opposite Gryazny Street,
in the house of Neslind.

Brother, my precious friend! all is settled! I am sentenced to four years' hard labour in the fortress (I believe, of Orenburg) and after that to serve as a private. To-day, the 22nd of December, we were taken to the Semionov Drill Ground. There the sentence of death was read to all of us, we were told to kiss the Cross, our swords were broken over our heads, and our last toilet was made (white shirts). Then three were tied to the pillar for execution. I was the sixth. Three at a time were called out; consequently, I was in the second batch and no more than a minute was left me to live. I remembered you, brother, and all yours; during the last minute you, you alone, were in my mind, only then I realised how I love you, dear brother mine! I also managed to embrace Plescheyev and Durov who stood close to me and to say good-bye to them. Finally the retreat was sounded, and those tied to the pillar were led back, and it was announced to us that His Imperial Majesty granted us our lives. Then followed the present sentences. Palm alone has been pardoned, and returns with his old rank to the army.

I was just told, dear brother, that to-day or to-morrow we are to be sent off. I asked to see you. But I was told that this was impossible; I may only write you this letter: make haste and give me a reply as soon as you can. I am afraid that you may somehow have got to know of our death-sentence. From the windows of the prison-van, when we were taken to the Semionov Drill Ground, I saw a multitude of people; perhaps the news reached you, and you suffered for me. Now you will be easier on my account. Brother! I have not become downhearted or low-spirited. Life is everywhere life, life in ourselves, not in what is outside us. There will be people near me, and to be a *man* among people and remain a man for ever, not to be downhearted nor to fall in whatever misfortunes may befall me—this is life; this is the task of life. I have realised this. This idea has entered into my flesh and into my blood. Yes, it's true! The head which was creating, living with the highest life of art, which had realised and grown used to the highest needs of the spirit, that head has already been cut off from my shoulders. There remain the memory and the images created but not yet incarnated by me. They will lacerate me, it is true! But there remains in me my heart and the same flesh and blood which can also love, and suffer, and desire, and remember, and this, after all, is life. *On voit le soleil!* Now, good-bye, brother! Don't grieve for me!

Now about material things: my books (I have the Bible still) and several sheets of my manu-script, the rough plan of the play and the novel (and the finished story *A Child's Tale*) have been taken away from me, and in all probability will be got by you. I also leave my overcoat and old clothes, if you send to fetch them. Now, brother, I may perhaps have to march a long distance. Money is needed. My dear brother, when you receive this letter, and if there is any possibility of getting some money, send it me at once. Money I need now more than air (for one particular purpose). Send me also a few lines. Then if the money from Moscow comes,—remember me and do not desert me. Well, that is all! I have debts, but what can I do?

Kiss your wife and children. Remind them of me continually; see that they do not forget me. Perhaps, we shall yet meet some time! Brother, take care of yourself and of your family, live quietly and carefully. Think of the future of your children... Live positively. There has never yet been working in me such a healthy abundance of spiritual life as now. But will my body endure? I do not know. I am going away sick, I suffer from scrofula. But never mind! Brother, I have already gone through so much in life that now hardly anything can frighten me. Let come what may! At the first opportunity I shall let you know about myself. Give the Maikovs my farewell and last greetings. Tell them that I thank them all for their constant interest in my fate. Say a few words for me, as warm as possible, as your heart will prompt you, to Eugenia Petrovna. I wish her much happiness, and shall ever remember her with grateful respect. Press the hands of Nikolay Apollonovich and Apollon Maikov, and also of all the others. Find Yanovsky. Press his hand, thank him. Finally, press the hands of all who have not forgotten me. And those who have forgotten me—remember me to them also. Kiss our brother Kolya. Write a letter to our brother Andrey and let him know about me. Write also to Uncle and Aunt. This I ask you in my own name, and greet them for me. Write to our sisters: I wish them happiness.

And maybe, we shall meet again some time, brother! Take care of yourself, go on living, for the love of God, until we meet. Perhaps some time we shall embrace each other and recall our youth, our golden time that was, our youth and our hopes, which at this very instant I am tearing out from my heart with my blood, to bury them.

Can it indeed be that I shall never take a pen into my hands? I think that after the four years there may be a possibility. I shall send you every-thing that I may write, if I write anything, my God! How many imaginations, lived through by me, created by me anew, will perish, will be ex-tinguished in my brain or will be spilt as poison in my blood! Yes, if I am not allowed to write, I shall perish. Better fifteen years of prison with a pen in my hands!

Write to me more often, write more details, more, more facts. In every letter write about all kinds of family details, of trifles, don't forget. This will give me hope and life. If you knew how your letters revived me here in the fortress. These last two months and a half, when it was forbidden to write or receive a letter, have been very hard on me. I was ill. The fact that you did not send me money now and then worried me on your account; it meant you yourself were in great need! Kiss the children once again; their lovely little faces do not leave my mind. Ah, that they may be happy! Be happy yourself too, brother, be happy!

But do not grieve, for the love of God, do not grieve for me! Do believe that I am not down-hearted, do remember that hope has not deserted me. In four years there will be a mitigation of my fate. I shall be a private soldier,—no longer a prisoner, and remember that some time I shall embrace you. I was to-day in the grip of death for three-quarters of an hour; I have lived it through with that idea; I was at the last instant and now I live again!

If any one has bad memories of me, if I have quarreled with any one, if I have created in any one an unpleasant impression—tell them they should forget it, if you manage to meet them. There is no gall or spite in my soul; I should dearly love to embrace any one of my former friends at this moment. It is a comfort, I experienced it to-day when saying good-bye to my dear ones before death. I thought at that moment that the news of the execution would kill you. But now be easy, I am still alive and shall live in the future with the thought that some time I shall embrace you. Only this is now in my mind.

What are you doing? What have you been thinking to-day? Do you know about us? How cold it was to-day!

Ah, if only my letter reaches you soon. Other-wise I shall be for four months without news of you. I saw the envelopes in which you sent money during the last two months; the address was written in your hand, and I was glad that you were well.

When I look back at the past and think how much time has been wasted in vain, how much time was lost in delusions, in errors, in idleness, in ignorance of how to live, how I did not value time, how often I sinned against my heart and spirit,—my heart bleeds. Life is a gift, life is happiness, each minute might have been an age of happiness. *Si jeunesse savait!* Now, changing my life, I am being reborn into a new form. Brother! I swear to you that I shall not lose hope, and shall preserve my spirit and heart in purity. I shall be reborn to a better thing. That is my whole hope, my whole comfort!

The life in prison has already sufficiently killed in me the demands of the flesh which were not wholly pure; I took little heed of myself before. Now privations are nothing to me, and, therefore, do not fear that any material hardship will kill me. This cannot be! Ah! To have health!

Good-bye, good-bye, my brother! When shall I write you again? You will receive from me as detailed an account as possible of my journey. If I can only preserve my health, then everything will be right!

Well, good-bye, good-bye, brother! I embrace you closely, I kiss you closely. Remember me without pain in your heart. Do not grieve, I pray you, do not grieve for me! In the next letter I shall tell you how I go on. Remember then what I have told you: plan out your life, do not waste it, arrange your destiny, think of your children. Oh, to see you, to see you! Good-bye! Now I tear myself away from everything that was dear; it is painful to leave it! It is painful to break oneself in two, to cut the heart in two. Good-bye! Good-bye! But I shall see you, I am convinced—I hope; do not change, love me, do not let your memory grow cold, and the thought of your love will be the best part of my life. Good-bye, good-bye, once more! Good-bye to all!

—Your brother

Fiodor Dostoevsky.

Dec. 22, 1849.

At my arrest several books were taken away from me. Only two of them were prohibited books. Won't you get the rest for yourself? But there is this request: one of the books was *The Work of Valerian Maikov*: his critical essays—Eugenia Petrovna's copy. It was her treasure, and she lent it me. At my arrest I asked the police officer to return that book to her, and gave him the address. I do not know if he returned it to her. Make enquiries! I do not want to take this memory away from her. Good-bye, good-bye, once more!

— Your

F. Dostoevsky.

Telephone
MUrray Hill 2-0500

425 LEXINGTON AVENUE
New York 17, N. Y.

THE WHITE HOUSE
MAY 14 11 36 AM '58
RECEIVED

May 13, 1958

The President
The White House
Washington, D. C.

My dear Mr. President:

I was sitting in the audience at the Summit Meeting of Negro
Leaders yesterday when you said we must have patience. On
hearing you say this, I felt like standing up and saying, "Oh
no! Not again."

I respectfully remind you sir, that we have been the most
patient of all people. When you said we must have self-
respect, I wondered how we could have self-respect and remain patient considering the treatment accorded us through
the years.

17 million Negroes cannot do as you suggest and wait for the
hearts of men to change. We want to enjoy now the rights
that we feel we are entitled to as Americans. This we cannot do unless we pursue aggressively goals which all other
Americans achieved over 150 years ago.

As the chief executive of our nation, I respectfully suggest
that you unwittingly crush the spirit of freedom in Negroes
by constantly urging forbearance and give hope to those pro-
segregation leaders like Governor Faubus who would take
from us even those freedoms we now enjoy. Your own experience with Governor Faubus is proof enough that forbearance and not eventual integration is the goal the pro-
segregation leaders seek.

In my view, an unequivocal statement backed up by action
such as you demonstrated you could take last fall in deal-

MAY 26 1958

17 MILLION NEGROES CANNOT WAIT FOR THE HEARTS OF MEN TO CHANGE

JACKIE ROBINSON to US
PRESIDENT DWIGHT D.
EISENHOWER
May 13th, 1958

Jackie Robinson was an exceptionally talented baseball player; in fact, such was his talent that in 1947 he obliterated an unwritten policy within baseball that had, until that point, prevented players of African descent from joining teams in either the minor or major leagues. He then went on to feature in six World Series and win multiple awards, not to mention his being inducted into the Baseball Hall of Fame in 1962. In 1957, he retired from the sport and instead took an active role in the political world, fighting, amongst other things, racial segregation. He sent this powerful letter to US President Eisenhower in 1958 in response to a speech in which he had called for patience from African-Americans in their fight for civil rights.

ing with Governor Faubus if it became necessary, would let
it be known that America is determined to provide -- in the
near future -- for Negroes -- the freedoms we are entitled to under the constitution.

Respectfully yours,

Jackie Robinson

Jackie Robinson

JR:cc

11 ALIVE...NEED SMALL BOAT... KENNEDY

JOHN F. KENNEDY to
ALLIED FORCES
August, 1943

On August 2nd 1943, whilst serving as commander of the *PT-109* torpedo boat during World War II, future US President John F. Kennedy and his crew were rammed by the Japanese destroyer *Amagiri* – their boat was instantly halved by the impact and two crew members were killed. Six days later, stranded in the Solomon Islands with his fellow survivors, Kennedy carved a desperate message into a coconut shell and handed it to Biuku Gasa and Eroni Kumana, two natives tasked with delivering it to the nearest Allied base 35 nautical miles away, by canoe. Amazingly, they succeeded, and as a result Kennedy and his men were soon rescued.

Kennedy later had the shell encased in plastic; it was then used as a paperweight in the Oval Office during his presidency.

NAURO ISL COMMANDER
NATIVE KNOWS POS'IT
HE CAN PILOT 11 ALIVE
NEED SMALL BOAT
KENNEDY

spike milligan

28th February, 1977

9 Orme Court,
LONDON. W. 2.

Stephen Gard Esq.,
Bunnaloo East Public School,
Thyra Road,
via. MOAMA. 2739.

Dear Stephen,

Questions, questions, questions - if you are disappointed in my
book 'MONTY', so am I.   I must be more disappointed than you
because I spent a year collecting material for it, and it was a
choice of having it made into a suit or a book.

There are lots of one liners in the book, but then when the German
Army are throwing bloody great lumps of hot iron at you, one only
has time for one liners, in fact, the book should really consist
of the following:

> "Oh fuck"

> "Look out"

> "Christ here's another"

> "Where did that fall"

> "My lorry's on fire"

> "Oh Christ, the cook is dead".

You realise a book just consisting of those would just be the end,
so my one liners are extensions of these brevities.

Then you are worried because as yet I have not mentioned my meeting
with Secombe and later Sellers, well by the end of the Monty book
I had as yet not met either Secombe or Sellers.   I met Secombe
in Italy, which will be in vol. 4., and I am arranging to meet
Peter Sellers on page 78 in vol. 5, in London.   I'm sorry I can't
put back the clock to meet Secombe in 1941, to alleviate your
disappointment I hope springs anew with the information I have
given you.

Another thing that bothers you is "cowardice in the face of the
enemy".   Well, the point is I suffer from cowardice in the face
of the enemy throughout the war - in the face of the enemy, also

in the legs, the elbows, and the wrists, in fact, after two years
in the front line a mortar bomb exploded by my head (or was it
my head exploded by a Mortar bomb), and it so frightened me, I
put on a tremendous act of stammering, stuttering, and shivering
this mixed with cries of "mother", and a free flow of dysentery
enabled me to be taken out of the line and down-graded to B.2.
But for that brilliant performance, this letter would be coming
to you from a grave in Italy.

Anymore questions from you and our friendship is at an end.

                              Sincerely,

                              Spike Milligan.

OH CHRIST, THE COOK IS DEAD

SPIKE MILLIGAN to
STEPHEN GARD
February 28th, 1977

In February 1977, a well-meaning teacher named Stephen Gard managed to elicit this wonderfully frosty letter from Spike Milligan after writing to the legendary comedian with a number of questions, many of which concerned *Monty*, the third instalment in a seven-part series of memoirs by Spike which focused on his life as a soldier in World War II. Gard explains his reasoning:

"My letter was written as a fan, but it did ask a lot of questions; questions that a lifetime of Goon Show *listening had raised in my mind. The one that obviously annoyed Spike was, 'Why do so many* Goon Shows, e.g. 'Tales of Men's Shirts', *harp on the theme of military cowardice? After the line "The prison camp was filled with British Officers who'd sworn to DIE rather than be captured," [audience laughter] why did you come to the mike and say "Thank you, fellow cowards!"? Is it because you yourself were accused of this?'*

"Of course, Spike's next book explained just this incident: his being blown up, his nerves being shattered, and his commanding officer's cruel and foolish response to Spike's distress and illness. I did complain that a little too much of Monty was taken up with Goonish dialogue. I had hoped to learn more about Spike himself. His later memoirs were more straightforward accounts, and much more helpful in understanding so interesting and complex a man.

"For the record, too, after receiving this wonderful missive from Spike, I wrote at once to say how much I admired him and his work, and in a weak attempt at Goon humour, included a snapshot of my wife and our cats, to prove that I was being sincere. Spike didn't reply, and I didn't expect him to."

```
To   :   H. R. Haldeman

From:    Bill Safire                    July 18, 1969.

-----------------------------------------------------------------

IN EVENT OF MOON DISASTER:

        Fate has ordained that the men who went to the moon to

explore in peace will stay on the moon to rest in peace.

        These brave men, Neil Armstrong and Edwin Aldrin, know

that there is no hope for their recovery.  But they also know that there

is hope for mankind in their sacrifice.

        These two men are laying down their lives in mankind's

most noble goal:  the search for truth and understanding.

        They will be mourned by their families and friends; they

will be mourned by their nation; they will be mourned by the people of

the world; they will be mourned by a Mother Earth that dared send two

of her sons into the unknown.

        In their exploration, they stirred the people of the world to

feel as one; in their sacrifice, they bind more tightly the brotherhood

of man.

        In ancient days, men looked at stars and saw their heroes in

the constellations.  In modern times, we do much the same, but our heroes

are epic men of flesh and blood.
```

IN EVENT OF MOON DISASTER

WILLIAM SAFIRE to H. R. HALDEMAN
July 18th, 1969

It is difficult to imagine a memo more chilling than this one, expertly written by presidential speechwriter William Safire on July 18th 1969, as the world waited anxiously for Apollo 11 to land safely on the surface of the moon. It was a contingency plan of sorts, containing a speech titled "IN EVENT OF MOON DISASTER", to be read out by US President Richard Nixon to a hushed public should astronauts Neil Armstrong and Buzz Aldrin become stranded on the moon, never to return, and instructions for the President to call and inform the "widows-to-be" of the tragedy. As we now know, the memo was never needed; all that remains is an eerie reminder that things could have gone terribly wrong and that those at the top were very much prepared for such an unthinkably bleak eventuality.

Others will follow, and surely find their way home. Man's search will not be denied. But these men were the first, and they will remain the foremost in our hearts.

For every human being who looks up at the moon in the nights to come will know that there is some corner of another world that is forever mankind.

PRIOR TO THE PRESIDENT'S STATEMENT:

The President should telephone each of the widows-to-be.

AFTER THE PRESIDENT'S STATEMENT, AT THE POINT WHEN NASA ENDS COMMUNICATIONS WITH THE MEN:

A clergyman should adopt the same procedure as a burial at sea, commending their souls to "the deepest of the deep," concluding with the Lord's Prayer.

THE MOST BEAUTIFUL
DEATH

LAURA HUXLEY to JULIAN
AND JULIETTE HUXLEY
December 8th, 1963

In 1960, as he was writing
Island, the utopian
counterpart to his classic
dystopian masterpiece,
Brave New World, celebrated
author Aldous Huxley was
diagnosed with cancer of the
larynx. On his deathbed three
years later, In November
1963, just as he was passing
away, Aldous – a man
who for many years, ever
since being introduced to
mescaline in 1953, had been
fascinated with the effects
of psychedelic drugs – asked
his wife of seven years, Laura,
to administer him with LSD.
She agreed. The next month,
Laura wrote to Aldous's
brother, Julian, and Julian's
wife, Juliette, and gave an
incredibly moving, detailed
account of Aldous's last days,
the draft of which you see
here courtesy of the Erowid
Center's Stolaroff Collection.

6233 Mulholland Highway
Los Angeles 28, California
December 8, 1963

Dearest Julian and Juliette:

There is so much I want to tell you about the last week of Aldous' life and
particularly the last day. What happened is important not only for us close and
loving but it is almost a conclusion, better, a continuation of his own work, and
therefore it has importance for people in general.

First of all I must confirm to you with complete subjective certainty that
Aldous had not consciously looked at the fact that he might die until the day he
died. Subconsciously it was all there, and you will be able to see this for yourselves
because beginning from November 15th until November 22nd I have much of
Aldous' remarks on tape, For these tapes I know we shall all be immensely grateful.
Aldous was never quite willing to give up his writing and dictate or makes notes on
a recorder. He used a Dictograph, only to read poetry or passages of literature; he
would listen to these in his quiet moments in the evening as he was going to sleep.
I have had a tape recorder for years, and I tried to use it with him sometimes, but it
was too bulky, and particularly now when we were always in the bedroom and the
bed had so much hospital equipment around it. (We had spoken about buying a
small one, but the market here is flooded with transis ter tape recorders, and most
of them are very bad. I didn't have time to look into it, and this remained just one
of those things like many others that we were going to do.) In the beginning of
November, when Aldous was in the hospital, my birthday occurred, so Jinny looked
carefully into all the machines, and presented me with the best of them – a small
thing, easy manageable and practically unnoticeable. After having practiced with it
myself a few days, I showed it to Aldous, who was very pleased with it, and from
the 15th on we used it a little every day recording his dreams and notes for future
writing.

The period from the 15th to the 22nd marked, it seems to me, a period
of intense mental activity for Aldous. We had diminished little by little the
tranquillizers he had been taking four times a day a drug called Sperine which is
akin, I understand, to Thorazin. We diminished it practically to nothing only used
painkillers like Percodon a little Amitol, and something for nausea. He took also a
few injections of 1/2 cc of Dilaudid,

Dearest Julian and Juliette:

There is so much I want to tell you about the last week of
Aldous' life and particularly the last day. What happened is
important not only for us close and loving but it is almost a
conclusion, better, a continuation of his own work, and there-
for it has importance for people in general.

First of all I must confirm to you with complete subjective
certainty that Aldous had not consciously looked at the fact that
he might die until the day he died. Subconsciously it was all
there, and you will be able to see this for yourselves because
beginning from November 15th until November 22nd I have much of
Aldous' remarks on tape. For these tapes I know we shall all be
immensely grateful. Aldous was never quite willing to give up
his writing and dictate or makes notes on a recorder. He used a
Dictagraph, only to read poetry or passages of literature; he
would listen to these in his quiet moments in the evening as he
was going to sleep. I have had a tape recorder for years, and
I tried to use it with him sometimes, but it was too bulky, and
particularly now when we were always in the bedroom and the bed
had so much hospital equipment around it. (We had spoken about
buying a small one, but the market here is flooded with transister
tape recorders, and most of them are very bad. I didn't have time
to look into it, and this remained just one of those things like
many others that we were going to do.) In the beginning of
November, when Aldous was in the hospital, my birthday occurred,
so Jinny looked carefully into all the machines, and presented me
with the best of them - a small thing, easy manageable and practically unnoticeable. After having practiced with it myself a few
days, I showed it to Aldous, who was very pleased with it, and
from the 15th on we used it a little every day recording his
dreams and notes for future writing.

The period from the 15th to the 22nd marked, it seems to me, a
period of intense mental activity for Aldous. We had diminished
little by little the tranquillizers - he had been taking four
times a day a drug called Sperine which is akin, I understand, to
Thorazin. We diminished it practically to nothing - only used
painkillers like Percoden - a little Amitol, and something for
nausea. He took also a few injections of 1/2 cc of Dilaudid,

which is a derivative of morphine, and which gave him many dreams, some of which you will hear on the tape. The doctor says this is a small intake of morphine.

Now to pick up my point again, in these dreams as well as sometimes in his conversation, it seemed obvious and transparent that subconsciously he knew that he was going to die. But not once consciously did he speak of it. This had nothing to do with the idea that some of his friends put forward, that he wanted to spare me. It wasn't this, because Aldous had never been able to play a part, to say a single lie; he was constitutionally unable to lie, and if he wanted to spare me, he could certainly have spoken to Jinny.

During the last two months I gave him almost daily an opportunity, an opening for speaking about death, but of course this opening was always one that could have been taken in two ways – either towards life or towards death, and he always took it towards life. We read the entire manual of Dr. Leary extracted from The Book of the Dead. He could have, even jokingly said don't forget to remind me his comment instead was only directed to the way Dr. Leary conducted his LSD sessions, and how he would bring people, who were not dead, back here to this life after the session. It is true he said sometimes phrases like, "If I get out of this," in connection to his new ideas for writing, and wondered when and if he would have the strength to work. His mind was very active and it seems that this Dilaudid had stirred some new layer which had not often been stirred in him.

The night before he died, (Thursday night) about eight o'clock, suddenly an idea occurred to him. "Darling," he said, "it just occurs to me that I am imposing on Jinny having somebody as sick as this in the house with the two children, this is really an imposition." Jinny was out of the house at the moment, and so I said, "Good, when she comes back I will tell her this. It will be a nice laugh." "No," he said with unusual insistence, "we should do something about it." "Well," I replied, keeping it light, "all right, get up. Let's go on a trip." "No", he said, "It is serious. We must think about it. All these nurses in the house. What we could do, we could take an apartment for this period. Just for this period." It was very clear what he meant. It was unmistakeably clear. He thought he might be so sick for another three of four weeks, and then he could come back and start his normal life again. This fact of starting his normal life occurred quite often. In the last three or four weeks he was several times appalled by his weakness, when he realized how much he had lost, and how long it would take to be normal again. Now this Thursday night he had remarked about taking an apartment with an unusual energy, but a few minutes later and all that evening I felt that he was going down, he was losing ground quickly. Eating

which is a derivative of morphine, and which gave him many dreams, some of which you will hear on the tape. The doctor says this is a small intake of morphine.

Now to pick up my point again, in these dreams as well as sometimes in his conversation, it seemed obvious and transparent that subconsciously he knew that he was going to die. But not once consciously did he speak of it. This had nothing to do with the idea that some of his friends put forward, that he wanted to spare me. It wasn't this, because Aldous had never been able to play a part, to say a single lie; he was constitutionall unable to lie, and if he wanted to spare me, he could certainly have spoken to Jinny.

During the last two months I gave him almost daily an opportunity, an opening for speaking about death, but of course this opening was always one that could have been taken in two ways - either towards life or towards death, and he always took it towards life. We read the entire manual of Dr. Leary extracted from The Book of the Dead. He could have, even jokingly said - don't forget to remind me - his comment instead was only directed to the way Dr. Leary conducted his LSD sessions, and how he would bring people, who were not dead, back here to this life after the session. It is true he said sometimes phrases like, "If I get out of this," in connection to his new ideas for writing, and wondered when and if he would have the strength to work. His mind was very active and it seems that this Dilaudid had stirred some new layer which had not often been stirred in him.

The night before he died, (Thursday night) about eight o'clock, suddenly an idea occurred to him. "Darling," he said, "it just occurs to me that I am imposing on Jinny having somebody as sick as this in the house with the two children, this is really an imposition." Jinny was out of the house at the moment, and so I said, "Good,when she comes back I will tell her this. It will be a nice laugh." "No," he said with unusual insistence, "we should do something about it." "Well," I replied, keeping it light, "all right, get up. Let's go on a trip." "No," he said, "It is serious. We must think about it. All these nurses in the house. What we could do, we could take an apartment for this period. Just for this period." It was very clear what he meant. It was unmistakeably clear. He thought he might be so sick for another three or four weeks, and then he could come back and start his normal life again. This fact of starting his normal life occurred quite often. In the last three or four weeks he was several times appalled by his weakness, when he realized how much he had lost, and how long it would take to be normal again. Now this Thursday night he had remarked about taking an apartment with an unusual energy, but a few minutes later and all that evening I felt that he was going down, he was losing ground quickly. Eating was almost out of the question. He had just taken a few spoonsful of liquid and puree, in fact every time that he took something, this would start the cough. Thursday night I called Dr. Bernstein, and told him the pulse was very high – 140, he had a little bit of fever and my whole feeling was one of immanence of death. But both the nurse and the doctor said they didn't think this was the case, but that if I wanted him the doctor would come up to see him that night. Then I returned to Aldous' room and we decided to give him an injection of Dilaudid. It was about nine o'clock, and he went to sleep and I told the doctor to come the next morning. Aldous slept until about two a.m. and then he got another shot, and I saw him again at six-thirty. Again I felt that life was leaving, something was more wrong than usual, although I didn't know exactly what, and a little later I sent you and Matthew and Ellen and my sister a wire. Then about nine a.m. Aldous began to be so agitated, so uncomfortable, so desperate really. He wanted to be moved all the time. Nothing was right. Dr. Bernstein came about that time and decided to give him a shot which he had given him once before, something that you give intravenously, very slowly – it takes five minutes to give the shot, and it is a drug that dilates the bronchial tubes, so that respiration is easier.

This drug made him uncomfortable the time before, it must have been three Fridays before, when he had that crisis I wrote you about. But then it helped him. This time it was quite terrible. He couldn't express himself but he was feeling dreadul, nothing was right, no position was right. I tried to ask him what was occurring. He had difficulty in speaking, but he managed to say, "Just trying to tell you makes it worse." He wanted to be moved all the time – "Move me." "Move my legs." "Move my arms." "Move my bed." I had one of those push-button beds, which moved up and down both from the head and the feet, and incessantly, at times, I would have him go up and down, up and down by pushing buttons. We did this again, and somehow it seemed to give him a little relief. but it was very, very little.

All of a sudden, it must have been then ten o'clock, he could hardly speak, and he said he wanted a tablet to write on, and for the first time he wrote – "If I die," and gave a direction for his will. I knew what he meant. He had signed his will as I told you about a week before, and in this will there was a transfer of a life insurance policy from me to Matthew. We had spoken of getting these papers of transfer, which the insurance company had just sent, and that actually arrived special delivery just a few minutes before. Writing was very, very difficult for him. Rosalind and Dr. Bernstein were there trying also to understand what he wanted. I said to him, "Do you mean that you want to make sure that the life insurance is transferred from me to Matthew?" He said, "Yes." I said, "The papers for the transfer have just arrived,

was almost out of the question. He had just taken a few spoonsful
of liquid and puree, in fact every time that he took something,
this would start the cough. Thursday night I called Dr. Bernstein,
and told him the pulse was very high – 140, he had a little bit of
fever and my whole feeling was one of immanence of death. But
both the nurse and the doctor said they didn't think this was the
case, but that if I wanted him the doctor would come up to see him
that night. Then I returned to Aldous' room and we decided to give
him an injection of Dilaudid. It was about nine o'clock, and he
went to sleep and I told the doctor to come the next morning.
Aldous slept until about two a.m. and then he got another shot,
and I saw him again at six-thirty. Again I felt that life was
leaving, something was more wrong than usual, although I didn't
know exactly what, and a little later I sent you and Matthew and
Ellen and my sister a wire. Then about nine a.m. Aldous began to
be so agitated, so uncomfortable, so desperate really. He wanted
to be moved all the time. Nothing was right. Dr. Bernstein came
about that time and decided to give him a shot which he had given
him once before, something that you give intravenously, very
slowly – it takes five minutes to give the shot, and it is a drug
that dilates the bronchial tubes, so that respiration is easier.

This drug made him uncomfortable the time before, it must have
been three Fridays before, when he had that crisis I wrote you
about. But then it helped him. This time it was quite terrible.
He couldn't express himself but he was feeling dreadul, nothing
was right, no position was right. I tried to ask him what was
occurring. He had difficulty in speaking, but he managed to say,
"Just trying to tell you makes it worse." He wanted to be moved
all the time – "Move me." "Move my legs." "Move my arms." "Move
my bed." I had one of those push-button beds, which moved up and
down both from the head and the feet, and incessantly, at times,
I would have him go up and down, up and down by pushing buttons.
We did this again, and somehow it seemed to give him a little
relief. but it was very, very little.

All of a sudden, it must have been then ten o'clock, he could
hardly speak, and he said he wanted a tablet to write on, and for
the first time he wrote – "If I die," and gave a direction for his
will. I knew what he meant. He had signed his will as I told you
about a week before, and in this will there was a transfer of a
life insurance policy from me to Matthew. We had spoken of getting
these papers of transfer, which the insurance company had just
sent, and that actually arrived special delivery just a few minutes
before. Writing was very, very difficult for him. Rosalind and
Dr. Bernstein were there trying also to understand what he wanted.
I said to him, "Do you mean that you want to make sure that the
life insurance is transferred from me to Matthew?" He said,
"Yes." I said, "The papers for the transfer have just arrived,

if you want to sign them you can sign them, but it is not necessary because you already made it legal in your will. He heaved a sigh of relief in not having to sign. I had asked him the day before even, to sign some important papers, and he had said, "Let's wait a little while," this, by the way, was his way now, for him to say that he couldn't do something. If he was asked to eat, he would say, "Let's wait a little while," and when I asked him to do some signing that was rather important on Thursday he said, "Let's wait a little while" He wanted to write you a letter – "and especially about Juliette's book, is lovely," he had said several times. And when I proposed to do it, he would say, "Yes, just in a little while" in such a tired voice, so totally different from his normal way of being. So when I told him that the signing was not necessary and that all was in order, he had a sigh of relief.

"If I die." This was the first time that he had said that with reference to NOW. He wrote it. I knew and felt that for the first time he was looking at this. About a half an hour before I had called up Sidney Cohen, a psychiatrist who has been one of the leaders in the use of LSD. I had asked him if he had ever given LSD to a man in this condition. He said he had only done it twice actually, and in one case it had brought up a sort of reconciliation with Death, and in the other case it did not make any difference. I asked him if he would advise me to give it to Aldous in his condition. I told him how I had offered it several times during the last two months, but he always said that he would wait until he was better. Then Dr. Cohen said, "I don't know. I don't think so. What do you think?" I said, "I don't know. Shall I offer it to him?" He said, "I would offer it to him in a very oblique way, just say 'what do you think about taking LSD [sometime again]?'" This vague response had been common to the few workers in this field to whom I had asked, "Do you give LSD in extremes?" ISLAND is the only definite reference that I know of. I must have spoken to Sidney Cohen about nine-thirty. Aldous' condition had become so physically painful and obscure, and he was so agitated he couldn't say what he wanted, and I couldn't understand. At a certain point he said something which no one here has been able to explain to me, he said, "Who is eating out of my bowl?" And I didn't know what this meant and I yet don't know. And I asked him. He managed a faint whimsical smile and said, "Oh, never mind, it is only a joke." And later on, feeling my need to know a little so I could do something, he said in an agonizing way, "At this point there is so little to share." Then I knew that he knew that he was going. However, this inability to express himself was only muscular – his brain was clear and in fact, I feel, at a pitch of activity.

Then I don't know exactly what time it was, he asked for his tablet and wrote, "Try LSD 100 intramuscular." Although as you see from this photostatic copy it is not very clear, I know that this is what he meant. I asked him and he confirmed it. Suddenly something became very clear to me. I knew that we were if you want to sign them you can sign them, but it is not necessary because you already made it legal in your will. He heaved a sigh of relief in not having to sign. I had asked him the day before even, to sign some important papers, and he had said, "Let's wait a little while." This, by the way, was his way now, for him to say that he couldn't do something. If he was asked to eat, he would say, "Let's wait a little while," and when I asked him to do some signing that was rather important on Thursday he said, "Let's wait a little while," He wanted to write you a letter - "and especially about Juliette's book, is lovely," he had said several times. And when I proposed to do it, he would say, "Yes, just in a little while." in such a tired voice, so totally different from his normal way of being. So when I told him that the signing was not necessary and that all was in order, he had a sigh of relief.

"If I die." This was the first time that he had said that with reference to NOW. He wrote it. I knew and felt that for the first time he was looking at this. About a half an hour before I had called up Sidney Cohen, a psychiatrist who has been one of the leaders in the use of LSD. I had asked him if he had ever given LSD to a man in this condition. He said that he had only done it twice actually, and in one case it had brought up a sort of reconciliation with Death, and in the other case it did not make any difference. I asked him if he would advise me to give it to Aldous in his condition. I told him how I had offered it several times during the last two months, but he always said that he would wait until he was better. Then Dr. Cohen said, "I don't know. I don't think so. What do you think?" I said, "I don't know. Shall I offer it to him?" He said, "I would offer it to him in a very ~~sometimes~~ oblique way, just say 'what do you think about taking LSD?'" This ~~again?~~ vague response had been common to the few workers in this field to whom I had asked, "Do you give LSD in extremes?" ISLAND is the only definite reference that I know of. I must have spoken to Sidney Cohen about nine-thirty. Aldous' condition had become so physically painful and obscure, and he was so agitated he couldn't say what he wanted, and I couldn't understand. At a certain point he said something which no one here has been able to explain to me, he said, "Who is eating out of my bowl?" And I didn't know what this meant and I yet don't know. And I asked him. He managed a faint whimsical smile and said, "Oh, never mind, it is only a joke." And later on, feeling my need to know a little so I could do something, he said in an agonizing way, "At this point there is so little to share." Then I knew that he knew that he was going. However, this inability to express himself was only muscular - his brain was clear and in fact, I feel, at a pitch of activity.

Then I don't know exactly what time it was, he asked for his tablet and wrote, "Try LSD 100 ~~mgms~~ intramuscular." Although as you see from this photostatic copy it is not very clear, I know that this is what he meant. I asked him and he confirmed it. Suddenly something became very clear to me. I knew that we were together again after this torturous talking of the last two months. I knew then, I knew what was to be done. I went quickly into the cupboard in the other room where Dr. Bernstein was, and the TV which had just announced the shooting of Kennedy. I took the LSD and said, "I am going to give him a shot of LSD, he asked for it." The doctor had a moment of agitation because you know very well the uneasiness about this drug in the medical mind. Then he said, "All right, at this point what is the difference." Whatever he had said, no "authority," not even an army of authorities could have stopped me then. I went into Aldous' room with the vial of LSD and prepared a syringe. The doctor asked me if I wanted him to give him the shot – maybe because he saw that my hands were trembling. His asking me that made me conscious of my hands, and I said, "No, I must do this." I quieted myself, and when I gave him the shot my hands were very firm. Then, somehow, a great relief came to us both. I believe it was 11:20 when I gave him his first shot of 100 microgrammes. I sat near his bed and I said, "Darling, maybe in a little while I will take it with you. Would you like me to take it also in a little while?" I said a little while because I had no idea of when I should or could take it, in fact I have not been able to take it to this writing because of the condition around me. And he indicated "yes." We must keep in mind that by now he was speaking very, very little. Then I said, "Would you like Matthew to take it with you also? And he said, "Yes." "What about Ellen?" He said, "Yes." Then I mentioned two or three people who had been working with LSD and he said, "No, no, basta, basta." Then I said, "What about Jinny?" And he said, "Yes," with emphasis. Then we were quiet. I just sat there without speaking for a while. Aldous was not so agitated physically. He seemed – somehow I felt he knew, we both knew what we were doing, and this has always been a great relief to Aldous. I have seen him at times during his illness very upset until he knew what he was going to do, then even if it was an operation or X-ray, he would make a total change. This enormous feeling of relief would come to him, and he wouldn't be worried at all about it, he would say let's do it, and we would go to it and he was like a liberated man. And now I had the same feeling – a decision had been made, he made the decision again very quickly. Suddenly he had accepted the fact of death; he had taken this moksha medicine in which he believed. He was doing what he had written in ISLAND, and I had the feeling that he was interested and relieved and quiet.

After half an hour, the expression on his face began to change a little, and I asked him if he felt the effect of LSD, and he indicated no. Yet, I think that a something had taken place already. This was one of Aldous' characteristics. He would always delay acknowledging the effect of any medicine, even when the effect was quite certainly there, unless the effect was very, very stong he would say no. Now, the expression of his face was beginning to look as it did every time that he had the moksha

together again after this torturous talking of the last two
months. I knew then, I knew what was to be done. I went quickly
into the cupboard in the other room where Dr. Bernstein was, and
the TV which had just announced the shooting of Kennedy. I took
the LSD and said, "I am going to give him a shot of LSD, he asked
for it." The doctor had a moment of agitation because you know
very well the uneasiness about this drug in the medical mind.
Then he said, "All right, at this point what is the difference."
Whatever he had said, no "authority," not even an army of
authorities could have stopped me then. I went into Aldous' room
with the vial of LSD and prepared a syringe. The doctor asked me
if I wanted him to give him the shot - maybe because he saw that
my hands were trembling. His asking me that made me conscious of
my hands, and I said, "No, I must do this." I quieted myself, and
when I gave him the shot my hands were very firm. Then, somehow,
a great relief came to us both. I believe it was 11:20 when I gave
him his first shot of 100 microgrammes. I sat near his bed and
I said, "Darling, maybe in a little while I will take it with you.
Would you like me to take it also in a little while?" I said a
little while because I had no idea of when I should or could take
it, in fact I have not been able to take it to this writing because
of the condition around me. And he indicated "yes." We must keep
in mind that by now he was speaking very, very little. Then I said,
"Would you like Matthew to take it with you also?" And he said,
"Yes." "What about Ellen?" He said, "Yes." Then I mentioned
two or three people who had been working with LSD and he said, "No,
no, basta, basta." Then I said, "What about Jinny?" And he said,
"Yes," with emphasis. Then we were quiet. I just sat there
without speaking for a while. Aldous was not so agitated physically. He seemed - somehow I felt he knew, we both knew what we
were doing, and this has always been a great relief to Aldous. I
have seen him at times during his illness very upset until he knew
what he was going to do, then even if it was an operation or
X-ray, he would make a total change. This enormous feeling of
relief would come to him, and he wouldn't be worried at all about
it, he would say let's do it, and we would go to it and he was
like a liberated man. And now I had the same feeling - a decision
had been made, he made the decision again very quickly. Suddenly
he had accepted the fact of death; he had taken this moksha
medicine in which he believed. He was doing what he had written
in ISLAND, and I had the feeling that he was interested and
relieved and quiet.

After half an hour, the expression on his face began to change
a little, and I asked him if he felt the effect of LSD, and he
indicated no. Yet, I think that a something had taken place
already. This was one of Aldous' characteristics. He would
always delay acknowledging the effect of any medicine, even when
the effect was quiet certainly there, unless the effect was very, very
stong he would say no. Now, the expression of his face was
beginning to look as it did every time that he had the moksha

medicine, when this immense expression of complete bliss and love would come over him. This was not the case now, but there was a change in comparison to what his face had been two hours ago. I let another half hour pass, and then I decided to give him another 100 mg. I told him I was going to do it, and he acquiesced. I gave him another shot, and then I began to talk to him. He was very quiet now; he was very quiet and his legs were getting colder; higher and higher I could see purple areas of cynosis. Then I began to talk to him, saying, "Light and free." Some of these things I told him at night in these last few weeks before he would go to sleep, and now I said it more convincingly, more intensely – "go, go, let go, darling; forward and up. You are going forward and up; you are going towards the light. Willing and consciously you are going, willingly and consciously, and you are doing this beautifully; you are doing this so beautifully – you are going towards the light; you are going towards a greater love; you are going forward and up. It is so easy; it is so beautiful. You are doing it so beautifully, so easily. Light and free. Forward and up. You are going towards Maria's love with my love. You are going towards a greater love than you have ever known. You are going towards the best, the greatest love, and it is easy, it is so easy, and you are doing it so beautifully." I believe I started to talk to him – it must have been about one or two o'clock. It was very difficult for me to keep track of time. The nurse was in the room and Rosalind and Jinny and two doctors – Dr. Knight and Dr. Cutler. They were sort of far away from the bed. I was very, very near his ears, and I hope I spoke clearly and understandingly. Once I asked him, "Do you hear me?" He squeezed my hand. He was hearing me. I was tempted to ask more questions, but in the morning he had begged me not to ask any more question, and the entire feeling was that things were right. I didn't dare to inquire, to disturb, and that was the only question that I asked, "Do you hear me?" Maybe I should have asked more questions, but I didn't.

Later on I asked the same question, but the hand didn't move any more. Now from two o'clock until the time he died, which was five-twenty, there was complete peace except for once. That must have been about three-thirty or four, when I saw the beginning of struggle in his lower lip. His lower lip began to move as if it were going to be a struggle for air. Then I gave the direction even more forcefully. "It is easy, and you are doing this beautifully and willingly and consciously, in full awareness, in full awareness, darling, you are going towards the light." I repeated these or similar words for the last three or four hours. Once in a while my own emotion would overcome me, but if it did I immediately would leave the bed for two or three minutes, and would come back only when I could dismiss my emotion. The twitching of the lower lip lasted only a little bit, and it seemed to respond completely to what I was saying. "Easy, easy, and you are doing this willingly and consciously and beautifully –

medicine, when this immense expression of complete bliss and love would come over him. This was not the case now, but there was a change in comparison to what his face had been two hours ago. I let another half hour pass, and then I decided to give him another 100 mg. I told him I was going to do it, and he acquiesced. I gave him another shot, and then I began to talk to him. He was very quiet now; he was very quiet and his legs were getting colder; higher and higher I could see purple areas of cynosis. Then I began to talk to him, saying, "Light and free." Some of these things I told him at night in these last few weeks before he would go to sleep, and now I said it more convincingly, more intensely - "go, go, let go, darling; forward and up. You are going forward and up; you are going towards the light. Willing and consciously you are going, willingly and consciously, and you are doing this beautifully; you are doing this so beautifully - you are going towards the light; you are going towards a greater love; you are going forward and up. It is so easy; it is so beautiful. You are doing it so beautifully, so easily. Light and free. Forward and up. You are going towards Maria's love with my love. You are going towards a greater love than you have ever known. You are going towards the best, the greatest love, and it is easy, it is so easy, and you are doing it so beautifully." I believe I started to talk to him - it must have been about one or two o'clock. It was very difficult for me to keep track of time. The nurse was in the room, and Rosalind and Jinny and two doctors - Dr. Knight and Dr. Cutler. They were sort of far away from the bed. I was very, very near his ears, and I hope I spoke clearly and understandingly. Once I asked him, "Do you hear me?" He squeezed my hand. He was hearing me. I was tempted to ask more questions, but in the morning he had begged me not to ask any more question, and the entire feeling was that things were right. I didn't dare to inquire, to disturb, and that was the only question that I asked, "Do you hear me?" Maybe I should have asked more questions, but I didn't.

Later on I asked the same question, but the hand didn't move any more. Now from two o'clock until the time he died, which was five-twenty, there was complete peace except for once. That must have been about three-thirty or four, when I saw the beginning of struggle in his lower lip. His lower lip began to move as if it were going to be a struggle for air. Then I gave the direction even more forcefully. "It is easy, and you are doing this beautifully and willingly and consciously, in full awareness, in full awareness, darling, you are going towards the light." I repeated these or similar words for the last three or four hours. Once in a while my own emotion would overcome me, but if it did I immediately would leave the bed for two or three minutes, and would come back only when I could dismiss my emotion. The twitching of the lower lip lasted only a little bit, and it seemed to respond completely to what I was saying. "Easy, easy, and you are doing this willingly and consciously and beautifully -

going forward and up, light anf free, forward and up towards the light, into the light, into complete love." The twitching stopped, the breating became slower and slower, and there was absolutely not the slightest indication of contraction, of struggle. it was just that the breathing became slower – and slower – and slower, and at five-twenty the breathing stopped.

I had been warned in the morning that there might be some up–setting convulsions towards the end, or some sort of contraction of the lungs, and noises. People had been trying to prepare me for some horrible physical reaction that would probably occur. None of this happened, actually the ceasing of the breathing was not a drama at all, because it was done so slowly, so gently, like a piece of music just finishing in a sempre piu piano dolcemente. I had the feeling actually that the last hour of breathing was only the conditioned reflex of the body that had been used to doing this for 69 years, millions and millions of times. There was not the feeling that with the last breath, the spirit left. It had just been gently leaving for the last four hours. In the room the last four hours were two doctors, Jinny, the nurse, Rosalind Roger Gopal – you know she is the great friend of Krishnamurti, and the directress of the school in Ojai for which Aldous did so much. They didn't seem to hear what I was saying. I thought I was speaking loud enough, but they said they didn't hear it. Rosalind and Jinny once in a while came near the bed and held Aldous' hand. These five people all said that this was the most serene, the most beautiful death. Both doctors and nurse said they had never seen a person in similar physical condition going off so completely without pain and without struggle.

We will never know if all this is only our wishful thinking, or if it is real, but certainly all outward signs and the inner feeling gave indication that it was beautiful and peaceful and easy.

And now, after I have been alone these few days, and less bombarded by other people's feelings, the meaning of this last day becomes clearer and clearer to me and more and more important. Aldous was, I think (and certainly I am) appalled at the fact that what he wrote in ISLAND was not taken seriously. It was treated as a work of science fiction, when it was not fiction because each one of the ways of living he described in ISLAND was not a product of his fantasy, but something that had been tried in one place or another and some of them in our own everyday life. If the way Aldous died were known, it might awaken people to the awareness that not only this, but many other facts described in ISLAND are possible here and now. Aldous' asking for moksha medicine while dying is a confirmation of his work, and as such is of importance not only to us, but to the world. It is true we will have some people saying that he was a drug addict all his life and that he ended as one, but it is history that Huxleys stop ignorance before ignorance can stop Huxleys.

light, into the light, into complete love." The twitching
stopped, the breating became slower and slower, and there was
absolutely not the slightest indication of contraction, of struggle.
it was just that the breathing became slower - and slower - and
slower, and at five-twenty the breathing stopped.

I had been warned in the morning that there might be some
up-setting convulsions towards the end, or some sort of contraction
of the lungs, and noises. People had been trying to prepare me for
some horrible physical reaction that would probably occur. None
of this happened, actually the ceasing of the breathing was not a
drama at all, because it was done so slowly, so gently, like a
piece of music just finishing in a sempre piu piano dolcemente.
I had the feeling actually that the last hour of breathing was
only the conditioned reflex of the body that had been used to
doing this for 69 years, millions and millions of times. There
was not the feeling that with the last breath, the spirit left.
It had just been gently leaving for the last four hours. In the
room the last four hours were two doctors, Jinny, the nurse,
Rosalind   Roger Gopal - you know she is the great friend of
Krishnamurti, and the directress of the school in Ojai for which
Aldous did so much. They didn't seem to hear what I was saying.
I thought I was speaking loud enough, but they said they didn't
hear it. Rosalind and Jinny once in a while came near the bed
and held Aldous' hand. These five people all said that this was
the most serene, the most beautiful death. Both doctors and nurse
said they had never seen a person in similar physical condition
going off so completely without pain and without struggle.

We will never know if all this is only our wishful thinking,
or if it is rea l, but certainly all outward signs and the inner
feeling gave indication that it was beautiful and peaceful and
easy.

And now, after I have been alone these few days, and less
bombarded by other people's feelings, the meaning of this last
day becomes clearer and clearer to me and more and more important.
Aldous was, I think (and certainly I am) appalled at the fact
that what he wrote in ISLAND was not taken seriously. It was
treated as a work of science fiction, when it was not fiction
because each one of the ways of living he described in ISLAND was
not a product of his fantasy, but something that had been tried
in one place or another and some of them in our own everyday
life. If the way Aldous died were known, it might awaken
people to the awareness that not only this, but many other facts
described in ISLAND are possible here and now. Aldous' asking
for moksha medicine while dying is a confirmation of his work,
and as much is of importance not only to us, but to the world.
It is true we will have some people saying that he was a drug
addict all his life and that he ended as one, but it is history
that Huxley's stop ignorance before ignoracne can stop Huxleys.

Even after our correspondence on the subject, I had many doubts about keeping Aldous in the dark regarding his condition. It seemed not just that, after all he had written and spoken about death, he should be let to go into it unaware. And he had such complete confidence in me – he might have taken it for granted that had death been near I certainly would have told him and helped him. So my relief at his sudden awakening at his quick adjusting is immense. Don't you feel this also.

Now, is his way of dying to remain our, and only our relief and consolation, or should others also benefit from it? What do you feel?

Even after our correspondence on the subject, I had many doubts about keeping Aldous in the dark regarding his condition. It seemed not just that, after all he had written and spoken about death, he should be let to go into it unaware. And he had such complete confidence in me - he might have taken it for granted that had death been near I certainly would have told him and helped him. So my relief at his sudden awakening at his quick adjusting is immense. Don't you feel this also.

Now, is his way of dying to remain our, and only our relief and consolation, or should others also benefit from it? What do you feel?

REGARDING YOUR DAM COMPLAINT

STEPHEN L. TVEDTEN to
DAVID L. PRICE
January 6th, 1998

In December 1997, as a result of an official complaint from a neighbour, a Michigan resident named Stephen Tvedten received, indirectly, a stern warning from the region's Department of Environmental Quality in the form of a letter – a letter in which he was given six weeks to remove two "unauthorized" and "hazardous" dams from the stream on his property or else face prosecution. Tvedten's amusing response, in which he makes a mockery of the complaint and refuses to comply on behalf of the beavers who built those dams, soon made the local news. The case was quickly dropped.

STATE OF MICHIGAN

December 17, 1997

CERTIFIED

Dear Mr. DeVries:

SUBJECT: DEQ File No. 97-59-0023-1 T11N, R10W, Sec. 20, Montcalm County

It has come to the attention of the Department of Environmental Quality that there has been recent unauthorized activity on the above referenced parcel of property. You have been certified as the legal landowner and/or contractor who did the following unauthorized activity:

Construction and maintenance of two wood debris dams across the outlet stream of Spring Pond. A permit must be issued prior to the start of this type of activity. A review of the Department's files show that no permits have been issued.

Therefore, the Department has determined that this activity is in violation of Part 301, Inland Lakes and Streams, of the Natural Resource and Environmental Protection Act, Act 451 of the Public Acts of 1994, being sections 324.30101 to 324.30113 of the Michigan Compiled Laws annotated. The Department has been informed that one or both of the dams partially failed during a recent rain event, causing debris dams and flooding at downstream locations. We find that dams of this nature are inherently hazardous and cannot be permitted. The Department therefore orders you to cease and desist all unauthorized activities at this location, and to restore the stream to a free-flow condition by removing all wood and brush forming the dams from the strewn channel. All restoration work shall be completed no later than January 31, 1998. Please notify this office when the restoration has been completed so that a follow-up site inspection may be scheduled by our staff. Failure to comply with this request, or any further unauthorized activity on the site, may result in this case being referred for elevated enforcement action. We anticipate and would appreciate your full cooperation in this matter.

Please feel free to contact me at this office if you have any questions.

Sincerely,

[Redacted]
District Representative
Land and Water Management Division

1/6/98

[Redacted]
District Representative
Land and Water Management Division
Grand Rapids District Office

Dear [Redacted]:

Re: DEQ File No. 97-59-0023; T11N, R10W, Sec 20; Montcalm County

Your certified letter dated 12/17/97 has been handed to me to respond to. You sent out a great deal of carbon copies to a lot of people, but you neglected to include their addresses. You will, therefore, have to send them a copy of my response.

First of all, Mr. Ryan DeVries is not the legal landowner and/or contractor at 2088 Dagget, Pierson, Michigan — I am the legal owner and a couple of beavers are in the (State unauthorized) process of constructing and maintaining two wood "debris" dams across the outlet stream of my Spring Pond. While I did not pay for, nor authorize their dam project, I think they would be highly offended you call their skillful use of natural building materials "debris". I would like to challenge you to attempt to emulate their dam project any dam time and/or any dam place you choose. I believe I can safely state there is no dam way you could ever match their dam skills, their dam resourcefulness, their dam ingenuity, their dam persistence, their dam determination and/or their dam work ethic.

As to your dam request the beavers first must fill out a dam permit prior to the start of this type of dam activity, my first dam question to you is: are you trying to discriminate against my Spring Pond Beavers or do you require all dam beavers throughout this State to conform to said dam request? If you are not discriminating against these particular beavers, please send me completed copies of all those other applicable beaver dam permits. Perhaps we will see if there really is a dam violation of Part 301, Inland Lakes and Streams, of the Natural Resource and Environmental Protection Act, Act 451 of the Public Acts of 1994, being sections 324.30101 to 324.30113 of the Michigan Compiled Laws annotated.

My first concern is — aren't the dam beavers entitled to dam legal representation? The Spring Pond Beavers are financially destitute and are unable to pay for said dam representation — so the State will have to provide them with a dam lawyer. The Department's dam concern that either one or both of the dams failed during a recent rain event causing dam flooding is proof we should leave the dam Spring Pond Beavers alone rather than harassing them and calling their dam names. If you want the dam stream "restored" to a dam free-flow condition — contact the dam beavers — but if you are going to arrest them (they obviously did not pay any dam attention to your dam letter — being unable to read English) — be sure you read them their dam Miranda first.

As for me, I am not going to cause more dam flooding or dam debris jams by interfering with these dam builders. If you want to hurt these dam beavers — be aware I am sending a copy of your dam letter and this response to PETA. If your dam Department seriously finds all dams of this nature inherently hazardous and truly will not permit their existence in this dam State — I seriously hope you are not selectively enforcing this dam policy — or once again both I and the Spring Pond Beavers will scream prejudice!

In my humble opinion, the Spring Pond Beavers have a right to build their dam unauthorized dams as long as the sky is blue, the grass is green and water flows downstream. They have more dam right than I to live and enjoy Spring Pond. So, as far as I and the beavers are concerned, this dam case can be referred for more dam elevated enforcement action now. Why wait until 1/31/98? The Spring Pond Beavers may be under the dam ice then, and there will be no dam way for you or your dam staff to contact/harass them then. In conclusion, I would like to bring to your attention a real environmental quality (health) problem; bears are actually defecating in our woods. I definitely believe you should be persecuting the defecating bears and leave the dam beavers alone. If you are going to investigate the beaver dam, watch your step! (The bears are not careful where they dump!)

Being unable to comply with your dam request, and being unable to contact you on your dam answering machine, I am sending this response to your dam office.

Sincerely,

Stephen L. Tvedten

cc: PETA

WHY EXPLORE SPACE?

DR. ERNST STUHLINGER to
SISTER MARY JUCUNDA
May 6th, 1970

In 1970, a Zambia-based nun
named Sister Mary Jucunda
wrote to the director of
science at NASA's Marshall
Space Flight Center, Dr.
Ernst Stuhlinger, and posed
a question related to his
ongoing research into a
piloted mission to Mars;
specifically, she asked how
he could possibly suggest
spending billions of dollars
on such a project at a time
when so many children
were starving here on
earth. Stuhlinger replied to
Sister Jucunda with both a
thoughtful, lengthy letter
and a copy of "Earthrise",
the iconic photograph
of earth taken from the
moon in 1968 by astronaut
William Anders. Stuhlinger's
response was so admired
by his colleagues that it was
later published by NASA for
wider consumption, bearing
the title, *Why Explore Space?*

May 6, 1970

Dear Sister Mary Jucunda:

Your letter was one of many which are reaching me every day, but it has touched me more deeply than all the others because it came so much from the depths of a searching mind and a compassionate heart. I will try to answer your question as best as I possibly can.

First, however, I would like to express my great admiration for you, and for all your many brave sisters, because you are dedicating your lives to the noblest cause of man: help for his fellowmen who are in need.

You asked in your letter how I could suggest the expenditures of billions of dollars for a voyage to Mars, at a time when many children on this Earth are starving to death. I know that you do not expect an answer such as "Oh, I did not know that there are children dying from hunger, but from now on I will desist from any kind of space research until mankind has solved that problem!" In fact, I have known of famined children long before I knew that a voyage to the planet Mars is technically feasible. However, I believe, like many of my friends, that travelling to the Moon and eventually to Mars and to other planets is a venture which we should undertake now, and I even believe that this project, in the long run, will contribute more to the solution of these grave problems we are facing here on Earth than many other potential projects of help which are debated and discussed year after year, and which are so extremely slow in yielding tangible results.

Before trying to describe in more detail how our space program is contributing to the solution of our Earthly problems, I would like to relate briefly a supposedly true story, which may help support the argument. About 400 years ago, there lived a count in a small town in Germany. He was one of the benign counts, and he gave a large part of his income to the poor in his town. This was much appreciated, because poverty was abundant during medieval times, and there were epidemics of the plague which ravaged the country frequently. One day, the count met a strange man. He had a workbench and little laboratory in his house, and he labored hard during the daytime so that he could afford a few hours every evening to work in his laboratory. He ground small lenses from pieces of glass; he mounted the lenses in tubes, and he used these gadgets to look at very small objects. The count was particularly fascinated by the tiny creatures that could be observed with the strong magnification, and which he had never seen before. He invited the man to move with his laboratory to the castle, to become a member of the count's household, and to devote henceforth all his time to the development and perfection of his optical gadgets as a special employee of the count.

The townspeople, however, became angry when they realized that the count was wasting his money, as they thought, on a stunt without purpose. "We are suffering from this plague," they said, "while he is paying that man for a useless hobby!" But

the count remained firm. "I give you as much as I can afford," he said, "but I will also support this man and his work, because I know that someday something will come out of it!"

Indeed, something very good came out of this work, and also out of similar work done by others at other places: the microscope. It is well known that the microscope has contributed more than any other invention to the progress of medicine, and that the elimination of the plague and many other contagious diseases from most parts of the world is largely a result of studies which the microscope made possible.

The count, by retaining some of his spending money for research and discovery, contributed far more to the relief of human suffering than he could have contributed by giving all he could possibly spare to his plague-ridden community.

The situation which we are facing today is similar in many respects. The President of the United States is spending about 200 billion dollars in his yearly budget. This money goes to health, education, welfare, urban renewal, highways, transportation, foreign aid, defense, conservation, science, agriculture and many installations inside and outside the country. About 1.6 percent of this national budget was allocated to space exploration this year. The space program includes Project Apollo, and many other smaller projects in space physics, space astronomy, space biology, planetary projects, Earth resources projects, and space engineering. To make this expenditure for the space program possible, the average American taxpayer with 10,000 dollars income per year is paying about 30 tax dollars for space. The rest of his income, 9,970 dollars, remains for his subsistence, his recreation, his savings, his other taxes, and all his other expenditures.

You will probably ask now: "Why don't you take 5 or 3 or 1 dollar out of the 30 space dollars which the average American taxpayer is paying, and send these dollars to the hungry children?" To answer this question, I have to explain briefly how the economy of this country works. The situation is very similar in other countries. The government consists of a number of departments (Interior, Justice, Health, Education and Welfare, Transportation, Defense, and others) and the bureaus (National Science Foundation, National Aeronautics and Space Administration, and others). All of them prepare their yearly budgets according to their assigned missions, and each of them must defend its budget against extremely severe screening by congressional committees, and against heavy pressure for economy from the Bureau of the Budget and the President. When the funds are finally appropriated by Congress, they can be spent only for the line items specified and approved in the budget.

The budget of the National Aeronautics and Space Administration, naturally, can contain only items directly related to aeronautics and space. If this budget were not approved by Congress, the funds proposed for it would not be available for something else; they would simply not be levied from the taxpayer, unless one of the other budgets had obtained approval for a specific increase which would then absorb the funds not spent for space. You realize from this brief discourse that support for hungry children, or rather a support in addition to what the United States is already contributing to this very worthy cause in the form of foreign aid, can be obtained only if the appropriate department submits a budget line item for this purpose, and if this line item is then approved by Congress.

You may ask now whether I personally would be in favor of such a move by our government. My answer is an emphatic yes. Indeed, I would not mind at all if my annual taxes were increased by a number of dollars for the purpose of feeding hungry children, wherever they may live.

I know that all of my friends feel the same way. However, we could not bring such a program to life merely by desisting from making plans for voyages to Mars. On the contrary, I even believe that by working for the space program I can make some contribution to the relief and eventual solution of such grave problems as poverty and hunger on Earth. Basic to the hunger problem are two functions: the production of food and the distribution of food. Food production by agriculture, cattle ranching, ocean fishing and other large-scale operations is efficient in some parts of the world, but drastically deficient in many others. For example, large areas of land could be utilized far better if efficient methods of watershed control, fertilizer use, weather forecasting, fertility assessment, plantation programming, field selection, planting habits, timing of cultivation, crop survey and harvest planning were applied.

The best tool for the improvement of all these functions, undoubtedly, is the artificial Earth satellite. Circling the globe at a high altitude, it can screen wide areas of land within a short time; it can observe and measure a large variety of factors indicating the status and condition of crops, soil, droughts, rainfall, snow cover, etc., and it can radio this information to ground stations for appropriate use. It has been estimated that even a modest system of Earth satellites equipped with Earth resources, sensors, working within a program for worldwide agricultural improvements, will increase the yearly crops by an equivalent of many billions of dollars.

The distribution of the food to the needy is a completely different problem. The question is not so much one of shipping volume, it is one of international cooperation. The ruler of a small nation may feel very uneasy about the prospect of having large quantities of food shipped into his country by a large nation, simply because he fears that along with the food there may also be an import of influence and foreign power. Efficient relief from hunger, I am afraid, will not come before the boundaries between nations have become less divisive than they are today. I do not believe that space flight will accomplish this miracle over night. However, the space program is certainly among the most promising and powerful agents working in this direction.

Let me only remind you of the recent near-tragedy of Apollo 13. When the time of the crucial reentry of the astronauts approached, the Soviet Union discontinued all Russian radio transmissions in the frequency bands used by the Apollo Project in order to avoid any possible interference, and Russian ships stationed themselves in the Pacific and the Atlantic Oceans in case an emergency rescue would become necessary. Had the astronaut capsule touched down near a Russian ship, the Russians would undoubtedly have expended as much care and effort in their rescue as if Russian cosmonauts had returned from a space trip. If Russian space travelers should ever be in a similar emergency situation, Americans would do the same without any doubt.

Higher food production through survey and assessment from orbit, and better food distribution through improved international relations, are only two examples of how profoundly the space program will impact life on Earth. I would like to quote two other examples: stimulation of technological development, and generation of scientific knowledge.

The requirements for high precision and for extreme reliability which must be imposed upon the components of a moon-travelling spacecraft are entirely unprecedented in the history of engineering. The development of systems which meet these severe requirements has provided us a unique opportunity to find new material and methods, to invent better technical systems, to manufacturing procedures, to lengthen the lifetimes of instruments, and even to discover new laws of nature.

All this newly acquired technical knowledge is also available for application to Earth-bound technologies. Every year, about a thousand technical innovations generated in the space program find their ways into our Earthly technology where they lead to better kitchen appliances and farm equipment, better sewing machines and radios, better ships and airplanes, better weather forecasting and storm warning, better communications, better medical instruments, better utensils and tools for everyday life. Presumably, you will ask now why we must develop first a life support system for our moon-travelling astronauts, before we can build a remote-reading sensor system for heart patients. The answer is simple: significant progress in the solutions of technical problems is frequently made not by a direct approach, but by first setting a goal of high challenge which offers a strong motivation for innovative work, which fires the imagination and spurs men to expend their best efforts, and which acts as a catalyst by including chains of other reactions.

Spaceflight without any doubt is playing exactly this role. The voyage to Mars will certainly not be a direct source of food for the hungry. However, it will lead to so many new technologies and capabilities that the spin-offs from this project alone will be worth many times the cost of its implementation.

Besides the need for new technologies, there is a continuing great need for new basic knowledge in the sciences if we wish to improve the conditions of human life on Earth. We need more knowledge in physics and chemistry, in biology and physiology, and very particularly in medicine to cope with all these problems which threaten man's life: hunger, disease, contamination of food and water, pollution of the environment.

We need more young men and women who choose science as a career and we need better support for those scientists who have the talent and the determination to engage in fruitful research work. Challenging research objectives must be available, and sufficient support for research projects must be provided. Again, the space program with its wonderful opportunities to engage in truly magnificent research studies of moons and planets, of physics and astronomy, of biology and medicine is an almost ideal catalyst which induces the reaction between the motivation for scientific work, opportunities to observe exciting phenomena of nature, and material support needed to carry out the research effort.

Among all the activities which are directed, controlled, and funded by the American government, the space program is certainly the most visible and probably the most debated activity, although it consumes only 1.6 percent of the total national budget, and 3 per mille (less than one-third of 1 percent) of the gross national product. As a stimulant and catalyst for the development of new technologies, and for research in the basic sciences, it is unparalleled by any other activity. In this respect, we may even say that the space program is taking over a function which for three or four thousand years has been the sad prerogative of wars.

How much human suffering can be avoided if nations, instead of competing with their bomb-dropping fleets of airplanes and rockets, compete with their moon-travelling space ships! This competition is full of promise for brilliant victories, but it leaves no room for the bitter fate of the vanquished, which breeds nothing but revenge and new wars.

Although our space program seems to lead us away from our Earth and out toward the moon, the sun, the planets, and the stars, I believe that none of these celestial objects will find as much attention and study by space scientists as our Earth. It will become a better Earth, not only because of all the new technological and scientific knowledge which we will apply to the betterment of life, but also because we are developing a far deeper appreciation of our Earth, of life, and of man.

The photograph which I enclose with this letter shows a view of our Earth as seen from Apollo 8 when it orbited the moon at Christmas, 1968. Of all the many wonderful results of the space program so far, this picture may be the most important one. It opened our eyes to the fact that our Earth is a beautiful and most precious island in an unlimited void, and that there is no other place for us to live but the thin surface layer of our planet, bordered by the bleak nothingness of space. Never before did so many people recognize how limited our Earth really is, and how perilous it would be to tamper with its ecological balance. Ever since this picture was first published, voices have become louder and louder warning of the grave problems that confront man in our times: pollution, hunger, poverty, urban living, food production, water control, overpopulation. It is certainly not by accident that we begin to see the tremendous tasks waiting for us at a time when the young space age has provided us the first good look at our own planet.

Very fortunately though, the space age not only holds out a mirror in which we can see ourselves, it also provides us with the technologies, the challenge, the motivation, and even with the optimism to attack these tasks with confidence. What we learn in our space program, I believe, is fully supporting what Albert Schweitzer had in mind when he said: "I am looking at the future with concern, but with good hope."

My very best wishes will always be with you, and with your children.

Very sincerely yours,

Ernst Stuhlinger

Associate Director for Science

I AM VERY REAL

KURT VONNEGUT to
CHARLES MCCARTHY
November 16th, 1973

Since first being published
in 1967, and despite being
considered one of the
great modern novels, Kurt
Vonnegut's time-hopping,
semi-autobiographical, anti-
war classic, *Slaughterhouse-
Five*, has been, and
continues to be, banned
from classrooms and
libraries the world over due
to what is often described
by those who censor it as
its "obscene" content. This
view wasn't held by Bruce
Severy, a then 26-year-old
English teacher at Drake
High School, North Dakota,
who in 1973 decided to use
the novel as a teaching aid
in his classroom, much to
the delight of his students.
Unfortunately for them, the
head of the school board,
Charles McCarthy, had other
ideas: the next month, he
demanded that all 32 copies
be burned in the school's
furnace.

On November 16th, an angry
and disappointed Vonnegut
wrote to McCarthy and made
his feelings known. His
brilliant and powerful letter
failed to generate a reply.

November 16, 1973

Dear Mr. McCarthy:

I am writing to you in your capacity as chairman of the Drake School Board. I am
among those American writers whose books have been destroyed in the now famous
furnace of your school.

Certain members of your community have suggested that my work is evil. This is
extraordinarily insulting to me. The news from Drake indicates to me that books
and writers are very unreal to you people. I am writing this letter to let you know
how real I am.

I want you to know, too, that my publisher and I have done absolutely nothing to
exploit the disgusting news from Drake. We are not clapping each other on the
back, crowing about all the books we will sell because of the news. We have declined
to go on television, have written no fiery letters to editorial pages, have granted
no lengthy interviews. We are angered and sickened and saddened. And no copies
of this letter have been sent to anybody else. You now hold the only copy in your
hands. It is a strictly private letter from me to the people of Drake, who have done
so much to damage my reputation in the eyes of their children and then in the eyes
of the world. Do you have the courage and ordinary decency to show this letter to
the people, or will it, too, be consigned to the fires of your furnace?

I gather from what I read in the papers and hear on television that you imagine
me, and some other writers, too, as being sort of ratlike people who enjoy making
money from poisoning the minds of young people. I am in fact a large, strong
person, fifty-one years old, who did a lot of farm work as a boy, who is good with
tools. I have raised six children, three my own and three adopted. They have all
turned out well. Two of them are farmers. I am a combat infantry veteran from
World War II, and hold a Purple Heart. I have earned whatever I own by hard
work. I have never been arrested or sued for anything. I am so much trusted
with young people and by young people that I have served on the faculties of the
University of Iowa, Harvard, and the City College of New York. Every year I
receive at least a dozen invitations to be commencement speaker at colleges and
high schools. My books are probably more widely used in schools than those of any
other living American fiction writer.

If you were to bother to read my books, to behave as educated persons would, you
would learn that they are not sexy, and do not argue in favor of wildness of any
kind. They beg that people be kinder and more responsible than they often are.
It is true that some of the characters speak coarsely. That is because people speak
coarsely in real life. Especially soldiers and hardworking men speak coarsely, and
even our most sheltered children know that. And we all know, too, that those words
really don't damage children much. They didn't damage us when we were young.
It was evil deeds and lying that hurt us.

After I have said all this, I am sure you are still ready to respond, in effect, "Yes, yes—but it still remains our right and our responsibility to decide what books our children are going to be made to read in our community." This is surely so. But it is also true that if you exercise that right and fulfill that responsibility in an ignorant, harsh, un-American manner, then people are entitled to call you bad citizens and fools. Even your own children are entitled to call you that.

I read in the newspaper that your community is mystified by the outcry from all over the country about what you have done. Well, you have discovered that Drake is a part of American civilization, and your fellow Americans can't stand it that you have behaved in such an uncivilized way. Perhaps you will learn from this that books are sacred to free men for very good reasons, and that wars have been fought against nations which hate books and burn them. If you are an American, you must allow all ideas to circulate freely in your community, not merely your own.

If you and your board are now determined to show that you in fact have wisdom and maturity when you exercise your powers over the education of your young, then you should acknowledge that it was a rotten lesson you taught young people in a free society when you denounced and then burned books—books you hadn't even read. You should also resolve to expose your children to all sorts of opinions and information, in order that they will be better equipped to make decisions and to survive.

Again: you have insulted me, and I am a good citizen, and I am very real.

Kurt Vonnegut

AN IDIOT OF THE 33RD DEGREE

MARK TWAIN to J. H. TODD
November 20th, 1905

Mark Twain, the inimitable author of, most famously, *Adventures of Huckleberry Finn*, saw more illness than most in his lifetime. In 1872, he lost a 19-month-old son, Langdon, to diphtheria; in 1896, he lost a daughter, Susy, to meningitis; and in 1904, his wife, Olivia, passed away from heart failure. So when, just a year after being widowed, he received both a letter and pamphlet from a seller of "The Elixir of Life", a supposedly magical medicine that could cure all of the above and more, he had every right to be angry and desperate to respond. So he did just that, furiously and in style. The version you see here was a draft, immediately dictated to his secretary.

Nov. 20. 1905

J. H. Todd
1212 Webster St.
San Francisco, Cal.

Dear Sir,

Your letter is an insoluble puzzle to me. The handwriting is good and exhibits considerable character, and there are even traces of intelligence in what you say, yet the letter and the accompanying advertisements profess to be the work of the same hand. The person who wrote the advertisements is without doubt the most ignorant person now alive on the planet; also without doubt he is an idiot, an idiot of the 33rd degree, and scion of an ancestral procession of idiots stretching back to the Missing Link. It puzzles me to make out how the same hand could have constructed your letter and your advertisements. Puzzles fret me, puzzles annoy me, puzzles exasperate me; and always, for a moment, they arouse in me an unkind state of mind toward the person who has puzzled me. A few moments from now my resentment will have faded and passed and I shall probably even be praying for you; but while there is yet time I hasten to wish that you may take a dose of your own poison by mistake, and enter swiftly into the damnation which you and all the other patent medicine assassins have so remorselessly earned and do so richly deserve.

Adieu, adieu, adieu!

Mark Twain

Nov. 20. 1905

JosH. Todd –

1212 Webster St.

Dear Sir   San Francisco
                              Cal.

          Your letter is an insoluble
puzzle to me. The hand writing
is good + exhibits considerable
character, + there are even
traces of intelligence in what
you say, in it, get the letter
+ the accompanying adver-
tisements profess to be the
work of the same hand.
          The person who wrote the
advertisements is without doubt the
most ignorant person now
alive on the planet; also without doubt he is an idiot, an
idiot of the 33rd degree, +
scion of an ancestral procession
of idiots stretching back to the
Missing Link. It puzzles me
to make out how the same
hand could have constructed

207

& your letter & your advertisements.
Puzzles fret me, puzzles
annoy me, puzzles exasperate
me; & always, for a moment,
they arouse in me an unkind
state of mind toward the person
who has puzzled me. A few
moments from now my
resentment will have faded
& passed, & I shall probably
even be praying for you; but
while there is yet time I
hasten to wish you may
take a dose of your own
poison by mistake, & enter
swiftly into the damnation
which you & all the other
patent medicine assassins
have so remorselessly earned
& so richly deserve.

Adieu, adieu, adieu!

Mark Twain

HANG ON, MY LOVE, AND GROW BIG AND STRONG

IGGY POP to LAURENCE
February, 1995

It took nine months for Iggy Pop to reply to 21-year-old Laurence's fan letter, but really the timing couldn't have been more perfect, as on the morning his thoughtful note *did* arrive at her home in Paris, Laurence's family were being evicted by bailiffs. Laurence recalls that moment back in 1995:

"By the time I finished I was in tears. Not only had Iggy Pop received the letter I had sent him nine months before – which I could have missed if he'd sent it a day later – but he had read the whole 'fucking' 20 pages, including the bit about my Adidas dress (a semi-innocent allusion on my part), and all the rest; my description of being the child of an acrimonious divorce with the string of social workers, lawyers, greedy estate agents and bailiffs at the door, the fear, the anger, the frustration, the love."

Although brief, Iggy's empathetic, handwritten response addressed Laurence's problems with both grace and eloquence, and really can't be praised enough.

dear laurence,

thankyou for your gorgeous and charming letter, you brighten up my dim life. i read the whole fucking thing, dear. of course, i'd love to see you in your black dress and your white socks too. but most of all i want to see you take a deep breath and do whatever you must to survive and find something to be that you can love. you're obviously a bright fucking chick, w/ a big heart too and i want to wish you a (belated) HAPPY HAPPY HAPPY 21st b'day and happy spirit. i was very miserable and fighting hard on my 21st b'day, too. people booed me on the stage, and i was staying in someone else's house and i was scared. it's been a long road since then, but pressure never ends in this life. 'perforation problems' by the way means to me also the holes that will always exist in any story we try to make of our lives. so hang on, my love, and grow big and strong and take your hits and keep going.

all my love to a really beautiful girl.
that's you laurence.

iggy pop

dear laurence,

thankyou for your gorgeous and charming letter, you brighten up my bim life. i read the whole fucking thing, bear. of course, i'd love to see you in your black dress + your white socks too. but most of all i want to see you take a ~~deep breath~~ breath + do whatever you must to survive + find something to be that you can love. you're obviously a bright fucking chick, w/ a big heart too + i want to wish you a (belated) HAPPY HAPPY HAPPY 21ˢᵗ b'day + a HAPPY spirit. i was very miserable + fighting hard on my 21ˢᵗ b'day, too. people booed me on the stage, + i was staying in someone else's house and i was scared.

its been a long road since then,
but pressure never ends in this life.

perforation problems' by the way
means to me also the holes that
will always exist in any story
we try to make of our ~~to~~ lives.
so hang on, my love, + grow big
+ strong + take your hits + keep going.
all my love to a really beautiful
girl
that's you Florence!

I WROTE A BOOK CALLED *THE GODFATHER*

MARIO PUZO to MARLON BRANDO
January 23rd, 1970

In 1970, before Francis Ford Coppola had taken his place in the director's chair, *The Godfather* author Mario Puzo scribbled and sent the following letter to Marlon Brando, the one man he was determined to see take on the role of Vito Corleone in the forthcoming movie adaptation of his novel. Although Brando was keen, the studio refused Puzo's request to cast him, due largely to the actor's reputation as a live wire with notoriously overbearing demands and a diminishing box office. Then Coppola came on board, filmed Brando in character as the Don, and screened it for the executives at Paramount. They quickly changed their tune.

The Godfather went on to break records and win multiple awards. Brando's magnificent turn as Vito Corleone netted him an Oscar for Best Actor, which he famously refused.

MARIO PUZO
866 MANOR LANE
BAY SHORE, LONG ISLAND
NEW YORK, N. Y. 11706

Jan 23

Dear Mr Brando

I wrote a book called THE GODFATHER which has had some success and I think you're the only actor who can play the ~~part~~ Godfather with that quiet force and irony (the book is an ironical comment on American society) the part requires. I hope you'll read the book and like it well enough to use whatever power you can to get the role.

I'm writing Paramount to the same effect for whatever good that will do.

I know this was presumptuous of me but the least I can do for the book is try. I really think you'd be tremendous. Needless to say I've been an admirer of your art.

Mario Puzo

A mutual friend, Jeff Brown, gave me your address

The book is an ironical comment on American Society

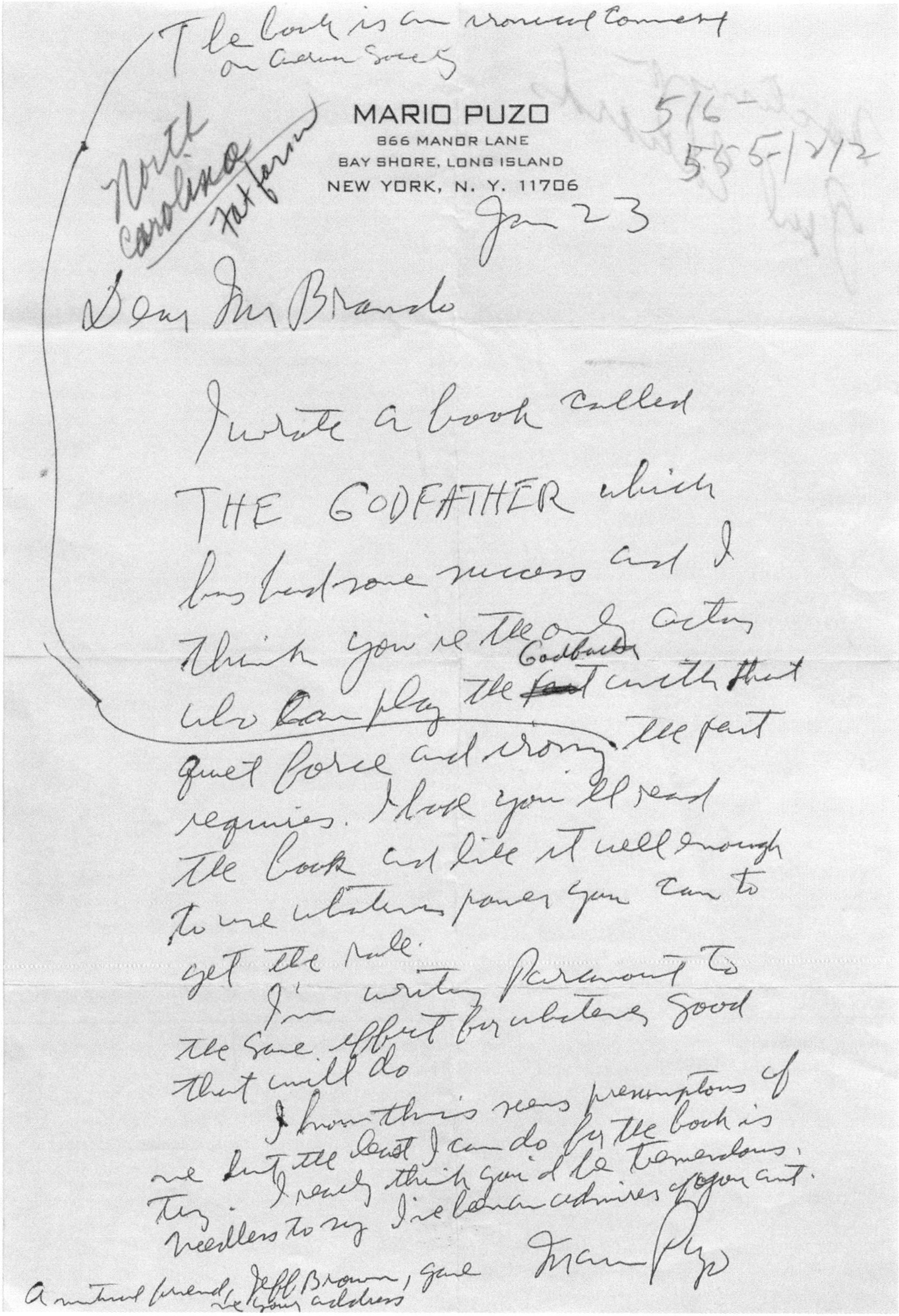

MARIO PUZO
866 MANOR LANE
BAY SHORE, LONG ISLAND
NEW YORK, N. Y. 11706

North Carolina fat farm

516-555-1212

Jan 23

Dear Mr Brando

I wrote a book called THE GODFATHER which has had some success and I think you're the only actor who can play the ~~part~~ Godfather with that quiet force and irony the part requires. I hope you'll read the book and like it well enough to use whatever power you can to get the role.

I'm writing Paramount to the same effect for whatever good that will do.

I know this seems presumptuous of me but the least I can do for the book is try. I really think you'd be tremendous. Needless to say I've been an admirer of your art.

Mario Puzo

A mutual friend, Jeff Brown, gave me your address

MORTON THIOKOL, INC.   COMPANY PRIVATE

Wasatch Division

Interoffice Memo

31 July 1985
2870:FY86:073

TO: R. K. Lund
         Vice President, Engineering

CC: B. C. Brinton, A. J. McDonald, L. H. Sayer, J. R. Kapp

FROM: R. M. Boisjoly
         Applied Mechanics - Ext. 3525

SUBJECT: SRM O-Ring Erosion/Potential Failure Criticality

This letter is written to insure that management is fully aware of the seriousness of the current O-Ring erosion problem in the SRM joints from an engineering standpoint.

The mistakenly accepted position on the joint problem was to fly without fear of failure and to run a series of design evaluations which would ultimately lead to a solution or at least a significant reduction of the erosion problem. This position is now drastically changed as a result of the SRM 16A nozzle joint erosion which eroded a secondary O-Ring with the primary O-Ring never sealing.

If the same scenario should occur in a field joint (and it could), then it is a jump ball as to the success or failure of the joint because the secondary O-Ring cannot respond to the clevis opening rate and may not be capable of pressurization. The result would be a catastrophe of the highest order - loss of human life.

An unofficial team (a memo defining the team and its purpose was never published) with leader was formed on 19 July 1985 and was tasked with solving the problem for both the short and long term. This unofficial team is essentially nonexistent at this time. In my opinion, the team must be officially given the responsibility and the authority to execute the work that needs to be done on a non-interference basis (full time assignment until completed).

It is my honest and very real fear that if we do not take immediate action to dedicate a team to solve the problem with the field joint having the number one priority, then we stand in jeopardy of losing a flight along with all the launch pad facilities.

R. M. Boisjoly

Concurred by:

J. R. Kapp, Manger
Applied Mechanics

COMPANY PRIVATE

THE RESULT WOULD BE A CATASTROPHE

ROGER BOISJOLY to R. K. LUND
July 31st, 1985

On January 28th 1986, just 73 seconds after launch, a tragedy was witnessed by millions as Space Shuttle *Challenger* broke apart over the coast of Florida and ended the lives of all seven of its crew members. A subsequent investigation determined that the accident had been caused by the failure of an O-ring – essentially a rubber seal on one of the shuttle's solid rocket boosters – brought on, in part, by extremely cold weather around the time of launch. But the disaster wasn't a shock to all involved. Six months prior to launch, this memo was sent by Roger Boisjoly, an engineer working at Morton Thiokol, the manufacturers of the solid rocket boosters, to the company's Vice President. In it, he predicted the problem and warned of a potential "catastrophe of the highest order".

Tragically, Boisjoly's warning went unheeded. He later attempted to halt the launch, unsuccessfully.

ALL THE LADIES LIKE WHISKERS

GRACE BEDELL to
ABRAHAM LINCOLN
October 15th, 1860

In 1860, having recently seen a picture of him without facial hair, an 11-year-old girl named Grace Bedell decided to write to Republican candidate and future US President Abraham Lincoln, with a single suggestion that would surely win him the affections of the voting public. That suggestion was simply to grow a beard. To her amazement and delight, Lincoln soon replied; better still, she met him in person a few months later, as he travelled victoriously to Washington, DC by train – and he now had a beard.

"He climbed down and sat down with me on the edge of the station platform," Grace later recalled. "'Gracie,' he said, 'look at my whiskers. I have been growing them for you.' Then he kissed me. I never saw him again."

Westfield Chautauque Co NY
Oct 15–1860

Hon A B Lincoln

    Dear Sir

      My father has just home from the fair and brought home your picture and Mr. Hamlin's. I am a little girl only 11 years old, but want you should be President of the United States very much so I hope you wont think me very bold to write to such a great man as you are. Have you any little girls about as large as I am if so give them my love and tell her to write to me if you cannot answer this letter. I have got 4 brothers and part of them will vote for you any way and if you let your whiskers grow I will try and get the rest of them to vote for you you would look a great deal better for your face is so thin. All the ladies like whiskers and they would tease their husbands to vote for you and then you would be President. My father is going to vote for you and if I was a man I would vote for you to but I will try to get every one to vote for you that I can I think that rail fence around your picture makes it look very pretty I have got a little baby sister she is nine weeks old and is just as cunning as can be. When you direct your letter direct to Grace Bedell Westfield Chautauque County New York.

    I must not write any more answer this letter right off Good bye

                Grace Bedell

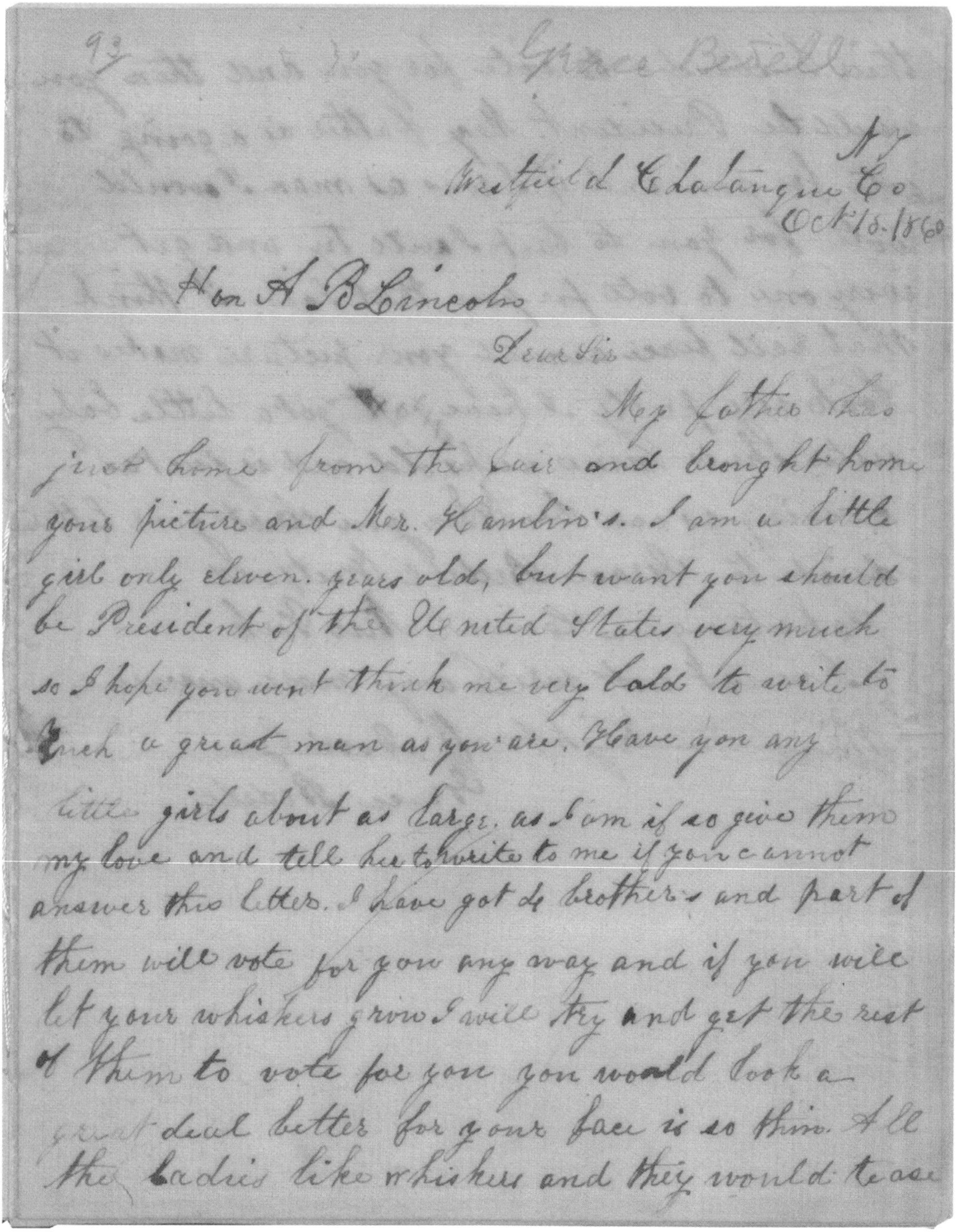

Westfield Chatauque Co N.Y.
Oct 15. 1860

Hon A B Lincoln

Dear Sir

My father has
just home from the fair and brought home
your picture and Mr. Hamlin's. I am a little
girl only eleven years old, but want you should
be President of the United States very much
so I hope you wont think me very bold to write to
such a great man as you are. Have you any

little girls about as large as I am if so give them
my love and tell her to write to me if you cannot
answer this letter. I have got 4 brothers and part of
them will vote for you any way and if you will
let your whiskers grow I will try and get the rest
of them to vote for you you would look a
great deal better for your face is so thin. All
the ladies like whiskers and they would tease

their husbands to vote for you and then you would be President. My father is a going to vote for you and if I was a man I would vote for you to but I will try and get every one to vote for you that I can I think that rail fence around your picture makes it look very pretty I have got a little baby sister she is nine weeks old and is just as cunning as can be. When you direct your letter diret to Grace Bedell Westfield Chatange County New York

I must not write any more answer this letter right off Good bye

Grace Bedell

Springfield, Ill. Oct 19, 1860

Miss Grace Bedell
        My dear little Miss
                Your very agreeable letter of the 15th is received—
I regret the necessity of saying I have no daughters— I have three sons— one
seventeen, one nine, and one seven years of age— They, with their mother,
constitute my whole family—
As to the whiskers, having never worn any, do you not think people would call it a
piece of silly affectation if I were to begin it now?
                                Your very sincere well wisher
                                        A. Lincoln

Springfield, Ills. Oct 19. 1860

Miss. Grace Bedell

My dear little Miss.

Your very agreeable letter of the 15th is received—

I regret the necessity of saying I have no daughter— I have three sons— one seventeen, one nine, and one seven, years of age— They, with their mother, constitute my whole family—

As to the whiskers having never worn any, do you not think people would call it a piece of silly affectation if I were to begin it now?—

Your very sincere well-wisher

A. Lincoln

219

AMERICAN GOTHIC PRODUCTIONS, INC.

February 13, 1987

Mr. Leslie Barany
UGLY PUBLISHING INTERNATIONAL

Dear Mr. Barany:

I regret that the intense pressure to complete "ALIENS" did not afford me the time to reply to your letter of 3/11/86, which was on behalf of your client, Mr. H.R. Giger.

In that letter you describe Mr. Giger's 'initial sense of disappointment' at not being contacted for "ALIENS" in view of his, quite correct, intense sense of authorship of the creatures and designs. Ironically, it was the production design of "ALIEN", with its bizarre, psycho-sexual landscape of the subconscious as created by Mr. Giger, that initially attracted me to the project of a sequel. However, having been a production designer myself before becoming a director, I felt I had to put my own unique stamp on the project. Otherwise, it would have had little meaning for me at that point in my career, when I had a number of original concepts and creations which I could have pursued, with equal financial reward and an even greater degree of authorship.

I found that creating a sequel can be an uneasy exercise in balancing creative impulses, the desire to create a whole new canvas, with the need to pay proper hommage to the original. Mr. Giger's visual stamp was so powerful and pervasive in "ALIEN" (a major contributor to its success, I believe) that I felt the risk of being overwhelmed by him and his world, if we had brought him into a production where in a sense, he had more reason to be there than I did.

Because 20th Century Fox liked the story I presented to them, they gave me the opportunity to create the world I had seen in my mind as I wrote. I took that opportunity, and enlisted the aid of special effects designers, sculptors and technicians with whom I had worked before which, of course, is a natural course when one must guarantee a schedule and budget.

An additional deciding factor was Mr. Giger's conflicting involvement in "POLTERGEIST II" which unfortunately did not utilize his vision nearly as well as "ALIEN".

2

I offer all this commentary by way of apology and explanation in the hope that Mr. Giger can find it possible to forgive me for abducting his 'first-born'. If so, there may come a time when we can collaborate in mutual respect on some completely new and original project where the only limitation is his superb imagination.

I am, first and always, a fan of his work (a signed litho of the alien egg commissioned during "ALIEN" is one of my prized possessions).

Sincerely.

JAMES F. CAMERON

JC:lw

I FELT THE RISK OF BEING OVERWHELMED BY GIGER

JAMES CAMERON to LESLIE BARANY
February 13th, 1987

Considering the hugely positive reaction to his incredible Oscar-winning work on the film's predecessor, it's little wonder that H. R. Giger was "disappointed" not to be contacted when production began on *Aliens*, the second instalment in what is still one of the most successful movie franchises in cinema's history. Indeed, Giger, the celebrated Swiss artist who famously designed the beautifully horrific Alien itself in the late 1970s, vocalised his displeasure and, via his agent, Leslie Barany, even wrote to the sequel's director, James Cameron. Three months later, Cameron explained his decision by way of this fascinating and remarkably honest letter.

HOW COULD YOU GO AHEAD OF ME?

A WIDOW to EUNG-TAE LEE
June 1st, 1586

In 1998, shortly after excavating an ancient tomb in Andong City, South Korea, archaeologists were stunned to find the coffin of Eung-Tae Lee – a 16th-century male, now mummified, who, until his death at the age of 30, had been a member of Korea's ancient Goseong Yi clan. Resting on his chest was this incredibly moving letter, written by his pregnant widow and addressed to the father of their unborn child; also found in the tomb, placed beside his head, were some sandals, woven from hemp bark and his distraught wife's own hair.

The letter and tomb's discovery generated enormous interest in Korea and the story has since been retold in novels, films and even operas. A statue of Eung-Tae Lee's pregnant wife now stands near his grave.

To Won's Father

June 1, 1586

You always said, "Dear, let's live together until our hair turns gray and die on the same day." How could you pass away without me? Who should I and our little boy listen to and how should we live? How could you go ahead of me?

How did you bring your heart to me and how did I bring my heart to you? Whenever we lay down together you always told me, "Dear, do other people cherish and love each other like we do? Are they really like us?" How could you leave all that behind and go ahead of me?

I just cannot live without you. I just want to go to you. Please take me to where you are. My feelings toward you I cannot forget in this world and my sorrow knows no limit. Where would I put my heart in now and how can I live with the child missing you?

Please look at this letter and tell me in detail in my dreams. Because I want to listen to your saying in detail in my dreams I write this letter and put it in. Look closely and talk to me.

When I give birth to the child in me, who should it call father? Can anyone fathom how I feel? There is no tragedy like this under the sky.

You are just in another place, and not in such a deep grief as I am. There is no limit and end to my sorrows that I write roughly. Please look closely at this letter and come to me in my dreams and show yourself in detail and tell me. I believe I can see you in my dreams. Come to me secretly and show yourself. There is no limit to what I want to say and I stop here.

워닉 아븨님젼 샹백

병슐 뉴월 초...

I AM THE SERVANT OF THE KING

AYYAB to AMENHOTEP IV
Circa 1340 BC

In the late 1800s, locals in Armana discovered a collection of clay tablets in the ruins of the ancient Egyptian city of Akhetaten, all covered in an unintelligible script now known to be Akkadian cuneiform – an extinct, Middle Eastern language imprinted into wet clay as far back as 2600 BC. These stunning tablets were in fact diplomatic correspondence of old, sent between kings and officials of neighbouring lands; to this day 382 have been found. This particular example was written between 1350 and 1335 BC by Ayyab – king of the city of Aštartu in the Canaan region – and sent to Amenhotep IV, then Pharaoh of the eighteenth dynasty of ancient Egypt.

Justified War

To the king, my lord.

Message of Ayyab, your servant.

I fall at the feet of my lord 7 times and 7 times. I am the servant of the king, my lord, the dirt at his feet. I have heard what the king, my lord, wrote to me through Atahmaya. Truly, I have guarded very carefully, the cities of the king, my lord. Moreover, note that it is the ruler of Hasura who has taken 3 cities from me. From the time I heard and verified this, there has been waging of war against him. Truly, may the king, my lord, take cognizance, and may the king, my lord, give thought to his servant.

I SHALL ALWAYS BE NEAR YOU

SULLIVAN BALLOU to
SARAH BALLOU
July 14th, 1861

In 1861, as the American
Civil War approached, a
32-year-old lawyer named
Sullivan Ballou left his wife
of five years and two sons
at home and joined the
war effort as a major in the
Union Army. On July 14th of
that year, acutely aware that
particularly perilous times
were ahead, he wrote, but
didn't send, the following
beautiful letter to his wife, in
which he eloquently warned
her of the dangers he faced
and spoke of his love for
both his family and country.
Sadly, two weeks after
penning his letter, Sullivan
was killed in the First Battle
of Bull Run – the first major
conflict of a war that lasted
four years and cost the lives
of more than 600,000 people
– along with 93 of his men.
The letter was later found
amongst his belongings and
then delivered to his widow,
but has since been lost; this
copy, thought to have been
transcribed by a relative, is
held at the Abraham Lincoln
Presidential Library.

Sarah, who was 24 when
her husband died, never
remarried. She passed away
at 80 years of age and is now
buried alongside Sullivan in
Providence, Rhode Island.

Headquarters
Camp Clark
Washington D. C.

July 14th 1861

My Very dear Wife

The indications are very strong that we shall move in a few days perhaps tomorrow and lest I should not be able to write you again I feel impelled to write a few lines that may fall under your eye when I am am no more. Our movement may be one of a few days duration and be full of pleasure. And it may be one of severe conflict and death to me "Not my will but thine O God be done" if it is necessary that I should fall on the battle field for my Country I am ready. I have no misgivings about or lack of confidence in the cause in which I am engaged, and my courage does not halt or falter. I know how American Civilization now leans upon the triumph of the Government and how great a debt we owe to those who went before us through the blood and suffering of the Revolution; and I am willing perfectly willing to lay down all my joys in this life to help maintain this Government and to pay that debt.

But my dear wife, when I know that with my own joys I lay down nearly all of yours,– and replace them in this life with care and sorrow– when, after having eaten for long years the bitter fruit of orphanage myself, I must offer it as their only sustenance to my dear little children, is it weak or dishonorable that while the banner of purpose flotes calmly and proudly in the breeze, underneath my unbounded love for you my dear wife and children should struggle in fierce though useless contest with my love of Country

I cannot describe to you my feelings on this calm summer night when two thousand men are sleeping around me, many of them enjoying the last perhaps before that of Death. And I suspicious that Death is creeping behind me with his fatal dart am communing with God my Country and thee. I have sought most closely and diligently and often in my breast for a wrong motive in thus hazarding the happiness of all that I love and I could not find one. A pure love of my Country and of the principles I have advocated before the people and the name of honour that I love more than I fear death, have called upon me and I have obeyed.

Sarah my love for you is deathless it seems to bind me with mighty cables that nothing but Omnipotence can break. And yet my love of Country comes over me like a strong wind and bears me irresistibly with all those chains to the battle field the memories of all the blissful moments I have enjoyed with you come crowding over me, and I feel most deeply grateful to God and you that I have enjoyed them so long. And how hard it is for me to give them up; and burn to ashes the hopes of future years when God willing we might still have loved and loved together and see our boys grow up to honourable manhood around us. I know I have but few and small claimes upon Divine Providence but something whispers to me perhaps it is the wafted prayer of my little Edgar that I shall return to my loved ones unharmed. If I do not my dear Sarah never forget how much I loved you nor that when my last breath escapes me on the battlefield it will whisper your name

Forgive my many faults and the many pains I have caused you. How thoughtless how foolish I have sometimes been! How gladly would I wash out with my tears every little spot upon your happiness and strugle with all the misfortunes of this world to shield you and my children from harm but I cannot I must watch you from the spirit world and hover near you while you buffet the stormes with your precious little freight – and wait with sad patience till we meet to part no more

But Oh Sarah! If the dead can come back to this earth and flit unseen around those they love I shall be always with you in the brightest day and the darkest night amidst your happiest sceans and gloomiest hours <u>always</u> <u>always</u> and when the soft breeze fans your cheek it shall be my breath or the cool air your throbbing temple it shall be my spirit passing by. Sarah, do not mourn me dead think I am gone and wait for me for we shall meet again.

As for my little boys they will grow as I have done and never know a fathers love and care.

Little Willie is to young to remember me long but my blue eyed Edgar will keep my frolics with him among the dimmest memories of his childhood

Sarah I have unlimited confidence in your maternal care and your development of their characters. Tell my two Mothers I call Gods blessings upon them

Oh! Sarah I wait for you <u>then</u> come to me and lead thither my children

Sullivan

Copy of a letter from Sullivan Ballou to
his wife before the battle of Bull Run

Headquarters
Camp Clark
Washington D. C.

July 14th 1861

My Very dear Wife

The indications are very strong that we
shall move in a few days perhaps tomorrow. And lest I should
not be able to write you again I feel impelled to write you
a few lines that may fall under your eye when I am am no
more. Our movement may be one of a few days duration and
be full of pleasure. And it may be one of severe conflict and death
to me. "Not my will but thine O God be done" if it is neces
-sary that I should fall on the battle field for my Country I
am ready. I have no misgivings about or lack of confidence
in the Cause in which I am engaged, and my courage does
not halt or falter. I know how American Civilization now
bears upon the triumph of the Government and how great
a debt we owe to those who went before us through the blood
and suffering of the Revolution; and I am willing perfectly
willing to lay down all my joys in this life to help
maintain this Government and to pay that debt.
But my dear wife, when I know that with my own joys I lay
down nearly all of yours,— and replace them in this life with care

228

and sorrow when after having eaten for long years the bitter fruit of orphenage myself. I must offer it as their onely sustenance to my dear little children. is it weak or dishonourable that while the banner of purpose flotes calmly and proudly in the breeze. underneath my unbounded love for you my dear wife and children should struggle in fierce though useless contest with my love of Country

I cannot discribe to you my feelings on this calm summer night when two thousand men are sleeping around me. many of them enjoying the last perhaps before that of Death. And I suspicious that Death is creeping behind me with his fatal dart am communeing with God my Cou"try and thee. I have sought most closely and dilegently and often in my brest for a wrong motive in thus hazerding the happiness of all that I love and I could not find one. A pure love of my Country and of the princefels, I have advocated before the people and the name of honour that I love more than I fear death. have called upon me and I have obeyed.

Sarah my love for you is deathless it seemes to bind me with mighty Cables that nothing but Omnipotence can break And yet my love of Country comes over me like a strong wind and bears me irresistibly with all those chains to the battle field the memories of all the blissful moments I have enjoyed with you come crouding over me. and I feel most deeply grateful to God and you that I have enjoyed them so long. And how

hard it is for me to give them up! and burn to ashes the
the hopes of future years when God willing we might still
have lived and loved together and see our boys grow up to hon
-ourable manhood around us. I know I have but few claims
upon Divine Providence but something whispers to me perhaps it
is the wafted prayer of my little Edgar that I shall return to my
loved ones unharmed. If I do not my dear Sarah never forget
how much I loved you nor that when my last breath escapes me
on the battlefield it will whisper your name
Forgive my many faults and the many pains I have caused you
How thoughtless how foolish I have sometimes been! How gladly
would I wash out with my tears every little spot upon your happiness
and strugle with all the misfortunes of this world to shield you
and my children from harm but I cannot I must watch
you from the spirit world and hover near you while you buffet
t the stormes with your precious little freight - and wait with
sad paitience till we meet to part no more
But Oh Sarah! if the dead can come back to this earth and flit
unseen around those they love I shall be always with you in
the brightest day and the darkest night amidst your happies
t sceans and gloomiest hours always always and when the
soft breeze fans your cheek it shall be my breath as the cool
air your throbbing temple it shall be my spirit passing by -
Sarah. do not mourn me dead think I am gone and wait
for me for we shall meet again.
As for my little boys they will grow up as I have done and

230

never know a fathers love and care

Little Willie is to young to remember me long but
my blue-eyed Edgar will keep my frolics with him
among the dimmest memories of his childhood

Sarah I have unlimited confidence in your maternal care
and your developement of their characters. Tell my
two Mothers I call Gods blessings upon them

Oh! Sarah I wait for you then come to me and lead
Hither my children

                    Sullivan

I'M STILL SOMEPLACE

UNCLE LYNN to PEGGY,
DOROTHY, CHUCK AND
DICK JONES
Unknown

In his wonderful book, *Chuck Reducks*, the late Chuck Jones – a true legend in the world of animation who, amongst countless other achievements, created such classic characters as Wile E. Coyote and Road Runner, and also directed what is widely considered to be one of the best cartoons ever made: *What's Opera, Doc?* – credits his beloved "Uncle Lynn" with teaching him "everything [he] would need to know about animated cartoon writing" during his early years, also painting him as a hugely positive influence in his life in general and an "ideal uncle" whom he "worshipped". Uncle Lynn also knew how to write. One day, soon after the sad death of the Jones's dear family dog, Teddy, Uncle Lynn sent this heartwarming letter to young Chuck and his siblings.

Dear Peggy and Dorothy and Chuck and Dick,

I had a telephone call last night. "Is this Uncle Lynn?" someone asked.

"Why yes," I said. "My name is Lynn Martin. Are you some unregistered nephew?"

"This is Teddy." He sounded a little impatient with me. "Teddy Jones, Teddy Jones the resident dog of 115 Wadsworth Avenue, Ocean Park, California. I'm calling long distance."

"Excuse me," I said. "I really don't mean to offend you, but I've never heard you talk before—just bark, or whine, or yell at the moon."

"Look who's talking," Teddy sniffed, a really impatient sniff if ever I've heard one. "Look, Peggy and Dorothy and Chuck and Dick seem to be having a very rough time of it because they think I'm dead." Hesitate. "Well, I suppose in a way I am."

I will admit that hearing a dog admit that he was dead was a new experience for me, and not a totally expected one. "If you're dead," I asked, not being sure of just how you talk to a dead dog, "how come you're calling me?" There was another irritated pause. Clearly he was getting very impatient with me.

"Because," he said, in as carefully a controlled voice as I've ever heard from a dog. "Because when you are alive, even if the kids don't know exactly where you are, they know you're someplace. So I just want them to know I may be sort of dead, but I'm still someplace."

"Maybe I should tell them you're in Dog Heaven, Teddy, Maybe to make 'em feel—"

"Oh, don't be silly." Teddy cleared his throat. "Look, where are you?"

"Oh, no, you don't. We're trying to find out where you are," I barked.

"Hey, I didn't know you could bark." He sounded impressed with my command of the language.

"Wait just a minute," I said. "You had to know where I am, or you couldn't have called me on the telephone, right?"

"Boy, you know so little," said Teddy. "I simply said I called you long distance. Who said anything about a telephone? They asked me if I knew where you were, and I said you were someplace else, besides 115 Wadsworth Avenue. So they dialled someplace else and here I am and here you are."

"Can I call you back?" I asked dazedly. "Maybe that'll give me a clue."

"Be reasonable," said Teddy. "How can you call me back when neither you nor I know where I am?"

"Oh, come on, give me a clue," I begged desperately. "For instance, are there other dogs around there? I've got to tell the kids something."

"Hold it," said Teddy, apparently looking around. "I did see a pug/schnauzer with wings a minute ago. The wings could lift the schnauzer part of him off the ground, but the pug part just sort of dragged through the grass bumping into fireplugs."

"Fireplugs?"

"Orchards of them, hundreds of 'em. Yellow, red, white, striped. Unfortunately, I don't seem to have to pee anymore. I strain a lot, but all I get is air.

Perfumed air," he added proudly.

"Sounds like Dog Heaven to me," I said. "Are there trees full of lamb chops and stuff like that?"

"You know," Teddy sighed. "For a fair to upper-middle-class uncle, you do have some weird ideas. But the reason I called you was Peggy, Dorothy, Chuck, and Dick trust you and will believe anything you say, which in my opinion is carrying the word 'gullible' about as far as it will stretch. Anyway, gullible or not, they trust you, so I want you to tell them that I'm still their faithful, noble, old dog, and—except for the noble part—that I'm in a place where they can't see me but I can see them, and I'll always be around keeping an eye, an ear, and a nose on them. Tell them that just because they can't see me doesn't mean I'm not there. Point out to them that during the day you can't see the latitudes and you can't really see a star, but they're both still there. So get a little poetic and ask them to think of me as 'good-dog,' the good old Teddy, the Dog Star from the horse latitudes, and not to worry, I'll bark the britches off anybody or anything that bothers them. Just because I bit the dust doesn't mean I can't bite the devils."

That's what he said. I never did find out exactly where he was, but I did find out where he wasn't—not ever very far from Peggy, Dorothy, Chuck and old Dick Jones.

Sincerely,
Lynn Martin, Uncle at Large

THE BIRTH OF
BONFIRE NIGHT

UNKNOWN to WILLIAM
PARKER, 4TH BARON
MONTEAGLE
October 26th, 1605

On October 26th 1605, William Parker, 4th Baron Monteagle, received a letter in which he was advised, anonymously, to stay away from Parliament the following week as a "terrible blowe" was expected to meet all those present. That terrible blow was in fact the Gunpowder Plot, a plan to destroy the Houses of Parliament organised by a group of people that included Guy Fawkes, a man now familiar to millions and whose failures we celebrate on November 5th of each year. Rather than burn the letter after reading as suggested, Parker passed it to the Earl of Salisbury, who then informed King James of the planned atrocity. As a result, in the early hours of November 5th, Fawkes was discovered underneath Parliament along with 36 barrels of gunpowder and the plot was foiled.

For the next 254 years it was compulsory in Britain to celebrate the plot's failure, with most choosing to burn an effigy of Fawkes on a bonfire.

My lord, out of the love I beare to some of youere frends, I have a care of youre preservacion, therefore I would aduyse you as you tender your life to devise some excuse to shift youer attendance at this parliament, for God and man hath concurred to punishe the wickedness of this tyme, and thinke not slightly of this advertisement, but retire yourself into your country, where you may expect the event in safety, for though there be no apparance of anni stir, yet I saye they shall receive a terrible blowe this parliament and yet they shall not seie who hurts them this cowncel is not to be contemned because it may do yowe good and can do yowe no harme for the dangere is passed as soon as yowe have burnt the letter and i hope God will give yowe the grace to mak good use of it to whose holy proteccion i comend yowe.

my lord out of the loue i beare to some of youer frends
i haue a caer of youer preseruacion therfor i would
aduyse yowe as yowe tender youer lyf to deuyse some
excuse to shift of youer attendance at this parleament
for god and man hathe concurred to punishe the wickednes
of this tyme and thinke not slightlye of this aduertisment
but retyere youre self into youer contri whaere yowe
maye expect the event in safti for thowghe theare be no
apparance of anni stir yet i saye they shall receyue a terrible
blowe this parleament and yet they shall not seie who
hurts them this councel is not to be contemned because
it maye do yowe good and can do yowe no harme for the
dangere is passed as soon as yowe haue burnt the letter
and i hope god will give yowe the grace to mak good
use of it to whose holy proteccion i comend yowe

IT'S UP TO YOU NOW

BETTE DAVIS to B. D.
HYMAN
1987

In 1983, at the end of an
amazing career during
which she was nominated
for a then record-breaking
ten Academy Awards for
acting, two of which she
won, legendary Hollywood
actress Bette Davis was
diagnosed with breast
cancer. Surgery followed,
as did a number of strokes
which left her partially
paralysed. Then, in 1985, her
daughter Barbara released
a controversial book titled
My Mother's Keeper, which
exposed their supposedly
troubled relationship and
generally painted Davis in
a terrible light. Two years
later, Davis published her
memoirs – at the very
end was this letter to her
daughter.

Dear Hyman,

You ended your book with a letter to me. I have decided to do the same.

There is no doubt you have a great potential as a writer of fiction. You have always been a great storyteller. I have often, lo these many years, said to you, "B.D., that is not the way it was. You are imagining things."

Many of the scenes in your book I have played on the screen. It could be you have confused the "me" on the screen with "me" who is your mother.

I have violent objections to your quotes of mine regarding actors I have worked with. For the most part, you have cruelly misquoted me. Ustinov I was thrilled to work with and I have great admiration of him as a person and as an actor. You have stated correctly my reactions to working with Faye Dunaway. She was a most exasperating co-star. But to quote me as having said Sir Laurence Olivier was not a good actor is most certainly one of the figments of your imagination. Few actors have ever reached the towering heights of his performances.

You constantly inform people that you wrote this book to help me understand you and your way of life better. Your goal was not reached. I am now utterly confused as to who you are or what your way of life is.

The sum total of your having written this book is a glaring lack of loyalty and thanks for the very privileged life I feel you have been given.

In one of your many interviews while publicizing your book, you said if you sell your book to TV you feel Glenda Jackson should play me. I would hope you would be courteous enough to ask me to play myself.

I have much to quarrel about in your book. I choose to ignore most of it. But not the pathetic creature you claim I have been because of the fact that I did not play Scarlett in "Gone With the Wind." I could have, but turned it down. Mr. Selznick attempted to get permission from my boss, Jack Warner, to borrow Errol Flynn and Bette Davis to play Rhett Butler and Scarlett. I refused because I felt Errol was not good casting for Rhett. At that time only Clark Gable was right. Therefore, dear Hyman, send me not back to Tara, rather send me back to Witch Way, our home on the beautiful coast of Maine where once lived a beautiful human being by the name of B.D., not Hyman.

As you ended your letter in "My Mother's Keeper" — it's up to you now, Ruth Elizabeth — I am ending my letter to you the same way: It's up to you now, Hyman.

Ruth Elizabeth

P.S. I hope someday I will understand the title "My Mother's Keeper." If it refers to money, if my memory serves me right, I've been your keeper all these many years. I am continuing to do so, as my name has made your book about me a success.

FORGET YOUR PERSONAL TRAGEDY

ERNEST HEMINGWAY to
F. SCOTT FITZGERALD
May 28th, 1934

In 1925, following
publication of his magnum
opus, *The Great Gatsby*,
author F. Scott Fitzgerald
began work on his fourth
novel, *Tender Is the Night* – a
tale about the troubled lives
of Dick and Nicole Diver,
a couple based largely on
Gerald and Sara Murphy,
a wealthy, popular couple
who moved in the same
social circles as Fitzgerald
in the 1920s. It would be
another nine years before it
was complete, and on May
10th 1934, a month after its
publication, Fitzgerald wrote
to his friend and fellow
novelist, Ernest Hemingway,
to ask for his honest opinion
on what was to be his final
book.

Hemingway certainly didn't
hold back and replied with
a brutally honest letter that
contains valuable advice for
writers the world over.

Key West
28 May 1934

Dear Scott:

I liked it and I didn't. It started off with that marvelous description of Sara and Gerald (goddamn it Dos took it with him so I can't refer to it. So if I make any mistakes—). Then you started fooling with them, making them come from things they didn't come from, changing them into other people and you can't do that, Scott. If you take real people and write about them you cannot give them other parents than they have (they are made by their parents and what happens to them) you cannot make them do anything they would not do. You can take you or me or Zelda or Pauline or Hadley or Sara or Gerald but you have to keep them the same and you can only make them do what they would do. You can't make one be another. Invention is the finest thing but you cannot invent anything that would not actually happen.

That is what we are supposed to do when we are at our best—make it all up—but make it up so truly that later it will happen that way.

Goddamn it you took liberties with peoples' pasts and futures that produced not people but damned marvellously faked case histories. You, who can write better than anybody can, who are so lousy with talent that you have to—the hell with it. Scott for gods sake write and write truly no matter who or what it hurts but do not make these silly compromises. You could write a fine book about Gerald and Sara for instance if you knew enough about them and they would not have any feeling, except passing, if it were true.

There were wonderful places and nobody else nor none of the boys can write a good one half as good reading as one that doesn't come out by you, but you cheated too damned much in this one. And you don't need to.

In the first place I've always claimed that you can't think. All right, we'll admit you can think. But say you couldn't think; then you ought to write, invent, out of what you know and keep the people's antecedants straight. Second place, a long time ago you stopped listening except to the answers to your own questions. You had good stuff in too that it didn't need. That's what dries a writer up (we all dry up. That's no insult to you in person) not listening. That is where it all comes from. Seeing, listening. You see well enough. But you stop listening.

It's a lot better than I say. But it's not as good as you can do.

You can study Clausewitz in the field and economics and psychology and nothing else will do you any bloody good once you are writing. We are like lousy damned acrobats but we make some mighty fine jumps, bo, and they have all these other acrobats that won't jump.

For Christ sake write and don't worry about what the boys will say nor whether it will be a masterpiece nor what. I write one page of masterpiece to ninety one pages of shit. I try to put the shit in the wastebasket. You feel you have to publish crap to make money to live and let live. All write but if you write enough and as well as you can there will be the same amount of masterpiece material (as we say at Yale). You can't think well enough to sit down and write a deliberate masterpiece and if you could get rid of Seldes and those guys that nearly ruined you and turn them out as well as you can and let the spectators yell when it is good and hoot when it is not you would be all right.

Forget your personal tragedy. We are all bitched from the start and you especially have to hurt like hell before you can write seriously. But when you get the damned hurt use it—don't cheat with it. Be as faithful to it as a scientist—but don't think anything is of any importance because it happens to you or anyone belonging to you.

About this time I wouldn't blame you if you gave me a burst. Jesus it's marvellous to tell other people how to write, live, die etc.

I'd like to see you and talk about things with you sober. You were so damned stinking in N.Y. we didn't get anywhere. You see, Bo, you're not a tragic character. Neither am I. All we are is writers and what we should do is write. Of all people on earth you needed discipline in your work and instead you marry someone who is jealous of your work, wants to compete with you and ruins you. It's not as simple as that and I thought Zelda was crazy the first time I met her and you complicated it even more by being in love with her and, of course you're a rummy. But you're no more of a rummy than Joyce is and most good writers are. But Scott, good writers always come back. Always. You are twice as good now as you were at the time you think you were so marvellous. You know I never thought so much of Gatsby at the time. You can write twice as well now as you ever could. All you need to do is write truly and not care about what the fate of it is.

Go on and write.

Anyway I'm damned fond of you and I'd like to have a chance to talk sometimes. We had good times talking. Remember that guy we went out to see dying in Neuilly? He was down here this winter. Damned nice guy Canby Chambers. Saw a lot of Dos. He's in good shape now and he was plenty sick this time last year. How is Scotty and Zelda? Pauline sends her love. We're all fine. She's going up to Piggott for a couple of weeks with Patrick. Then bring Bumby back. We have a fine boat. Am going good on a very long story. Hard one to write.

Always your friend

Ernest

[Written on envelope: What about The Sun also and the movies? Any chance? I dint put in about the good parts. You know how good they are. You're write about the book of stories. I wanted to hold it for more. That last one I had in Cosmopolitan would have made it.]

I WAS MEANT TO BE A COMPOSER

SAMUEL BARBER to
MARGUERITE BARBER
1919

To this day, the late Samuel Barber remains one of the most influential composers of all time. In 1936, at 26, he wrote *Adagio for Strings*, one of the most popular classical works of the 20th century; in 1958 he was awarded the Pulitzer Prize for Music for his opera, *Vanessa*; just five years later he received another Pulitzer for his Piano Concerto. In fact, it seems Barber knew from a very young age that he was to be a composer: in 1919, when he was just nine years old, he nervously left on his desk a confessional letter addressed to his mother, in the hopes she would come across it. She did. A year later, Barber began to compose his first opera, *The Rose Tree*.

NOTICE to Mother and nobody else

Dear Mother: I have written this to tell you my worrying secret. Now don't cry when you read it because it is neither yours nor my fault. I suppose I will have to tell it now without any nonsense. To begin with I was not meant to be an athlete. I was meant to be a composer, and will be I'm sure. I'll ask you one more thing.— Don't ask me to try to forget this unpleasant thing and go play football.—Please— Sometimes I've been worrying about this so much that it makes me mad (not very),

Love,

Sam Barber II

PERMISSION TO LAND

BUANG-LY to USS *MIDWAY*
April 30th, 1975

On April 30th 1975, the Vietnam War effectively came to a close with the capture of South Vietnam's capital city by North Vietnamese forces – the "Fall of Saigon". Shortly before this happened, as the US evacuated as many American civilians as possible by helicopter in *Operation Frequent Wind*, crew aboard the USS *Midway* were surprised to see a small two-seat Cessna O-1 Bird Dog approach the vessel and then circle above. Flying that plane, having just escaped from Con Son Island with his wife and five children – also aboard – was South Vietnamese Air Force Major Buang-Ly. With fuel running low, Buang-Ly soon tried to communicate with the carrier by dropping handwritten notes from the plane; after numerous unsuccessful attempts, this particular note defied the strong winds and hit the crowded deck, attached to a heavy pistol. On it was a handwritten request to land on the carrier.

Rather than simply move them to one side after reading the note, the carrier's captain, Larry Chambers, immediately ordered all available crew to push as many UH-1 Huey helicopters off the deck and into the ocean as necessary, thus giving Buang-Ly and his family space in which to touchdown. He soon landed the Cessna perfectly, without tailhook, to huge applause.

Can you move the Helicopter to the other side, I can land on your runway, I can fly 1 hour more, we have enough time to mouve. Please rescue me.

Major Bung wife and 5 child

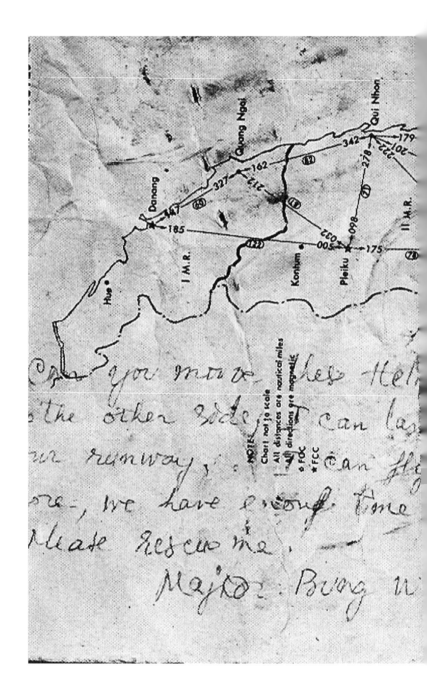

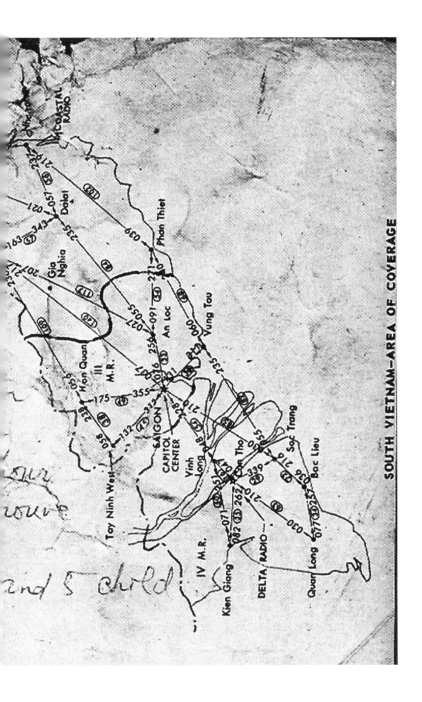

SOUTH VIETNAM—AREA OF COVERAGE

243

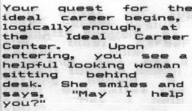

IDEAL CAREER CENTER

Your quest for the ideal career begins, logically enough, at the Ideal Career Center. Upon entering, you see a helpful looking woman sitting behind a desk. She smiles and says, "May I help you?"

>SAY YES I NEED A JOB

"Ah," she replies, "and where would you like to work, Los Angeles, Silicon Valley, or San Rafael?"

>SAY SAN RAFAEL

"Good choice," she says, "Here are some jobs you might be interested in," and gives you three brochures.

>EXAMINE BROCHURES

The titles of the three brochures are as follows: "HAL Computers: We've Got a Number For You," "Yoyodine Defense Technologies: Help Us Reach Our Destructive Potential," and "Lucasfilm, Ltd: Games, Games, Games!"

>OPEN LUCASFILM BROCHURE

SAY YES I NEED A JOB

TIM SCHAFER to DAVID FOX
1989

In 1989, at the end of a disastrous telephone interview in which he admitted to playing pirated versions of his prospective employer's games, aspiring computer game designer Tim Schafer was advised to send in his résumé and a covering letter relating to the role of Assistant Programmer/Designer at LucasArts, the video game developer founded by George Lucas in 1982. In an effort to win them over after such a bad first impression, Schafer decided to write his covering letter in the form of a text adventure game. The approach worked and just weeks later Schafer received a job offer and subsequently went on to write for, and program, two of the greatest adventure games ever released: *The Secret of Monkey Island* and its sequel, *Monkey Island 2: LeChuck's Revenge.*

The brochure says that Lucasfilm is looking for an imaginative, good-humored team player who has excellent communication skills, programming experience, and loves games. Under that description, oddly enough, is a picture of you.

>SEND RESUME

You get the job! Congratulations! You start right away!

>GO TO WORK

You drive the short commute to the Lucasfilm building and find it full of friendly people who show you the way to your desk.

>EXAMINE DESK

Your desk has on it a powerful computer, a telephone, some personal nicknacks, and some work to do.

>EXAMINE WORK

It is challenging and personally fulfilling to perform.

>DO WORK

As you become personally fulfilled, your score reaches 100, and this quest comes to an end. The adventure, however, is just beginning and so are your days at Lucasfilm.

THE END

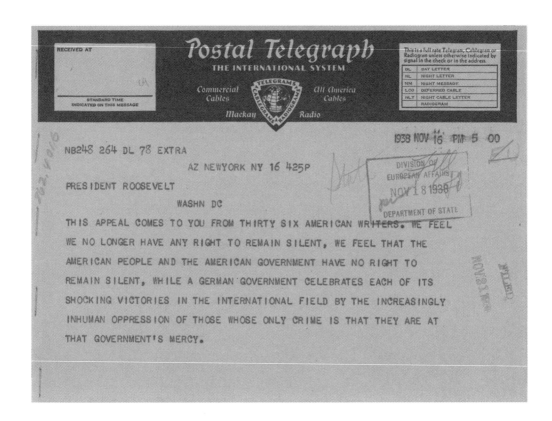

WE NO LONGER HAVE ANY RIGHT TO REMAIN SILENT

36 AMERICAN WRITERS to
US PRESIDENT FRANKLIN
D. ROOSEVELT
November 16th, 1938

In November 1938 millions looked on in shock as thousands of Jewish homes, businesses and synagogues were looted, trashed and even burnt to the ground in Germany during a coordinated series of attacks – known as *pogroms* – which left more than 90 Jews dead and many, many more in concentration camps. Worldwide condemnation was swift and on the 16th of that month, less than a week after what was dubbed Kristallnacht ("Crystal Night") had taken place, a star-studded and angry collective of 36 American writers sent a strongly worded telegram to President Franklin D. Roosevelt and urged him to cut all ties with Nazi Germany.

Postal Telegraph
THE INTERNATIONAL SYSTEM

Commercial Cables   All America Cables

Mackay   Radio

This is a full rate Telegram, Cablegram or Radiogram unless otherwise indicated by signal in the check or in the address.

DL	DAY LETTER
NL	NIGHT LETTER
NM	NIGHT MESSAGE
LCO	DEFERRED CABLE
NLT	NIGHT CABLE LETTER
	RADIOGRAM

1938 NOV 16 PM 5 00

NB248 2 NYC ROOSEVELT WASHN DC

THIRTY FIVE YEARS AGO A HORRIFIED AMERICA ROSE TO ITS FEET TO
PROTEST AGAINST THE KISHINEV POGROMS IN TSARIST RUSSIA. GOD
HELP US IF WE HAVE GROWN SO INDIFFIERENT TO HUMAN SUFFERING THAT
WE CANNOT RISE NOW IN PROTEST AGAINST THE POGROMS IN NAZI GERMANY.
WE DO NOT BELIEVE WE HAVE GROWN SO INDIFFERENT AND WE DO NOT
THINK THE WORLD SHOULD BE ALLOWED TO THINK WE HAVE. WE FEEL
THAT IT IS DEEPLY IMMORAL FOR THE AMERICAN PEOPLE TO CONTINUE
HAVING ECONOMIC RELATIONS WITH A GOVERNMENT THAT AVOWEDLY USES MASS
MURDER TO SOLVE ITS ECONOMIC PROBLEMS. WE ASK YOU TO SEVER
TRADE RELATIONS WITH NAZI GERMANY, TO DECLARE

Postal Telegraph
THE INTERNATIONAL SYSTEM

Commercial Cables   All America Cables

Mackay   Radio

This is a full rate Telegram, Cablegram or Radiogram unless otherwise indicated by signal in the check or in the address.

DL	DAY LETTER
NL	NIGHT LETTER
NM	NIGHT MESSAGE
LCO	DEFERRED CABLE
NLT	NIGHT CABLE LETTER
	RADIOGRAM

1938 NOV 16 PM 5 00

NB248 3 NYC ROOSEVELT WASHN DC

AN EMBARGO ON ALL NAZI GERMAN GOODS, SIGNED

NEWTON ARVIN PEARL BUCK S N BEHRMAN NORAH BENJAMIN VAN WYCK BROOKS
JOHN CHAMBERLIN ALAN CAMPBELL MARC CONNELLY ROBERT CANTWELL PAUL DE
KRUIF MAJOR GEORGE FIELDING ELIOT EDNA FERBER MARJORIE FISHCER
JOHN GUNTHER DASHIELL HAMMETT SIDNEY HOWARD LILLIAN HELLMAN
ROBINSON JEFFERS GEORGE S KAUFMAN LOUIS KRONENBERGER PARE LORENZ
OLIVER LA FARGE EUGENE O'NEILL CLIFFORD ODETS DOROTHY PARKER
MURDOCK PEMBERTON GEORGE SELDES ISIDOR SCHNEIDER JOHN STEINBECK
ROBERT SHERWOOD DOROTHY THOMPSON THORNTON WILDER FRANCES WINWAR
W S WOODWARD HELEN WOODWARD LESNE ZUGSMITH.

KIPLING'S HINTS ON SCHOOLBOY ETIQUETTE

RUDYARD KIPLING
to EDITORS OF THE
*HORSMONDEN SCHOOL
BUDGET*
Easter Monday, 1898

In 1898, in a ballsy effort to attract talent to their tiny publication, the editors of the *Horsmonden School Budget* – a fortnightly magazine published at Horsmonden School in Kent, England, "by boys, for boys" – aimed for the stars and sent a copy to the acclaimed author of *The Jungle Book*, Rudyard Kipling, along with a letter in which he was asked to contribute an article for their next issue. To the astonishment of everyone involved, Kipling replied with a letter of his own – a letter which contained a request for payment and a list of six "Hints on Schoolboy Etiquette", all of which were indeed printed in a subsequent issue. The cheque the editors sent in return was never cashed by Kipling and is now on display at his former family home in Burwash, England.

Capetown,
Easter Monday, 1898.

To the Editors, School Budget.

Gentlemen,—I am in receipt of your letter of no date, together with copy of the School Budget, February 14; and you seem to be in possession of all the cheek that is in the least likely to do you any good in this world or the next. And, furthermore, you have omitted to specify where your journal is printed and in what county of England Horsmonden is situated.

But, on the other hand, and notwithstanding, I very much approve of your 'Hints on Schoolboy Etiquette,' and have taken the liberty of sending you a few more, as following :

(1) If you have any doubts about a quantity, cough. In three cases out of five this will save you being asked to 'say it again.'

(2) The two most useful boys in a form are (a) the master's favourite, pro tem., (b) his pet aversion. With a little judicious management (a) can keep him talking through the first half of the construe, and (b) can take up the running for the rest of the time. N.B.—A syndicate should arrange to do (b's) imposts in return for this service.

(3) A confirmed guesser is worth his weight in gold on a Monday morning.

(4) Never shirk a master out of bounds. Pass him with an abstracted eye, and at the same time pull out a letter and study it earnestly. He may think it is a commission for someone else.

(5) When pursued by the native farmer, always take to the nearest ploughland. Men stick in furrows that boys can run over.

(6) If it is necessary to take other people's apples, do it on a Sunday. You can then put them inside your topper, which is better than trying to button them into a 'tight Eton.'

You will find this advice worth enormous sums of money, but I shall be obliged with a cheque or postal order for 6d., at your earliest convenience, if the contribution should be found to fill more than one page.—

Faithfully yours,

Rudyard Kipling.

SEX DOES NOT THRIVE
ON MONOTONY

ANAÏS NIN to THE
COLLECTOR
Circa 1940

In 1932, months after first
meeting in Paris and despite
both being married, Cuban
diarist Anaïs Nin and hugely
influential novelist Henry
Miller began an incredibly
intense love affair that
would last for many years.
In the 1940s, at which
point Nin, Miller and a
collective of other writers
were earning $1 per page
writing erotic fiction for the
private consumption of an
anonymous client known
only as the "Collector",
Nin wrote a passionate
letter to this mysterious
figure and made known her
frustrations – frustrations
caused by his repeated
insistence that they "leave
out the poetry" and instead
"concentrate on sex".

Dear Collector:

We hate you. Sex loses all its power and magic when it becomes explicit, mechanical, overdone, when it becomes a mechanistic obsession. It becomes a bore. You have taught us more than anyone I know how wrong it is not to mix it with emotion, hunger, desire, lust, whims, caprices, personal ties, deeper relationships which change its color, flavor, rhythms, intensities.

You do not know what you are missing by your microscopic examination of sexual activity to the exclusion of others, which are the fuel that ignites it. Intellectual, imaginative, romantic, emotional. This is what gives sex its surprising textures, its subtle transformations, its aphrodisiac elements. You are shrinking your world of sensations. You are withering it, starving it, draining its blood.

If you nourished your sexual life with all the excitements and adventures which love injects into sensuality, you would be the most potent man in the world. The source of sexual power is curiosity, passion. You are watching its little flame die of asphyxiation. Sex does not thrive on monotony. Without feeling, inventions, moods, no surprises in bed. Sex must be mixed with tears, laughter, words, promises, scenes, jealousy, envy, all of the spices of fear, foreign travel, new faces, novels, stories, dreams, fantasies, music, dancing, opium, wine.

How much do you lose by this periscope at the tip of your sex, when you could enjoy a harem of discrete and never-repeated wonders? Not two hairs alike, but you will not let us waste words on a description of hair; not two odors, but if we expand on this, you cry "Cut the poetry." Not two skins with the same texture, and never the same light, temperature, shadows, never the same gesture; for a lover, when he is aroused by true love, can run the gamut of centuries of love lore, What a range, what changes of age, what variations of maturity and innocence, perversity and art, natural and graceful animals.

We have sat around for hours and wondered how you look. If you have closed your senses around silk, light, color, odor, character, temperament, you must by now be completely shriveled up. There are so many minor senses, all running like tributaries into the mainstream of sex, nourishing it. Only the united beat of sex and heart together can create ecstasy.

Anaïs Nin

THE ATTORNEY GENERAL STATE OF ALABAMA
MONTGOMERY, ALABAMA 36130

WILLIAM J. BAXLEY
ATTORNEY GENERAL

GEORGE L. BECK
DEPUTY ATTORNEY GENERAL

E. RAY ACTON
EXECUTIVE ASSISTANT

WALTER S. TURNER
CHIEF ASSISTANT ATTORNEY GENERAL

LUCY H. RICHARDS
CONFIDENTIAL ASSISTANT

JACK D. SHOWS
CHIEF INVESTIGATOR

February 20, 1976

"Dr." Edward R. Fields
National States Rights Party
P. O. Box 1211
Marietta, Georgia 30061

Dear "Dr." Fields:

My response to your letter of February 19, 1976, is – kiss my ass.

Sincerely,

BILL BAXLEY
Attorney General

KISS MY ASS

BILL BAXLEY to EDWARD R. FIELDS
February 20th, 1976

In 1970, shortly after being elected Attorney General of Alabama, 29-year-old Bill Baxley reopened the case of the 16th Street Church bombing, a racially motivated act of terrorism that resulted in the deaths of four African-American girls in 1963 and a fruitless investigation, which marked a turning point in the Civil Rights Movement. Baxley's unwavering commitment to the case attracted much hostility, particularly from local Klansmen, and in 1976 he received a threatening letter of protest from white supremacist Edward R. Fields – founder of the National States' Rights Party and "Grand Dragon" of the New Order Knights of the Ku Klux Klan – in which he was accused of reopening the case for tactical reasons.

Baxley's magnificent letter of reply was both succinct and unambiguous.

The next year, a member of the United Klans of America named Robert Chambliss was found guilty of the 16th Street Church murders. He remained in prison until his death in 1985.

THE HEILIGENSTADT TESTAMENT

LUDWIG VAN BEETHOVEN
to HIS BROTHERS
October 6th, 1802

Ludwig van Beethoven was one of the most famous composers of all time – a true musical genius whose accomplishments still influence and astonish to this day, centuries after his death. His life's work seems even more impressive on learning that he started to lose his hearing in his late twenties, a development which brought on bouts of depression and suicidal thoughts, which in turn saw him distance himself from friends and family. At the age of 32, he wrote this, the "Heiligenstadt Testament", a heartbreaking letter to be opened by his brothers after his death in which he explains his antisocial behaviour and affliction. Despite his deafness, Beethoven continued to compose until the end of his life; he passed away in 1827, 25 years after writing this letter.

For my brothers Carl and [Johann] Beethoven

Oh you men who think or say that I am malevolent, stubborn, or misanthropic, how greatly do you wrong me. You do not know the secret cause which makes me seem that way to you. From childhood on, my heart and soul have been full of the tender feeling of goodwill, and I was even inclined to accomplish great things. But, think that for six years now I have been hopelessly afflicted, made worse by senseless physicians, from year to year deceived with hopes of improvement, finally compelled to face the prospect of a lasting malady (whose cure will take years or, perhaps, be impossible).

Though born with a fiery, active temperament, even susceptible to the diversions of society, I was soon compelled to isolate myself, to live life alone. If at times I tried to forget all this, oh, how harshly was I flung back by the doubly sad experience of my bad hearing. Yet it was impossible for me to say to people, "Speak Louder, shout, for I am deaf". Oh, how could I possibly admit an infirmity in the one sense which ought to be more perfect in me than others, a sense which I once possessed in the highest perfection, a perfection such as few in my profession enjoy or ever have enjoyed. — Oh I cannot do it; therefore forgive me when you see me draw back when I would have gladly mingled with you.

My misfortune is doubly painful to me because I am bound to be misunderstood; for me there can be no relaxation with my fellow men, no refined conversations, no mutual exchange of ideas. I must live almost alone, like one who has been banished. I can mix with society only as much as true necessity demands. If I approach near to people a hot terror seizes upon me, and I fear being exposed to the danger that my condition might be noticed. Thus it has been during the last six months which I have spent in the country. By ordering me to spare my hearing as much as possible, my intelligent doctor almost fell in with my own present frame of mind, though sometimes I ran counter to it by yielding to my desire for companionship.

But what a humiliation for me when someone standing next to me heard a flute in the distance and I heard nothing, or someone standing next to me heard a shepherd singing and again I heard nothing. Such incidents drove me almost to despair; a little more of that and I would have ended my life. It was only my art that held me back. Oh, it seemed to me impossible to leave the world until I had forth all that I felt was within me. So I endured this wretched existence, truly wretched for so susceptible a body, which can be thrown by a sudden change from the best condition to the worst. Patience, they say, is what I must now choose for my guide, and I have done so — I hope my determination will remain firm to endure until it pleases the inexorable Parcae to break the thread. Perhaps I shall get better, perhaps not; I am ready. — Forced to become a philosopher already in my twenty-eighth year, oh, it is not easy, and for the artist much more difficult than for anyone else. Divine One, thou seest my inmost soul thou knowest that therein dwells the love of mankind and the desire to do good. Oh, fellow men, when at some point you read this, consider then that you have done me injustice. Someone who has had misfortune may console himself to find a similar case to his, who despite all the limitations of Nature nevertheless did everything within his powers to become accepted among worthy artist and men.

You, my brothers Carl and Johann, as soon as I am dead, if Dr. Schmid is still alive, ask him in my name to describe my malady, and attach this written documentation to his account of my illness so that so far as it is possible at least the world may become reconciled to me after my death. At the same time, I declare you two to be the heirs to my small fortune (if so it can be called); divide it fairly, bear with and help each other. What injury you have done me you know was long ago forgiven. To you, brother Carl, I give special thanks for the attachment you have shown me of late. It is my wish that you may have a better and freer life than I have had. Recommend virtue to your children; it alone, not money, can make them happy. I speak from experience; this was what upheld me in time of misery. Thanks for it and to my art, I did not end my life by suicide — Farewell and love each other.

I thank all my friends, particularly Prince Lichnowsky and Professor Schmid; I would like the instruments from Prince L. to be preserved by one of you, but not to be the cause of strife between you, and as soon as they can serve you a better purpose, then sell them. How happy I shall be if I can still be helpful to you in my grave — so be it. With joy I hasten towards death. If it comes before I have had the chance to develop all my artistic capacities, it will still be coming too soon despite my harsh fate, and I should probably wish it later — yet even so I should be happy, for would it not free me from the state of endless suffering? Come when thou wilt, I shall meet thee bravely. Farewell and do not wholly forget me when I am dead; I deserve this from you, for during my lifetime I was thinking of you often and of ways to make you happy; please be so —

Ludwig van Beethoven

Heiligenstadt,
October 6th, 1802

für meine Brüder Carl und Beethowen

O ihr Menschen die ihr mich für Feindseelig störisch oder
Misantropisch haltet oder erkläret, wie unrecht thut ihr mir,
ihr wißt nicht die geheime ursache von dem, was euch so
scheinet, mein Herz und mein Sinn waren von Kindheit
an für das zarte gefühl des Wohlwollens, selbst große
Handlungen zu verrichten dazu war ich immer aufgelegt,
aber bedenket nur daß seit 6 jahren ein heilloser
Zustand mich befallen, durch unvernünftige Ärzte verschlimmert,
von jahr zu jahr in der Hofnung gebessert zu werden,
betrogen, endlich zu dem überblick eines dauernden
Übels (dessen Heilung vieleicht jahre dauern oder
gar unmöglich ist) gezwungen, mit einem feurigen
Lebhaften Temperamente gebohren selbst empfäng-
lich für die Zerstreuungen der Gesellschaft, muste ich früh
mich absondern, einsam mein Leben zubringen, wollte
ich auch zuweilen mich einmal über alles das hinaussezen
o wie hart wurde ich dan durch die verdoppelte traurige
Erfahrung meines schlechten Gehör's dann zurück-
gestoßen, und doch war's mir noch nicht möglich den
Menschen zu sagen: sprecht lauter, schreit, denn
ich bin Taub, ach wie wär es möglich daß ich dann die
Schwäche eines Sinnes angeben sollte, der bey mir in
einem Vollkommenern Grade als bey andern seyn sollte
einen Sinn den ich einst in der grösten Vollkommenheit
besaß, in einer Vollkommenheit, wie ihn wenige von
meinem Fache gewiß haben noch gehabt haben – o ich
kann es nicht, drum verzeiht, wenn ihr mich da zurück-
weichen sehen werdet, wo ich mich gerne unter euch mischte,
doppelt Wehe thut mir mein unglück, indem ich dabey verkannt
werden muß, für mich darf Erholung in Menschlicher Gesellschaft, feinere unterredungen, wechselseitige Ergießun-
gen nicht statt haben, ganz allein fast nur so viel
als es die höchste Nothwendigkeit fodert, darf ich mich in Gesellschaft einlassen, wie ein Verbannter muß ich leben, nahe ich mich
einer Gesellschaft, so überfällt mich eine heiße Ängstlich-
keit, indem ich befürchte in Gefahr gesezt zu werden, meinen
Zustand merken zu laßen – so war es denn auch
dieses halbe Jahr, was ich auf dem Lande zubrachte,
von meinem Vernünftigen Arzte aufgefordert, so viel
als möglich mein Gehör zu schonen, kam er fast meiner
jezigen natürlichen Disposition entgegen, obschon, vom Triebe
zur Gesellschaft manchmal hingerissen, ich mich dazu verleiten
ließ, aber welche Demüthigung wenn jemand neben mir
stund und von weitem eine Flöte hörte und ich nichts
hörte, oder jemand den Hirten Singen hörte, und ich auch nichts hörte,

ich wolle meinen Dienst, doch ich durch Samionen stellt
Invorderein glauben nidigte — Labt wohl und
Liebt auch — allen Freunden bleibe ich, besonderh
Euch glichnorstte und hoher Schmidt. —

Heiglnstadt
am 6ten October
1802

Ludwig van Beethoven

PAY IT FORWARD

BENJAMIN FRANKLIN to
BENJAMIN WEBB
April 22nd, 1784

Benjamin Franklin was an incredible man with more strings to his bow than most. As well as being a Founding Father of the United States of America, Franklin was, in alphabetical order, an activist, author, businessman, diplomat, humorist, inventor, musician, politician, printer and scientist. He was also, judging by this letter written to Benjamin Webb in 1784, a very early proponent – one of the first in modern times, in fact – of a concept in which debtors are encouraged to repay their loan or favour not to the original lender, but rather to others of a similar need along with similar instructions for repayment, thus creating a chain of goodwill that spreads through society. At the time of Franklin's letter this philosophy was nameless; now, it is widely known as "paying it forward".

Passy, April 22d, 1784.

Dear Sir,

   I received yours of the 15th Instant, and the Memorial it inclosed. The account they give of your situation grieves me. I send you herewith a Bill for Ten Louis d'ors. I do not pretend to *give* such a Sum; I only *lend* it to you. When you shall return to your Country with a good Character, you cannot fail of getting into some Business, that will in time enable you to pay all your Debts. In that Case, when you meet with another honest Man in similar Distress, you must pay me by lending this Sum to him; enjoining him to discharge the Debt by a like operation, when he shall be able, and shall meet with another opportunity. I hope it may thus go thro' many hands, before it meets with a Knave that will stop its Progress. This is a trick of mine for doing a deal of good with a little money. I am not rich enough to afford *much* in good works, and so am obliged to be cunning and make the most of a *little*. With best wishes for the success of your Memorial, and your future prosperity,

   I am, dear Sir, your most obedient servant,

B. Franklin.

EDDIE'S HOUSE

JIM BERGER to FRANK
LLOYD WRIGHT
June 19th, 1956

After his death in 1959, following an illustrious 70-year career during which he designed upwards of 1,000 structures and completed over 500 buildings, Frank Lloyd Wright was recognised by the American Institute of Architects as the "greatest American architect of all time". He was, by all accounts, a true master of his craft. His smallest and perhaps most unusual project came in 1956 and began with a letter from Jim Berger, the 12-year-old son of a previous client of Wright's. The young boy's request was simple: he wanted to commission the design of a house for his dog, Eddie; one which would complement the family home. Incredibly, Wright agreed and supplied a full set of drawings for "Eddie's House" the next year. Construction on this tiny piece of architectural history was eventually completed by Jim's father in 1963.

June 19, 1956

Dear Mr. Wright

I am a boy of twelve years. My name is Jim Berger. You designed a house for my father whose name is Bob Berger. I have a paper route which I make a little bit of money for the bank, and for expenses.

I would appreciate it if you would design me a dog house, which would be easy to build, but would go with our house. My dog's name is Edward, but we call him Eddie. He is four years old or in dog life 28 years. He is a Labrador retriever. He is two and a half feet high and three feet long. The reasons I would like this dog house is for the winters mainly. My dad said if you design the dog house he will help me build it. But if you design the dog house I will pay you for the plans and materials out of the money I get from my route.

Respectfully yours,

Jim Berger

June 19, 19

Dear Mr. Wright

    I am a boy of twelve years. My nama
Jim Berger. You designed a house for
father whose name is Bob Berger. I
have a paper route which I make a
little bit of money for the bank, and
expenses.

    I would appreciate it if you wou
design me a dog house, which wou
be easy to build, but would go with
our house. My dog's name is Edward,
we call him Eddie. He is four year
old or in dog life 88 years. He is a
Labrador retriever. He is two an
half feet high and three feet long.
reasons I would like this dog hou
is for the winters mainly. My dad
said if you would help me build it, but
will pay you for the plans and mat
out of the money I get from my ro

                Respectfully yours,
                Jim Burger

My dad said if you design the dog house he w
help me build it

But if your design the dog house I will
you for the plans and matrel

TALIESIN

Jim Berger
Box 437
San Anselmo
California

Dear Jim: A house for Eddie is an opportunity. Someday
I shall design one but just now I am too busy to concentrate
on it. You write me next November to Phoenix, Arizona and
I may have something then.

Truly yours,

Frank Lloyd Wright

June 28th, 1956

Dear Jim:

A house for Eddie is an opportunity. Someday I shall design one but just now I am too busy to concentrate on it. You write me next November to Phoenix, Arizona and I may have something then.

Truly yours,

Frank Lloyd Wright

June 28th, 1956

Dear Mr Wright

I wrote you June 19, 1956 about designing my dog Eddie a dog house to go with the house you designed for my dad. You told me to write you again in November so I ask you again, could you design me a dog house.

Respectfully yours,

Jim Berger

Box 437
San Andreas Calif
November 1, 1956
Calif

Dear Mr Wright

I wrote you June 19, 1956 about designing my dog Eddie a dog house to go with the house you designed for my dad in November. You told me to write you again. So I ask you again could you design me a dog house.

Respectfully yours;
Jim Berger

I WAS READY TO SINK INTO THE EARTH WITH SHAME

FORM LETTER
AD 856

It is somewhat reassuring to know that over a thousand years ago, much like today, certain human beings were frequently making drunken fools of themselves at dinner parties and waking up the next day filled with regret. In fact, this was such a regular occurrence in one region of China that a standard form letter of apology was created by the area's beautifully named "Dunhuang Bureau of Etiquette", copies of which were signed by hungover local officials and handed, with heads bowed, to disappointed dinner hosts – a ready-made apology for the previous night's bad behaviour. This particular version has been dated to AD 856.

Yesterday, having drunk too much, I was intoxicated as to pass all bounds; but none of the rude and coarse language I used was uttered in a conscious state. The next morning, after hearing others speak on the subject, I realised what had happened, whereupon I was overwhelmed with confusion and ready to sink into the earth with shame. It was due to a vessel of my small capacity being filled for the nonce too full. I humbly trust that you in your wise benevolence will not condemn me for my transgression. Soon I will come to apologize in person, but meanwhile I beg to send this written communication for your kind inspection. Leaving much unsaid, I am yours respectfully.

厶官動止萬福即此厶蒙免所守　限展拜未由空增馳暴　之至奉狀不

宣謹狀　　谷書　　久{}

芳猷未遂披展忽辱　榮問溁慰勤誠時候依惟　厶官動止萬福

即此厶蒙推免限以官守拜　謁未由瞻瞩之誠益增勤慕　謹奉迴狀不

宣謹狀　　酒熱相迎書

四海雜相迎書語　　酒熱相迎書

家臨清春晬始新熟深思　　已知御慕同還不耻逢門幸垂過訪一否

解悶便請速來即當幸也謹奉狀不宣謹狀

久不相見迎書　　春仰多時無由披叙念具空酒輒敢

諠邀幸蒙顧同歡請垂降顧　　壽停候　　不宣謹狀

醉後失禮謝書　　昨日多飲醉甚歐{}{}言詞都不醒

覺朝来見諸人說方知其由無地容身慙怵尤積本緣小器到次滿盈

仁明不賜罪責書面謝先狀　　謹申伏惟監察

深及炊伏望

不宣謹狀

歲日相迎書　　　戲歲初開元正啓　袛入新政故万物同軍業

131 Mount Vernon St.,
Boston
July 28th

SORROW PASSES AND WE REMAIN

HENRY JAMES to GRACE NORTON
July 28th, 1883

In July 1883, Henry James, the famed novelist responsible for writing, most notably, *The Portrait of a Lady*, received a worryingly emotional letter from Grace Norton, a friend of some years and successful essayist who, following a recent death in the family, had seemingly become depressed and was desperate for direction. James, no stranger to depression himself, responded with a stunning letter which, despite beginning, "...I hardly know what to say to you", contains some of the greatest, most compassionate advice ever put to paper – a feat made all the more impressive on learning that it was written just months after the deaths of his own parents.

My dear Grace,

Before the sufferings of others I am always utterly powerless, and the letter you gave me reveals such depths of suffering that I hardly know what to say to you. This indeed is not my last word—but it must be my first. You are not isolated, verily, in such states of feeling as this—that is, in the sense that you appear to make all the misery of all mankind your own; only I have a terrible sense that you give all and receive nothing—that there is no reciprocity in your sympathy—that you have all the affliction of it and none of the returns. However—I am determined not to speak to you except with the voice of stoicism.

I don't know *why* we live—the gift of life comes to us from I don't know what source or for what purpose; but I believe we can go on living for the reason that (always of course up to a certain point) life is the most valuable thing we know anything about and it is therefore presumptively a great mistake to surrender it while there is any yet left in the cup. In other words consciousness is an illimitable power, and though at times it may seem to be all consciousness of misery, yet in the way it propagates itself from wave to wave, so that we never cease to feel, though at moments we appear to, try to, pray to, there is something that holds one in one's place, makes it a standpoint in the universe which it is probably good not to forsake. You are right in your consciousness that we are all echoes and reverberations of the *same*, and you are noble when your interest and pity as to everything that surrounds you, appears to have a sustaining and harmonizing power. Only don't, I beseech you, *generalize* too much in these sympathies and tendernesses—remember that every life is a special problem which is not yours but another's, and content yourself with the terrible algebra of your own. Don't melt too much into the universe, but be as solid and dense and fixed as you can. We all live together, and those of us who love and know, live so most. We help each other—even unconsciously, each in our own effort, we lighten the effort of others, we contribute to the sum of success, make it possible for others to live. Sorrow comes in great waves—no one can know that better than you—but it rolls over us, and though it may almost smother us it leaves us on the spot and we know that if it is strong we are stronger, inasmuch as it passes and we remain. It wears us, uses us, but we wear it and use it in return; and it is blind, whereas we after a manner see. My dear Grace, you are passing through a darkness in which I myself in my ignorance see nothing but that you have been made wretchedly ill by it; but it is only a darkness, it is not an end, or *the* end. Don't think, don't feel, any more than you can help, don't conclude or decide—don't do anything but *wait*. Everything will pass, and serenity and *accepted* mysteries and disillusionments, and the tenderness of a few good people, and new opportunities and ever so much of life, in a word, will remain. You will do all sorts of things yet, and I will help you. The only thing is not to *melt* in the meanwhile. I insist upon the necessity of a sort of mechanical condensation—so that however fast the horse may run away there will, when he pulls up, be a somewhat agitated but perfectly identical G. N. left in the saddle. Try not to be ill—that is all; for in that there is a future. You are marked out for success, and you must not fail. You have my tenderest affection and all my confidence.

Ever your faithful friend—
Henry James

October 11, 1981

Mr. Jeff Walker,
The Lado Company,
4000 Warner Boulevard,
Burbank,
Calif. 91522.

Dear Jeff:

I happened to see the Channel 7 TV program "Hooray for Hollywood" tonight with the segment on BLADE RUNNER. (Well, to be honest, I didn't happen to see it; someone tipped me off that BLADE RUNNER was going to be a part of the show, and to be sure to watch.) Jeff, after looking --and especially after listening to Harrison Ford discuss the film-- I came to the conclusion that this indeed is not science fiction; it is not fantasy; it is exactly what Harrison said: futurism. The impact of BLADE RUNNER is simply going to be overwhelming, both on the public and on creative people -- and, I believe, on science fiction as a field. Since I have been writing and selling science fiction works for thirty years, this is a matter of some importance to me. In all candor I must say that our field has gradually and steadily been deteriorating for the last few years. Nothing that we have done, individually or collectively, matches BLADE RUNNER. This is not escapism; it is super realism, so gritty and detailed and authentic and goddam convincing that, well, after the segment I found my normal present-day "reality" pallid by comparison. What I am saying is that all of you collectively may have created a unique new form of graphic, artistic expression, never before seen. And, I think, BLADE RUNNER is going to revolutionize our conceptions of what science fiction is and, more, can be.

Let me sum it up this way. Science fiction has slowly and ineluctably settled into a monotonous death: it has become inbred, derivative, stale. Suddenly you people have come in, some of the greatest talents currently in existence, and now we have a new life, a new start. As for my own role in the BLADE RUNNER project, I can only say that I did not know that a work of mine or a set of ideas of mine could be escalated into such stunning dimensions. My life and creative work are justified and completed by BLADE RUNNER. Thank you...and it is going to be one hell of a commercial success. It will prove invincible.

Cordially,

Philip K. Dick

IT WILL PROVE INVINCIBLE

PHILIP K. DICK to JEFF WALKER
October 11th, 1981

In 1968, author Philip K. Dick's post-apocalyptic science fiction novel, *Do Androids Dream of Electric Sheep?* – the story of a bounty hunter, Rick Deckard, whose job is to find and "retire" rogue androids – was published, almost immediately generating interest from film studios keen to adapt it for the big screen. Early talks and screenplay drafts failed to impress Dick; however, in 1981, by which time Ridley Scott was on board to direct a script rewritten by David Peoples, he caught a glimpse of the forthcoming film, now titled *Blade Runner*, which changed his mind entirely. That same evening, he excitedly wrote this letter to the production company responsible and shared his thoughts. The tragedy is that Philip K. Dick passed away five months after sending this letter, without seeing the finished film. It is now regarded by many as the greatest science fiction film ever made.

THANK YOU BOB

FREDERIC FLOM to BOB
HOPE
February 24th, 1973

In 1997, as a result of his
tireless efforts to entertain
American troops and
campaign on their behalf,
an act of congress was
signed which resulted in
widely adored entertainer
Bob Hope becoming the
world's "first and only
honorary veteran of the
US armed forces". Few
things illustrate the effect
of Hope's humanitarian
work more than this letter
written in 1973 by a US pilot
named Frederic Flom. When
he wrote it, Flom was days
away from being released
as a prisoner of war, an
unimaginable six and a half
years after being captured
in Vietnam; after hearing of
Hope's POW-related work
from another captured pilot,
Flom felt the need to write
Bob a letter of thanks.

24 Feb, '73

Dear Mr. Hope,

Just another fan letter from a different address. I am an F-105 pilot, shot down over North Viet Nam on 8 August, 1966. I have been held captive since that time, but will finally be released in three days. We have almost no contact with the outside world in here, however, some word has gotten in, via POWs shot down in '72, concerning some of the activities of the American people, & you in particular, on behalf of the POWs. That is what prompted this note.

I want to thank you for all you have done or attempted to do on our behalf. You are truly a POW's friend, & are deserving of more than just a letter from each of us. There have been many a dark & lonesome night when we have felt all but forgotten. It thrills our hearts & makes us glow with pride to learn that the American people have not forgotten us, & that a celebrity such as yourself has active concern. I extend to you & all of America my deep appreciation & I know I speak for all of us.

There is something great about our nation & its people. A celebrity can have a large effect in influencing its thinking & attitude. This effect can be positive or negative, good or bad. Thank you Bob, for being such a large part of America & our wonderful way of life.

Best of luck to you,

Fred Flom

NEW RUBBISH DIALOGUE

ALEC GUINNESS to ANNE KAUFMAN
April 19th, 1976

When Alec Guinness wrote this letter to his dear friend, Anne Kaufman, in April 1976, and spoke so enthusiastically about his new play, *Yahoo*, he was known to most as a very dependable Academy Award-winning actor who regularly starred in the films of David Lean, the acclaimed English director of such classics as *Lawrence of Arabia* and *The Bridge on the River Kwai*. However, it's the upcoming role to which he briefly but so amusingly alludes in this otherwise unremarkable letter – the part of Obi-Wan Kenobi in *Star Wars*, a film that boasted "rubbish dialogue" and a co-star momentarily named Tennyson Ford – that went on to introduce him to a far larger audience of avid fans, and which ultimately brought him huge financial reward.

Easter Monday '76

My dear Anne

The sun has shone all over Easter and that has meant out-of-door life; bees humming in the cherry blossom; Walter on guard against birds having it off in hedges; daffodils wilting; balsam poplars scenting the air; baby ants on the march into the grubby kitchen; good wine to drink, and all fairly idyllic except for the presence of my provoking, irritating and unbalanced daughter-in-law. And her squabbling children. The children are more or less alright, I suppose, except for their foul manners and nasal cockney accents. Merula has now got them for the next ten days and I bet that once their parents have gone on their (separate) holidays the children will prove angelic. That has been the pattern before. I have returned to London this evening for my stint at the studio for the rest of the week. Can't say I'm enjoying the film, – new rubbish dialogue reaches me every other day on wadges of pink paper – and <u>none</u> of it makes my character clear or even bearable. I just think, thankfully, of the lovely bread, which will help me keep going until next April even if 'Yahoo' collapses in a week.

Thank you for you your card about that. Strachan and I have tried to probe where it is 'arch' – and I have decided either that Queen's English and U.S. usage of the word are at variances, or that you (forgivably) misread the tone of some of it – which is somewhat belligerent and harsh and far from coy. I <u>do</u> think the first half is a bit <u>cool</u>, and I'm not sure how to remedy that, except by possibly throwing in some coarse stuff and hitting up the ironies. – Anyway, it was nice of you to read it, and good of you to take it seriously. – We have settled on a youngish designer called Bernard Culshaw – I've only seen one set of his, and that about six years ago, but think he's got the right style and understanding. Eileen Atkins has expressed <u>enthusiasm</u> for it and promises to play Vanessa (et al) if a possible film she's keen on doesn't materialise. We shall know in two weeks. <u>If</u> she does it I'll feel more confident than with the alternative, who is good on T.V. but something of an unknown quantity in the theatre. My chum Mark Kingston will play the other man. Stella is still a blank in our minds –- but the casting of Vanessa must be done first.

Dined a week ago with your little mum, who was looking better and in better spirits than I've known her in years. Bright but not brittle, and in full command – so it seemed – of her life. Gavin was present (with broken foot) and a garrulous French woman with Islamic leanings. A friend of the Shit of Persia.

The Ehrenpreis Swift volumes (1 & 2) arrived safely and I'm in to them. Rather dry and too academic but full of useful information. I can't remember what you said about Vol 3, and can't put my hand on your letter. It doesn't exist? It's out of print? It was never written? But what the Hell do I owe you anyway? Please! – I have a lot of dollars dwindling slowly in L.A. – You are welcome to some of them. And who knows what my next demand may be! Probably toilet paper.

<u>Tuesday</u>

Another bright day has dawned. A letter from Nancy Green in the post. – A nightmarish night going round and round in my head my invitation with [*unknown name*] (a-in-law). Isn't it wretched how difficult unpleasant thoughts are to shake off. I had to sit up and read for ½ hour at 2. am. to exorcise myself. – Garson Kanin plagues me about 'Mr. Maugham' but 'Yahoo', if it does nothing else, has enabled me to side-step that one.

      I must off to studio and work with a dwarf (very sweet, – and he has to wash in a bidet) and your fellow countrymen Mark Hamill and Tennyson (that <u>can't</u> be right) Ford – Ellison (? – No!*) – well, a rangey, languid young man who is probably intelligent and amusing. But Oh, God, God, they make me feel <u>ninety</u> – and treat me as if I was 106.

Love,

Alec

* Harrison Ford – ever heard of him?

Easter Monday '76

My dear Anne

The sun has shone all over Easter and that has meant out-of-door life; bees humming in the cherry blossom; Walter on guard against birds having it off in hedges; daffodils wilting; balsam poplars scenting the air; baby ants on the march into the grubby kitchen; good wine to drink, and all fairly idyllic except for the presence of my provoking, irritating and unbalanced daughter-in-law. And her squabbling children. The children are more or less alright, I suppose, except for their foul manners and nasal cockney accents. Merula has now got them for the next ten days and I bet that once their parents have gone on their (separate) holidays the children will prove angelic. That has been the pattern before. I have returned to London this evening for my stint at the studio for the rest of the week. Can't say I'm enjoying the film, — new rubbishy dialogue reaches me every other day on wadges of pink paper — and none of it makes my character clear or even bearable. I just think, thankfully, of the lovely bread, which will keep me going until next April even if 'Yahoo' collapses in a week.

Thank you for your card about that. Strachan and I have tried to probe where it is 'arch' — and I have decided either that Queen's English and U.S. usage of the word are at variance, or that you (forgivably) misread the tone of some of it — which is somewhat belligerent and harsh and far from coy. I do think the first half is a bit cool, and I'm not sure how to remedy that, except by possibly throwing in some coarse stuff and hitting up the ironies — Anyway, it was nice of you to read it, and good of you to take it seriously. — We have settled on a youngish designer called Bernard Culshaw — I've only seen one set of his, and that about six years ago, but think he's got the right style and understanding. Eileen Atkins has expressed enthusiasm for it and promises to play Vanessa (et al) if a possible film she's keen on doesn't materialise. We shall know in two weeks. If she does it I'll feel more confident than with the alternative, who is good on T.V. but something of an unknown quantity in the theatre.

3

ALEC GUINNESS

My chum Mark Kingston will play the other man. Stella is still a blank in our minds — but the casting of Vanessa must be done first.

Dined a week ago with your little mum, who was looking better and in better spirits than I've known her in years. Bright but not brittle, and in full command — so it seemed — of her life. Gavin was present (with broken foot) and a garrulous French woman with Islamic leanings. A friend of the Shit of Persia.

The Ehrenpreis Swift volumes (1 & 2) arrived safely and I'm in to them. Rather dry and too academic but full of useful information. I cant remember what you said about Vol 3, and cant put my hand on your letter. It doesnt exist? Its out of print? It was never written? But what the Hell do I owe you anyway? Please! — I have a lot of dollars dwindling slowly in L. A. — you are welcome to some of them. And who knows what my next demand may be! Probably toilet paper.

Tuesday 4

Another bright day has dawned. A letter from Nancy Green in the post. — A nightmarish night going round and round in my head my irritation with Andrée (d-in-law). but it's wretched how difficult unpleasant thoughts are to shake off. I had to sit up and read for 1/2 hour at 2. am. to exorcise myself. — Garson Kanin plagues me about 'Mr. Maugham' but 'Yahoo', if it does nothing else, has enabled me to side-step that one.

I must off to studio and work with a dwarf (very sweet, — and he has to wash in a bidet) and your fellow countrymen Mark Hamill and Tennyson (that can't be right) Ford — Ellison (? — No! *) — well, a rangey, languid young man who is probably intelligent and amusing. But Oh, God, God, they make me feel <u>ninety</u> — and treat me as if I was 106.

Love,

Alec.

* <u>Harrison</u> Ford — ever heard of him?

I REFUSE TO BE CHEATED OUT OF MY DEATHBED SCENE

REBECCA WEST to
H. G. WELLS
March, 1913

In 1912, in what was a scathing review of his latest novel, *Marriage*, author and journalist Rebecca West called the great H. G. Wells, "the Old Maid of novelists". Naturally, his response to such a slight was to invite her out to dinner; she agreed, they dined, and then fell in love. The often explosive affair that resulted lasted for some months, until, in March 1913, Wells – 26 years her senior and already a married man – broke off their relationship. West was distraught and responded with this intense letter. However, she didn't carry out her threat – in fact they soon got back together and went on to have a son, Andrew, in 1914. The couple split up permanently nine years later.

Dear H. G.,

During the next few days I shall either put a bullet through my head or commit something more shattering to myself than death. At any rate I shall be quite a different person. I refuse to be cheated out of my deathbed scene.

I don't understand why you wanted me three months ago and don't want me now. I wish I knew why that were so. It's something I can't understand, something I despise. And the worst of it is that if I despise you I rage because you stand between me and peace. Of course you're quite right. I haven't anything to give you. You have only a passion for excitement and for comfort. You don't want any more excitement and I do not give people comfort. I never nurse them except when they're very ill. I carry this to excess. On reflection I can imagine that the occasion on which my mother found me most helpful to live with was when I helped her out of a burning house.

I always knew that you would hurt me to death some day, but I hoped to choose the time and place. You've always been unconsciously hostile to me and I have tried to conciliate you by hacking away at my love for you, cutting it down to the little thing that was the most you wanted. I am always at a loss when I meet hostility, because I can love and I can do practically nothing else. I was the wrong sort of person for you to have to do with. You want a world of people falling over each other like puppies, people to quarrel and play with, people who rage and ache instead of people who burn. You can't conceive a person resenting the humiliation of an emotional failure so much that they twice tried to kill themselves: that seems silly to you. I can't conceive of a person who runs about lighting bonfires and yet nourishes a dislike of flame: that seems silly to me.

You've literally ruined me. I'm burned down to my foundations. I may build myself again or I may not. You say obsessions are curable. They are. But people like me swing themselves from one passion to another, and if they miss smash down somewhere where there aren't any passions at all but only bare boards and sawdust. You have done for me utterly. You know it. That's why you are trying to persuade yourself that I am a coarse, sprawling, boneless creature, and so it doesn't matter. When you said, "You've been talking unwisely, Rebecca," you said it with a certain brightness: you felt that you had really caught me at it. I don't think you're right about this. But I know you will derive immense satisfaction from thinking of me as an unbalanced young female who flopped about in your drawing-room in an unnecessary heart-attack.

That is a subtle flattery. But I hate you when you try to cheapen the things I did honestly and cleanly. You did it once before when you wrote to me of "your—much more precious than you imagine it to be—self." That suggests that I projected a weekend at the Brighton Metropole with Horatio Bottomley. Whereas I had written to say that I loved you. You did it again on Friday when you said that what I wanted was some decent fun and that my mind had been, not exactly corrupted, but excited, by people who talked in an ugly way about things that are really beautiful. That was a vile thing to say. You once found my willingness to love you a beautiful and courageous thing. I still think it was. Your spinsterishness makes you feel that a woman desperately and hopelessly in love with a man is an indecent spectacle and a reversal of the natural order of things. But you should have been too fine to feel like that.

I would give my whole life to feel your arms round me again.

I wish you had loved me. I wish you liked me.

Yours,

Rebecca

P.S. Don't leave me utterly alone. If I live write to me now and then. You like me enough for that. At least I pretend to myself you do.

```
28213  EMICIN G

20TH FEB 1978

ATTENTION MICHAEL DEELEY AND BARRY SPIKINGS
EMI FILMS INC
BEVERLY HILLS. CALIF.
696231


HAVE LOOKED RATHER QUICKLY THROUGH THE SCRIPT OF
THE NEW MONTY PYTHON FILM AND AM AMAZED TO FIND THAT
IT IS NOT THE ZANY COMEDY USUALLY ASSOCIATED WITH HIS
FILMS. BUT IS OBSCENE AND SACRILEGIOUS, AND WOULD
CERTAINLY NOT BE IN THE INTEREST OF EMI'S IMAGE TO MAKE
THIS SORT OF FILM.

EVERY FEW WORDS THERE ARE OUTRAGEOUS SWEAR WORDS
WHICH IS NOT IN KEEPING WITH MONTY PYTHON'S IMAGE.

THIS IS VERY DISTRESSING TO ME AND IS A VERY SERIOUS
SITUATION AND I CANNOT, UNTIL WE KNOW EXACTLY WHAT WE
ARE DOING, ALLOW THIS FILM TO BE MADE.

I UNDERSTAND THIS VIEW IS ABSOLUTELY SUPPORTED BY BOB WEBSTER
AND JIMMY CARRERAS AND I HATE TO THINK WHAT JOHN READ'S VIEW
WOULD BE.

PLEASE ADVISE

BERNARD DELFONT



TIMED IN LONDON AT    16.37.


•
EMI FILMS BVHL

28213  EMICIN G"
```

OBSCENE AND SACRILEGIOUS

LORD BERNARD DELFONT
to MICHAEL DEELEY AND
BARRY SPIKINGS
February 20th, 1978

In February 1978, just a few weeks before filming was to start on *Monty Python's Life of Brian*, EMI Films unexpectedly withdrew all financial backing after its board's chairman, Lord Bernard Delfont, glanced at the "obscene and sacrilegious" script for the first time. This panicked memo, sent by Delfont to EMI's Michael Deeley and Barry Spikings, perfectly captures his horrified reaction. Luckily, the Monty Python team found an incredibly keen new backer in

Beatles' guitarist George Harrison, who even mortgaged his house to finance what was ultimately a great investment. As for Delfont, his last-minute decision to jump ship lives on in the film itself, the very last lines of which are as follows:

"Who do you think pays for all this rubbish? They're not gonna make their money back; you know I told them, I said to them, Bernie, I said they'll never make their money back."

WRETCHED WOMAN!

JERMAIN LOGUEN to
SARAH LOGUE
March 28th, 1860

In 1834, 21-year-old Jarm
Logue managed to steal
his master's horse and ride
to Canada, thus escaping
the life of slavery into
which he and his siblings
had been born; sadly, his
mother, brother and sister
remained in Davidson
County, Tennessee, unable
to flee. Twenty-six years
later, by which time he
had settled down in New
York, changed his name to
Jermain Loguen, started
his own family, opened
numerous schools for black
children, become a reverend
and noted abolitionist, and
authored an autobiography,
Loguen received an
astonishingly shameless
letter from the wife of his
old owner in which she
brazenly demanded $1,000
as payment for the horse
on which he had bolted.
Loguen was enraged, to say
the least – his response,
however, stands as a
masterclass in restrained,
eloquent fury.

Maury Co., State of Tennessee,
February 20th, 1860.

To JARM:—I now take my pen to write you a few lines, to let you know how well
we all are. I am a cripple, but I am still able to get about. The rest of the family are
all well. Cherry is as well as Common. I write you these lines to let you the situation
we are in—partly in consequence of your running away and stealing Old Rock,
our fine mare. Though we got the mare back, she was never worth much after you
took her; and as I now stand in need of some funds, I have determined to sell you;
and I have had an offer for you, but did not see fit to take it. If you will send me
one thousand dollars and pay for the old mare, I will give up all claim I have to you.
Write to me as soon as you get these lines, and let me know if you will accept my
proposition. In consequence of your running away, we had to sell Abe and Ann and
twelve acres of land; and I want you to send me the money that I may be able to
redeem the land that you was the cause of our selling, and on receipt of the above
named sum of money, I will send you your bill of sale. If you do not comply with
my request, I will sell you to some one else, and you may rest assured that the time
is not far distant when things will be changed with you. Write to me as soon as you
get these lines. Direct your letter to Bigbyville, Maury County, Tennessee. You had
better comply with my request.

I understand that you are a preacher. As the Southern people are so bad,
you had better come and preach to your old acquaintances. I would like to know
if you read your Bible? If so can you tell what will become of the thief if he does
not repent? and, if the blind lead the blind, what will the consequence be? I deem
it unnecessary to say much more at present. A word to the wise is sufficient. You
know where the liar has his part. You know that we reared you as we reared our own
children; that you was never abused, and that shortly before you ran away, when
your master asked if you would like to be sold, you said you would not leave him to
go with any body.

Sarah Logue.

Syracuse, N.Y., March 28, 1860.

MRS. SARAH LOGUE:—Yours of the 20th of February is duly received, and I thank you for it. It is a long time since I heard from my poor old mother, and I am glad to know she is yet alive, and, as you say, "as well as common." What that means I don't know. I wish you had said more about her.

You are a woman; but had you a woman's heart you could never have insulted a brother by telling him you sold his only remaining brother and sister, because he put himself beyond your power to convert him into money.

You sold my brother and sister, ABE and ANN, and 12 acres of land, you say, because I ran away. Now you have the unutterable meanness to ask me to return and be your miserable chattel, or in lieu thereof send you $1000 to enable you to redeem the *land*, but not to redeem my poor brother and sister! If I were to send you money it would be to get my brother and sister, and not that you should get land. You say you are a *cripple*, and doubtless you say it to stir my pity, for you know I was susceptible in that direction. I do pity you from the bottom of my heart. Nevertheless I am indignant beyond the power of words to express, that you should be so sunken and cruel as to tear the hearts I love so much all in pieces; that you should be willing to impale and crucify us out of all compassion for your poor *foot* or *leg*. Wretched woman! Be it known to you that I value my freedom, to say nothing of my mother, brothers and sisters, more than your whole body; more, indeed, than my own life; more than all the lives of all the slaveholders and tyrants under Heaven.

You say you have offers to buy me, and that you shall sell me if I do not send you $1000, and in the same breath and almost in the same sentence, you say, "you know we raised you as we did our own children." Woman, did you raise your *own children* for the market? Did you raise them for the whipping-post? Did you raise them to be driven off in a coffle in chains? Where are my poor bleeding brothers and sisters? Can you tell? Who was it that sent them off into sugar and cotton fields, to be kicked, and cuffed, and whipped, and to groan and die; and where no kin can hear their groans, or attend and sympathize at their dying bed, or follow in their funeral? Wretched woman! Do you say you did not do it? Then I reply, your husband did, and *you* approved the deed—and the very letter you sent me shows that your heart approves it all. Shame on you.

But, by the way, where is your husband? You don't speak of him. I infer, therefore, that he is dead; that he has gone to his great account, with all his sins against my poor family upon his head. Poor man! gone to meet the spirits of my poor, outraged and murdered people, in a world where Liberty and Justice are MASTERS.

But you say I am a thief, because I took the old mare along with me. Have you got to learn that I had a better right to the old mare, as you call her, than MANASSETH LOGUE had to me? Is it a greater sin for me to steal his horse, than it was for him to rob my mother's cradle and steal me? If he and you infer that I forfeit all my rights to you, shall not I infer that you forfeit all your rights to me? Have you got to learn that human rights are mutual and reciprocal, and if you take my liberty and life, you forfeit your own liberty and life? Before God and High Heaven, is there a law for one man which is not a law for every other man?

If you or any other speculator on my body and rights, wish to know how I regard my rights, they need but come here and lay their hands on me to enslave me. Did you think to terrify me by presenting the alternative to give my money to you, or give my body to Slavery? Then let me say to you, that I meet the proposition with unutterable scorn and contempt. The proposition is an outrage and an insult. I will not budge one hair's breadth. I will not breathe a shorter breath, even to save me from your persecutions. I stand among a free people, who, I thank God, sympathize with my rights, and the rights of mankind; and if your emissaries and venders come here to re-enslave me, and escape the unshrinking vigor of my own right arm, I trust my strong and brave friends, in this City and State, will be my rescuers and avengers.

Yours, &c.,
J.W. Loguen

PSNY 3-7-41 25M

Original

U. NAVAL AIR STATION, KODIAK ALASKA
NAVAL COMMUNICATIONS

Heading	NPO NR 63 F L Z F5L 071830 C8Q TARI 0 B1

From:	CINCPAC	Date	7 DEC 41

To:	ALL SHIPS PRESENT AT HAWAIIN AREA.

Info:	~ U R G E N T ~

DEFERRED unless otherwise checked | ROUTINE......... | PRIORITY......... | AIRMAIL......... | MAILGRAM.........

AIRRAID ON REARLHARBOR X THIS IS NO DRILL

07014

RM 58 1910 7DEC

Comdg Off	Exec	Comm	Oper	Supply	Disb	Med'l	Aerog	Pers	Pub Wks	Mar Det	A & R	Files	FAD	NRAB	OOD	WDO		

A–Denotes action   I–Denotes information   X–Denotes copy only

THIS IS NO DRILL

CINCPAC to ALL SHIPS
December 7th, 1941

At 7.58 a.m. on December 7th 1941, having just witnessed a low-flying plane drop a bomb on Ford Island, Lieutenant Commander Logan C. Ramsey urgently ordered this telegram to be sent to all ships in the Hawaiian area. Ramsey had in fact just witnessed the very beginning of a coordinated attack on the United States naval base at Pearl Harbor, in which, over the course of two hours, the Japanese would ultimately destroy 169 US aircraft and either damage or sink 20 ships. As a result of the attack, 2,403 Americans perished. The next day, as a direct result of this attack, the US declared war on Japan and entered World War II.

DEAR 8 YEAR-OLD TERESA

WIL WHEATON to TERESA
JUSINO
2009

In 1988, aged just eight but already a huge fan of the teen actor due to his part in the universally adored *Stand By Me* and a recurring role in *Star Trek: The Next Generation*, an excited Teresa Jusino saved up the $12 membership fee and applied to join "WilPower", then 15-year-old Wil Wheaton's official fan club. To her dismay, however, the membership kit she had paid for failed to materialise; eventually, many months later, even her disappointment was forgotten.

In 2009, Teresa Jusino, now a 29-year-old writer, received – along with a package containing the very items she had waited patiently for 21 years earlier – an incredibly endearing letter of apology and belated welcome to Wil Wheaton's now defunct fan club, written by the man himself after being alerted to her story.

"He gets a big thank you from Twenty-Nine Year Old Me," said Teresa, shortly after being sent the letter. "Don't get me wrong. Eight Year Old Me is very, very pleased. But Twenty-Nine Year Old Me better knows the importance of a kind gesture, and hopes that her gratitude carries more weight."

Dear 8 year-old Teresa,

I wanted to apologize to you for making you wait so long to get your official WilPower fanclub membership kit. You see, 15 year-old me is very busy with work and school, and the people who were responsible for getting your membership kit mailed back to you must have made a mistake.

It's been a long time since the fan club did anything, but I've enclosed a membership card for you, as well as a wallet photo, and a picture that shows you how much I love Batman (HINT: It's a lot.)

WilPower members got updates about me and my work a few times a year, but the fan club stopped sending those out a long time ago. My latest update, though, goes like this: I got married, I have two boys who I love more than anything in the world, and I'm a writer now, just like you!

And now, 8 year-old Teresa, I want to tell you something very important before I sign off, so listen closely: When you grow up, you're going to be a great writer. I can't tell you how I know, but I hope you'll trust me; I just do. So stay in school, always do your best, and treat people the way you want to be treated.

Thank you for being part of my fan club,

(Signed)

Wil Wheaton

WHAT A DANDY CAR YOU MAKE

CLYDE BARROW to HENRY FORD
April 10th, 1934

From 1932 until its bloody conclusion in May 1934, Bonnie Parker, Clyde Barrow and an ever-changing gang of accomplices became a nationwide talking point as a result of a murderous crime spree which spanned the central United States. Naturally, such a high-profile criminal gang depended on high-powered transport to evade the authorities, and judging by the number he stole over the years, Barrow seemingly had a soft spot for Ford's V8-powered Model B. In fact, in 1934, both Bonnie and Clyde died in the car they had grown to depend on, showered with bullets as they attempted to flee from police. A month before that happened, Henry Ford received an admiring letter, purportedly from Barrow himself, which is now held at the Ford Museum; its authenticity has been debated for many years.

Tulsa Okla
10th April
Mr. Henry Ford
Detroit Mich.

Dear Sir:—

While I still have got breath in my lungs I will tell you what a dandy car you make. I have drove Fords exclusivly when I could get away with one. For sustained speed and freedom from trouble the Ford has got ever other car skinned and even if my business hasen't been strickly legal it don't hurt enything to tell you what a fine car you got in the V8 —

Yours truly
Clyde Champion Barrow

Tulsa Okla
10th April

Mr. Henry Ford
Detroit Mich,

Dear Sir:—
    While I still have got
breath in my lungs I
will tell you what a dandy
car you make. I have drove
Fords exclusivly when I could
get away with one, For sustained
speed and freedom from
trouble the Ford has got ever
other car skinned and even if
my business hasent been
strickly legal it don't hurt eny
thing to tell you what a fine
car you got in the V8 —
    Yours truly
    Clyde Champion Barrow

LOVE, DAD

RONALD REAGAN to
MICHAEL REAGAN
June, 1971

In June 1971, 26-year-old
Michael Reagan married
his 18-year-old fiancée in a
beautiful ceremony that took
place in Hawaii, but which
sadly couldn't be attended
by his dad, the future
President of the United
States, Ronald Reagan.
A few days before the
ceremony, however, Michael
did receive something
invaluable that would be
treasured for years to come:
a heartfelt, loving and sage
letter of fatherly advice
on the subject of love and
marriage.

"It was straight from Dad's
heart," Michael said of the
letter in his 2004 book, *In
the Words of Ronald Reagan.*
"Honest, old-fashioned, and
wise. I cried when I read it,
and I've read it many times
in the years since then."

Michael Reagan
Manhattan Beach, California
June 1971

Dear Mike:

Enclosed is the item I mentioned (with which goes a torn up IOU). I could stop here but I won't.

You've heard all the jokes that have been rousted around by all the "unhappy marrieds" and cynics. Now, in case no one has suggested it, there is another viewpoint. You have entered into the most meaningful relationship there is in all human life. It can be whatever you decide to make it.

Some men feel their masculinity can only be proven if they play out in their own life all the locker-room stories, smugly confident that what a wife doesn't know won't hurt her. The truth is, somehow, way down inside, without her ever finding lipstick on the collar or catching a man in the flimsy excuse of where he was till three A.M., a wife does know, and with that knowing, some of the magic of this relationship disappears. There are more men griping about marriage who kicked the whole thing away themselves than there can ever be wives deserving of blame. There is an old law of physics that you can only get out of a thing as much as you put in it. The man who puts into the marriage only half of what he owns will get that out. Sure, there will be moments when you will see someone or think back to an earlier time and you will be challenged to see if you can still make the grade, but let me tell you how really great is the challenge of proving your masculinity and charm with one woman for the rest of your life. Any man can find a twerp here and there who will go along with cheating, and it doesn't take all that much manhood. It does take quite a man to remain attractive and to be loved by a woman who has heard him snore, seen him unshaven, tended him while he was sick and washed his dirty underwear. Do that and keep her still feeling a warm glow and you will know some very beautiful music. If you truly love a girl, you shouldn't ever want her to feel, when she sees you greet a secretary or a girl you both know, that humiliation of wondering if she was someone who caused you to be late coming home, nor should you want any other woman to be able to meet your wife and know she was smiling behind her eyes as she looked at her, the woman you love, remembering this was the woman you rejected even momentarily for her favors.

Mike, you know better than many what an unhappy home is and what it can do to others. Now you have a chance to make it come out the way it should. There is no greater happiness for a man than approaching a door at the end of a day knowing someone on the other side of that door is waiting for the sound of his footsteps.

Love,
Dad

P.S. You'll never get in trouble if you say "I love you" at least once a day.

WE ARE SINKING FAST

TITANIC to SS *BIRMA*
April 15th, 1912

Shortly before midnight on April 14th 1912, four days into her maiden voyage, RMS *Titanic*, then the largest passenger ship in the world, collided with an iceberg and began to fill with seawater – within hours she had sunk to the bottom of the Atlantic Ocean. Numerous telegrams relayed news of the disaster as it unfolded, and here we have just two. The first, received by SS *Birma* at approximately 0140 hours on April 15th, is the last complete distress call to have left the ship's radio room; the second, sent by *White Star Line* a couple of hours later to the General Post Office of London (employers of the postal staff aboard RMS *Titanic*), incorrectly reported no loss of life following the collision. In actual fact a total of 1,517 people had perished.

C/O SOS SOS cqd cqd – MGY

We are sinking fast passengers being put into boats

MGY

–––––––––––

SECRETARY GENERAL POST OFFICE LDN =

UNDERWRITERS HAVE MESSAGE FROM NEWYORK THAT VIRGINIAN IS STANDING BY TITANIC AND THAT THERE IS NO DANGER OF LOSS OF LIFE = ISMAY .+

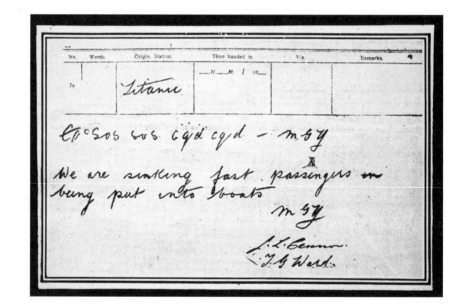

POST OFFICE TELEGRAPHS.

Office Stamp.

Handed in at   Office of Origin and Service Instructions.

Charges to pay ....

Words.   Received here

.M.

LPCOL M RL   27   4/21 =

4   57

SECRETARY GENERAL POST OFFICE LDN =

UNDERWRITERS HAVE MESSAGE FROM NEWYORK THAT VIRGINIAN

IS STANDING BY TITANIC AND THAT THERE IS NO DANGER OF

LOSS OF LIFE = ISMAY .+

Wt. 32321/207. 2,000,000. 2/12. Sch.12.

AN INCREDIBLE COINCIDENCE

ROBERT T. LINCOLN to
RICHARD W. GILDER
February 6th, 1909

On the evening of April 14th 1865, as he watched a play at Ford's Theatre in Washington, US President Abraham Lincoln was shot in the back of the head by 26-year-old John Wilkes Booth. He died the next morning. Forty-four years later, Lincoln's son, Robert, wrote this letter to Richard Gilder, editor of *The Century Magazine*, and described an incredible and largely undiscussed coincidence which had occurred all those years ago, shortly before the assassination of his father: whilst standing waiting for a train in New Jersey, Robert Lincoln had fallen into the gap between the moving train and platform, only to be quickly and heroically pulled to safety by a stranger. That stranger was in fact Edwin Booth, a famous actor who also happened to be the brother of John Wilkes Booth, the man who was soon to kill Robert's father.

PULLMAN BUILDING
   CHICAGO

February 6th, 1909.

My dear Mr. Gilder:

      I have your letter of February 4th, but the poems you mention in your postscript have not yet come. I will acknowledge them when they do. In the meantime I think it well to write to you about the other matters mentioned in your letter.

      In regard to the Lincoln portrait by Healy; I have conferred with Mr. Hempstead Washburne, and find that he has himself no knowledge of his father, Mr. E. B. Washburne, having ever owned the portrait of my father which is now in the possession of Senator Washburn. But he has a portrait of his father, and of several European Statesmen, which were painted by Mr. Healy for his father while he was our Minister at Paris. I find also that Mr. Healy's original portrait of my father made about 1860 is in the Newberry Library, in Chicago, and not in the Chicago Historical Society, as I wrote you before. I have accordingly made some slight changes in your copy on this subject.

      The account of my rescue by Mr. Edwin Booth, which I return to you, is essentially correct, but it is not accurate in its details. I do not know that it is worth changing – you can judge for yourself.

      The incident occurred while a group of passengers were late at night purchasing their sleeping car places from the conductor who stood on the station platform at the entrance of the car. The platform was about the height of the car floor, and there was of course a narrow space between the platform and the car body. There was some crowding, and I happened to be pressed by it against the car body while waiting my turn. In this situation the train began to move, and by the motion I was twisted off my feet, and dropped somewhat, with feet downward, into the open space, and was personally helpless, when my coat collar was vigorously seized and I was quickly pulled up and out to a secure footing on the platform. Upon turning to thank my rescuer I saw it was Edwin Booth, whose face was of course well known to me, and I expressed my gratitude to him, and in doing so, called him by name.

Very sincerely yours,
(Signed)

Richard Watson Gilder, Esq.,
   The Century Company,
      33 East 17th Street,
         New York City.

February 6th, 1909,

My dear Mr. Gilder:

I have your letter of February 4th, but the poems you mention in your postscript have not yet come. I will acknowledge them when they do. In the meantime I think it well to write you about the other matters mentioned in your letter.

In regard to the Lincoln portrait by Healy; I have conferred with Mr. Hempstead Washburne, and find that he has himself no knowledge of his father, Mr. E. B. Washburne, having ever owned the portrait of my father which is now in the possession of Senator Washburn. But he has a portrait of his father, and of several European Statesmen, which were painted by Mr. Healy for his father while he was our Minister at Paris. I find also that Mr. Healy's original portrait of my father made about 1860 is in the Newberry Library, in Chicago, and not in the Chicago Historical Society, as I wrote you before. I have accordingly made some slight changes in your copy on this subject.

The account of my rescue by Mr. Edwin Booth, which I return to you, is essentially correct, but it is not accurate in its details. I do not know that it is worth changing - you can judge for yourself.

The incident occurred while a group of passengers were late at night purchasing their sleeping car places from the conductor who stood on the station platform at the entrance of the car. The platform was about the height of the car floor, and there was of course a narrow space between the platform and the car body There was some crowding, and I happened to be pressed by it against the car body while waiting my turn.   In this situation the train began to move, and by the motion I was twisted off my feet, and had dropped somewhat, with feet downward, into the open space, and was personally helpless, when my coat collar was vigorously seized and I was quickly pulled up and out to a secure footing on the platform.   Upon turning to thank my rescuer I saw it was Edwin Booth, whose face was of course well known to me, and I expressed my gratitude to him, and in doing so, called him by name.

Very sincerely yours,

Richard Watson Gilder, Esq.,
The Century Company,
33 East 17th Street,
New York City.

PIXAR FILMS DON'T GET FINISHED, THEY JUST GET RELEASED

PETE DOCTER to ADAM
October 17th, 2008

Mid-2008, hoping at best to receive a signed photo from his idol in return, a young man named Adam wrote to Pete Docter, the award-winning screenwriter and director of Pixar's *Monsters, Inc.* who at that point was busy directing his next film, *Up*. In his letter, Adam spoke of his admiration for Docter and, as an amateur filmmaker and huge Pixar fan, mentioned his desire to work for the studio in the future. To his delight, a few months later the lovely handwritten and illustrated letter seen here arrived on Adam's doorstep.

10.17.08

Hey Adam!

First off, let me apologize for taking so long to respond to your very kind letter. Things are pretty nuts around here. You had asked for an autographed photo of me; I don't really have anything like that, not being famous. But here is a drawing of me for you.

I'm sure you can see the resemblance.

You are sure right about the importance of a good story in movies. Unfortunately, it's not as easy as it sounds. It takes a lot of work (and rework, and rework and rework) to get it right. And even then quite often we're not 100% pleased.

As John Lasseter likes to say, our films don't get finished, they just get <u>released</u>.

Hope you enjoy "UP" next year!

Pete Docter

Hey Adam!

First off, let me apologize for taking so long to respond to your very kind letter. Things are pretty nuts around here.

You had asked for an autographed photo of me; I don't really have anything like that, not being famous. But here is a drawing of me for you

↑ I'm sure you can see the resemblance →

10·17·08

- 2 -

You are sure right about the importance of a good story in movies. Unfortunately, It's not as easy as it sounds. It takes a lot of work (and rework, and rework and rework) to get it right. And even then quite often we're not 100% pleased. As John Lasseter likes to say, our films don't get finished, they just get released. Hope you enjoy "UP" next year!

Pete Docter

7-22-85

MAY WE ALL GET BETTER TOGETHER

CHARLES BUKOWSKI to
HANS VAN DEN BROEK
July 22nd, 1985

In 1985, following a
complaint from a local
reader, staff at the public
library in the Dutch city of
Nijmegen decided to remove
Charles Bukowski's 1983
collection of short stories,
Tales of Ordinary Madness,
from their shelves, whilst
declaring the book "very
sadistic, occasionally
fascist and discriminatory
against certain groups
(including homosexuals)".
Not everyone agreed with
the library's decision and in
the following weeks a local
journalist by the name of
Hans van den Broek wrote to
Bukowski and asked for his
opinion on such censorship.
It soon arrived.

Bukowski's magnificent
letter currently hangs
proudly in the Open Dicht
Bus, a mobile bookshop
based, more often than not,
in Eindhoven.

Dear Hans van den Broek:

Thank you for your letter telling me of the removal of one of my books from the Nijmegen library. And that it is accused of discrimination against black people, homosexuals and women. And that it is sadism because of the sadism.

The thing that I fear discriminating against is humor and truth.

If I write badly about blacks, homosexuals and women it is because of these who I met were that. There are many "bads"—bad dogs, bad censorship; there are even "bad" white males. Only when you write about "bad" white males they don't complain about it. And need I say that there are "good" blacks, "good" homosexuals and "good" women?

In my work, as a writer, I only photograph, in words, what I see. If I write of "sadism" it is because it exists, I didn't invent it, and if some terrible act occurs in my work it is because such things happen in our lives. I am not on the side of evil, if such a thing as evil abounds. In my writing I do not always agree with what occurs, nor do I linger in the mud for the sheer sake of it. Also, it is curious that the people who rail against my work seem to overlook the sections of it which entail joy and love and hope, and there are such sections. My days, my years, my life has seen up and downs, lights and darknesses. If I wrote only and continually of the "light" and never mentioned the other, then as an artist I would be a liar.

Censorship is the tool of those who have the need to hide actualities from themselves and from others. Their fear is only their inability to face what is real, and I can't vent any anger against them. I only feel this appalling sadness. Somewhere, in their upbringing, they were shielded against the total facts of our existence. They were only taught to look one way when many ways exist.

I am not dismayed that one of my books has been hunted down and dislodged from the shelves of a local library. In a sense, I am honored that I have written something that has awakened these from their non-ponderous depths. But I am hurt, yes, when somebody else's book is censored, for that book, usually is a great book and there are few of those, and throughout the ages that type of book has often generated into a classic, and what was once thought shocking and immoral is now required reading at many of our universities.

I am not saying that my book is one of those, but I am saying that in our time, at this moment when any moment may be the last for many of us, it's damned galling and impossibly sad that we still have among us the small, bitter people, the witch-hunters and the declaimers against reality. Yet, these too belong with us, they are part of the whole, and if I haven't written about them, I should, maybe have here, and that's enough.

     may we all get better together,
        yrs,
          (Signed)
          Charles Bukowski

7-22-85

Dear Hans van den Broek:

Thank you for your letter telling me of the removal of one of my books
from the Nijmegen library. And that it is accused of discrimination against
black people, homosexuals and women. And that it is sadism because of the
sadism.

The thing that I fear discriminating against is humor and truth.

If I write badly about blacks, homosexuals and women it is because of
those who I met were that. There are many "bads"--bad dogs, bad censorship;
there are even "bad" white males. Only when you write about "bad" white males
they don't complain about it. And need I say that there are "good" blacks,
"good" homosexuals and "good" women?

In my work, as a writer, I only photograph, in words, what I see. If
I write of "sadism" it is because it exists, I didn't invent it, and if
some terrible act occurs in my work it is because such things happen in our
lives. I am not on the side of evil, if such a thing as evil abounds. In
my writing I do not always agree with what occurs, nor do I linger in the
mud for the sheer sake of it. Also, it is curious that the people who rail
against my work seem to overlook the sections of it which entail joy and
love and hope, and there are such sections. My days, my years, my life HAS
seen up and downs, lights and darknesses. If I wrote only and continually
of the "light" and never mentioned the other, them as an artist I would be
a liar.

Censorship is the tool of those who have the need to hide actualities
from themselves and from others. Their fear is only their inability to face
what is real, and I can't vent any anger against them, I only feel this
appalling sadness. Somewhere, in their upbringings, they were shielded against
the total facts of our existence. They were only taught to look one way when
many ways exist.

I am not dismayed that one of my books has been hunted down and dislodged
from the shelves of a local library. In a sense, I am honored that I have
written something that has awakened these from their non-ponderous depths.
But I am hurt, yes, when somebody else's book is censored, for that book,
usually is a great book and there are few of those, and throughout the ages
that type of book has often generated into a classic, and what was once
thought shocking and immoral is now required reading at many of our universities.

I am not saying that my book is one of those, but I am saying that in
our time, at this moment any moment may be the last for most of us, it's
damned galling and impossibly sad that we still have among us the small,
bitter people, the witch-hunters and the declaimers against reality. Yet,
these too belong with us, they are a part of the whole, and if I haven't
written about them, I should, maybe have here, and that's enough.

may we all get better together.

yrs,

Charles Bukowski

WE ALL FEEL LIKE
THAT NOW AND THEN

SIR ARCHIBALD CLARK
KERR to LORD REGINALD
PEMBROKE
April 6th, 1943

At the height of World War
II on April 6th 1943, at
which point he was British
Ambassador to Moscow,
the famously eccentric Sir
Archibald Clark Kerr wrote
a letter to Foreign Office
minister Lord Reginald
Pembroke. This now classic
piece of correspondence,
which was prompted by
a Turkish diplomat with
the most unfortunate of
names, is indeed hilarious;
it also offers proof, if it
were needed, that name-
based punnery and mild
xenophobia did a roaring
trade long before the
internet was fired up.

H.M. EMBASSY
LONDON

Lord Pembroke
The Foreign Office
LONDON

6th April 1943

My Dear Reggie,

In these dark days man tends to look for little shafts of light that spill from
Heaven. My days are probably darker than yours, and I need, my God I do, all the
light I can get. But I am a decent fellow, and I do not wish to be mean and selfish
about what little brightness is shed upon me from time to time. So I propose to
share with you a tiny flash that has illuminated my sombre life and tell you that
God has given me a new Turkish colleague whose card tells me that he is called
Mustapha Kunt.

We all feel like that, Reggie, now and then, especially when Spring is upon
us, but few of us would care to put it on our cards. It takes a Turk to do that.

(Signed)

Sir Archibald Clerk Kerr,
H.M. Ambassador.

IT WAS HARD TO GIVE FIVE SONS TO THE NAVY

ALLETA SULLIVAN to US NAVY
January, 1943

In November 1942, during the three-day Naval Battle of Guadalcanal in the Solomon Islands, the USS *Juneau* sank after being struck by two Japanese torpedoes. As a result, 687 men were killed, five of whom were the Sullivan brothers – siblings who, ten months earlier, had enlisted at the same time on the understanding that they would serve together. Two months after their deaths, having heard worrying rumours about her sons, their mother, Alleta Sullivan, wrote a moving letter to the Bureau of Naval Personnel and asked for an update. She soon received a reply, not from the Bureau, but from US President Franklin D. Roosevelt.

As a result of the Sullivans' plight, the US military introduced the Sole Survivor Policy, which attempts to ensure that, should a family member be lost during military service, any remaining siblings be exempt from service.

Waterloo, Iowa
January 1943

Bureau of Naval Personnel

Dear Sirs:

I am writing you in regards to a rumor going around that my five sons were killed in action in November. A mother from here came and told me she got a letter from her son and he heard my five sons were killed.

It is all over town now, and I am so worried. My five sons joined the Navy together a year ago, Jan. 3, 1942. They are on the Cruiser, U.S.S. JUNEAU. The last I heard from them was Nov. 8th. That is, it was dated Nov 8th, U.S. Navy.

Their names are, George T., Francis Henry, Joseph E., Madison A., and Albert L. If it is so, please let me know the truth. I am to christen the U.S.S. TAWASA, Feb. 12th, at Portland, Oregon. If anything has happened to my five sons, I will still christen the ship as it was their wish that I do so. I hated to bother you, but it has worried me so that I wanted to know if it was true. So please tell me. It was hard to give five sons all at once to the Navy, but I am proud of my boys that they can serve and help protect their country. George and Francis served four years on the U.S.S. HOVEY, and I had the pleasure to go aboard their ship in 1937.

I am so happy the Navy has bestowed the honor on me to christen the U.S.S. TAWASA. My husband and daughter are going to Portland with me. I remain,

Sincerely,

Mrs. Alleta Sullivan
98 Adams Street
Waterloo, Iowa

My dear Mr. and Mrs. Sullivan:

The knowledge that your five gallant sons are missing in action against the enemy inspires me to write you this personal message. I realize full well there is little I can say to assuage your grief.

As Commander-in-Chief of the Army and Navy, I want you to know that the entire nation shares in your sorrow. I offer you the condolences and gratitude of our country. We who remain to carry on the fight must maintain spirit, in the knowledge that such sacrifice is not in vain.

The Navy Department has informed me of the expressed desire of your sons, George Thomas, Francis Henry, Joseph Eugene, Madison Abel, and Albert Leo, to serve in the same ship. I am sure that we all take heart in the knowledge that they fought side by side. As one of your sons wrote, "We will make a team together that can't be beat." It is this spirit which in the end must triumph.

Last March you, Mrs. Sullivan, were designated to sponsor a ship of the Navy, in recognition of your patriotism and that of your sons. I understand that you are now even more determined to carry on as sponsor. This evidence of unselfishness and of courage serves as a real inspiration for me, as I am sure it will for all Americans. Such acts of faith and fortitude in the face of tragedy convince me of the indomitable spirit and will of our people.

I send you my deepest sympathy in your hour of trial and pray that in Almighty God you will find the comfort and help that only He can bring.

Very sincerely yours,

(Signed)

Franklin D. Roosevelt

NOTHING GOOD GETS AWAY

JOHN STEINBECK to THOM STEINBECK
November 10th, 1958

John Steinbeck, born in 1902, was one of the most acclaimed authors of his generation, responsible for a body of work that boasts, most notably, *The Grapes of Wrath*, *East of Eden* and *Of Mice and Men* – all classics which have been read and adored by many millions in all corners of the globe, and which resulted in Steinbeck being awarded the Nobel Prize for Literature in 1962. Four years before that happened, his eldest son, 14-year-old Thomas, wrote home from boarding school and told of Susan, a young girl for whom he believed he had fallen. Steinbeck replied the same day with a wonderful, heartfelt letter of fatherly advice, on the subject of love, that couldn't have been more fitting.

Dear Thom:

We had your letter this morning. I will answer it from my point of view and of course Elaine will from hers.

First—if you are in love—that's a good thing—that's about the best thing that can happen to anyone. Don't let anyone make it small or light to you.

Second—There are several kinds of love. One is a selfish, mean, grasping, egotistical thing which uses love for self-importance. This is the ugly and crippling kind. The other is an outpouring of everything good in you—of kindness and consideration and respect—not only the social respect of manners but the greater respect which is recognition of another person as unique and valuable. The first kind can make you sick and small and weak but the second can release in you strength, and courage and goodness and even wisdom you didn't know you had.

You say this is not puppy love. If you feel so deeply—of course it isn't puppy love.

But I don't think you were asking me what you feel. You know better than anyone. What you wanted me to help you with is what to do about it—and that I can tell you.

Glory in it for one thing and be very glad and grateful for it.

The object of love is the best and most beautiful. Try to live up to it.

If you love someone—there is no possible harm in saying so—only you must remember that some people are very shy and sometimes the saying must take that shyness into consideration.

Girls have a way of knowing or feeling what you feel, but they usually like to hear it also.

It sometimes happens that what you feel is not returned for one reason or another—but that does not make your feeling less valuable and good.

Lastly, I know your feeling because I have it and I'm glad you have it.

We will be glad to meet Susan. She will be very welcome. But Elaine will make all such arrangements because that is her province and she will be very glad to. She knows about love too and maybe she can give you more help than I can.

And don't worry about losing. If it is right, it happens—The main thing is not to hurry. Nothing good gets away.

Love,

Fa

THE GREAT FIRE OF LONDON

JAMES HICKS to HIS
FELLOW POSTMASTERS
September 4th, 1666

Over 70,000 Londoners were left homeless in 1666 when, in the early hours of September 2nd, a fire that began in a bakery on Pudding Lane swiftly grew to consume and devastate the entire city. It is believed that approximately 13,000 residences burned to the ground. As London's first Post Office at Cloak Lane surrendered to what we now know as the Great Fire of London, Postmaster James Hicks quickly salvaged as much of the city's correspondence as physically possible and fled with his family to Barnet. Once there, still shaken, he sent this letter to his fellow Postmasters and informed them of the unfolding catastrophe.

To my good friends ye Postmasters betwixt London & Chester & so to Holly Head

Gentlemen,

it hath pleased Almighty God to visit this famous city of London with most raging fire which began on Sunday morning last about 2 a clock in Pudding Lane in a baker's house behind the Kings Head tavern in New Fish Street & though all the means possible was used yet it could not be obstructed but before night it had burnt most part of ye City with St Magnus Church & part of ye Bridge to Q Hith to the water side, Canon Street, Dowgate, & upon Monday struck up Gratious Street, Lombard Street, Cornhill, Poultry, Bartholomew Lane, Throgmorton Street, Lothbury, & the last night & this day rages through all parts of the city as far as Temple Bar, Holborn Bridge, Smithfield & by all conjecture is not by any means to be stopped from further ruin except God in his infinite wisdom prevent it. I am at ye Red Lyon in Barnet with my family, & God in reasonable good health, notwithstanding great loss and sufferings by the distraction of our office yet I am commanded to let you know yet what little come to your hands from any ministers of State yet again give you all quick and speedy dispatch to me hither yet I may convey you home to Court or such places as I may receive directions for, & I am also to intimate to you which letters are sent to you from Court & shall see them sent forwards from here to you with speedy care & conveyance & so soone as pleasith God to put an end to ye violence of this fire some place will be picked on for ye general correspondence as formerly of which you shall God willing have advice at present this is all

Your sorrowfull friend
James Hicks.

Barnet Sep. 4. 11 at night

To my good ffriends y[e] Postmasters betwixt London
& Chester & so to Holly head.

Gentlemen

  it hath pleased Al: God to lisit this famouscity of L[ndon] with most
raging fire wth began on Sunday morning last about 2 a clock in Pudding lane,
in a bakers house behind the Kgs head taverne in new ffish street & though all
the meanes possible was vsed yet it could not bee obstructed but before night
it had burnt most part of y[e] City wth st magnus church & part of y[e] Bridge
to L. Hith to the water side, Canon street, Dowgate, & vpon Munday struck
vp to Gratious street, Lumbard street, Cornhill, Poultry Bartholomew
lane. ffrogmorton street, Loathbury & the last night & this day rages
through all parts of the city as far as Temple Barr, Holburne bridge
Smithfield, & by all conjecture is not by any meanes to bee stopped
fro afurther ruine except god in his infinite wysdome prevent it
& am al y[e] Red Lyon in Barnett with my family & blisse god in reason
able good health, notwithstanding great losse & sufferings by this
distractions of o[r] office yet I am Comanded to let y[u] know y[t] what
letters come to yo hands fro any Ministers of state y[t] give give you
all quicke & speedy dispatch to mee hither y[t] I may Convey them home
to Court or such places as I may receive directions for, & I am also
to intimate to you y[t] w[t] letters are sent to y[u] fro Court I shall forw
them sfel forwards fro hence to you with Spedy Care & conveyance
& so soone as pleaseth god to put an end to y[e] violence of this fire
some place will bee pitch on for y[e] generall Correspondence as
formerly of w[th] you shall God willing heare advice at p[rese]nt this
is all

          yo[r] sorrowfull friend
          James Hicks.

Barnet sep. 4. 11 at night.

IT IS LIKE
CONFESSING A
MURDER

CHARLES DARWIN to
JOSEPH D. HOOKER
January 11th, 1844

In November 1859, Charles
Darwin's *On the Origin of
Species* was published. A
truly groundbreaking book
that would forever change
our perception of the
world instantly generated
widespread debate and
surprise due to Darwin's
central theory of evolution:
that a species, rather
than being unchanging,
will gradually transform
over time according to
its environment, the
most advantageous and
therefore attractive traits
of its individuals persisting.
Fifteen years earlier, when
Darwin first considered what
was later termed "natural
selection", he wrote a letter
to his friend, the botanist
Joseph D. Hooker, in which,
after discussing various
plants, shells and fossils, he
made mention of his world-
changing theory and likened
the revelation to "confessing
a murder".

Down. Bromley Kent

Thursday

My dear Sir

I must write to thank you for your last letter; I to tell you how much all your views
and facts interest me. — I must be allowed to put my own interpretation on what
you say of "not being a good arranger of extended views" — which is, that you
do not indulge in the loose speculations so easily started by every smatterer &
wandering collector. — I look at a strong tendency to generalize as an entire evil —

What limit shall you take on the Patagonian side — has d'Orbigny published, I
believe he made a large collection at the R. Negro, where Patagonia retains its
usual forlorn appearance; at Bahia Blanca & northward the features of Patagonia
insensibly blend into the savannahs of La Plata. — The Botany of S. Patagonia
(& I collected every plant in flower at the season when there) would be worth
comparison with the N. Patagonian collection by d'Orbigny. — I do not know
anything about King's plants, but his birds were so inaccurately habitated, that
I have seen specimen from Brazil, Tierra del & the Cape de Verde Isd all said to
come from the St. Magellan. — What you say of Mr Brown is humiliating; I had
suspected it, but cd not allow myself to believe in such heresy. — FitzRoy gave
him a rap in his Preface, & made me very indignant, but it seems a much harder
one wd not have been wasted. My crptogamic collection was sent to Berkeley; it
was not large; I do not believe he has yet published an account, but he wrote to me
some year ago that he had described & mislaid all his descriptions. Wd it not be
well for you to put yourself in communication with him; as otherwise some things
will perhaps be twice laboured over. — My best (though poor) collection of the
Crptogam. was from the Chonos Islands. —

Would you kindly observe one little fact for me, whether any species of plant,
peculiar to any isld, as Galapagos, St. Helena or New Zealand, where there are no
large quadrupeds, have hooked seeds, — such hooks as if observed here would be
thought with justness to be adapted to catch into wool of animals. —

Would you further oblige me some time by informing me (though I forget this will
certainly appear in your Antarctic Flora) whether in isld like St. Helena, Galapagos,
& New Zealand, the number of families & genera are large compared with the
number of species, as happens in coral-isld, & as I believe? in the extreme Arctic
land. Certainly this is case with Marine shells in extreme Arctic seas. — Do you
suppose the fewness of species in proportion to number of large groups in Coral-
islets., is owing to the chance of seeds from all orders, getting drifted to such new
spots? as I have supposed. —

Did you collect sea-shells in Kerguelen land, I shd like to know their character.?

Your interesting letters tempt me to be very unreasonable in asking you questions; but you must not give yourself any trouble about them, for I know how fully & worthily you are employed.

Besides a general interest about the Southern lands, I have been now ever since my return engaged in a very presumptuous work & which I know no one individual who wd not say a very foolish one. — I was so struck with distribution of Galapagos organisms &c &c & with the character of the American fossil mammifers, &c &c that I determined to collect blindly every sort of fact, which cd bear any way on what are species. — I have read heaps of agricultural & horticultural books, & have never ceased collecting facts — At last gleams of light have come, & I am almost convinced (quite contrary to opinion I started with) that species are not (it is like confessing a murder) immutable. Heaven forfend me from Lamarck nonsense of a "tendency to progression" "adaptations from the slow willing of animals" &c, — but the conclusions I am led to are not widely different from his — though the means of change are wholly so — I think I have found out (here's presumption!) the simple way by which species become exquisitely adapted to various ends. — You will now groan, & think to yourself 'on what a man have I been wasting my time in writing to.' — I shd, five years ago, have thought so. — I fear you will also groan at the length of this letter — excuse me, I did not begin with malice prepense.

Believe me my dear Sir
Very truly your's
C. Darwin

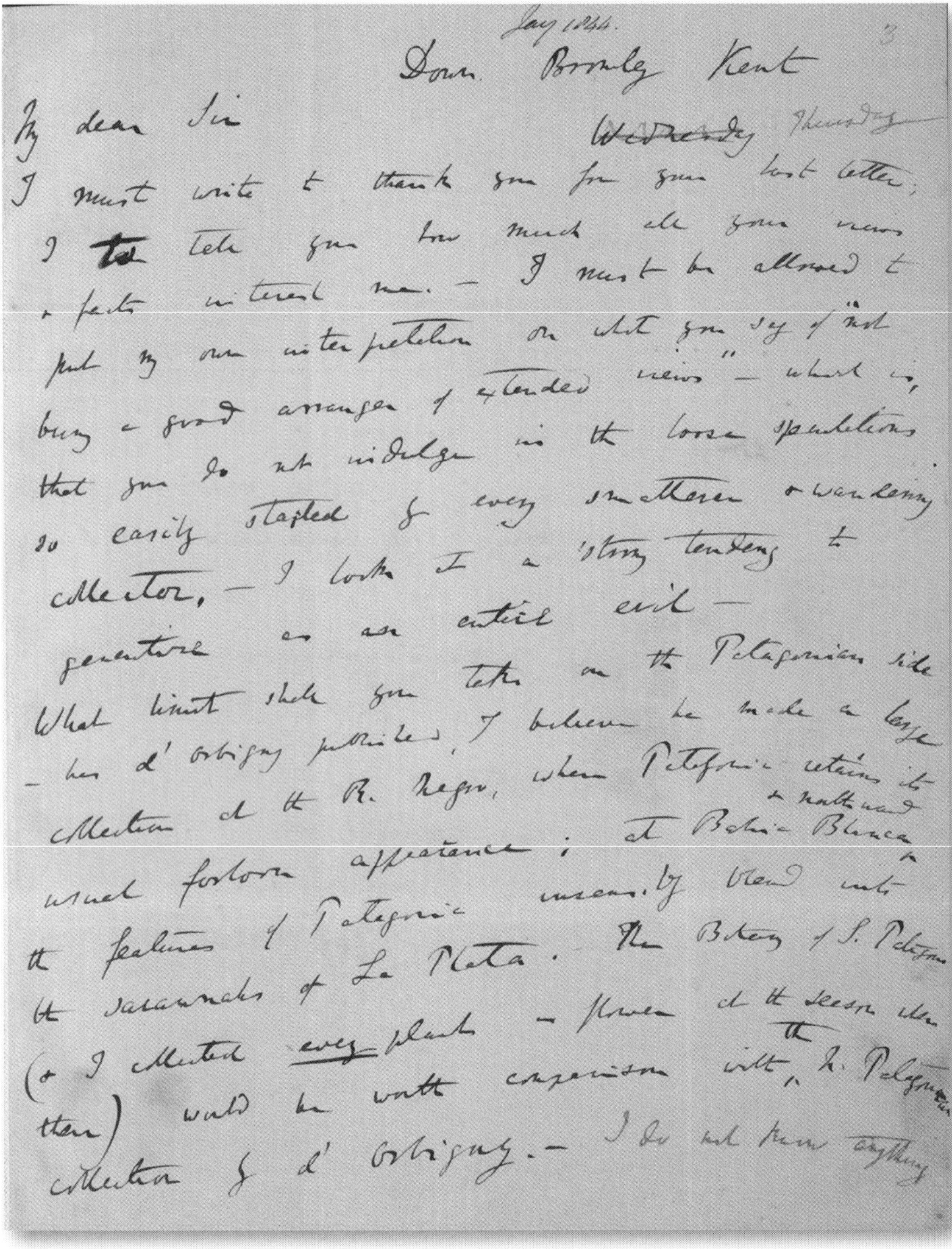

3

Jany 1844.

Down. Bromley Kent

My dear Sir

~~Wednesday~~ Thursday

I must write to thank you for your last letter; I ~~tell~~ tell you how much all your news & facts interest me. — I must be allowed to put my own interpretation on what you say of "not being a good arranger of extended views" — what is, that you do not indulge in the loose speculations so easily started by every smatterer & wandering collector, — I look at a "strong tendency to generalize" as an entire evil —

What limit shall you take on the Patagonian side — has d'Orbigny published, I believe he made a large collection at the R. Negro, when Patagonia retains its usual forlorn appearance; at Bahia Blanca & northward the features of Patagonia insensibly blend into the savannahs of La Plata. The Botany of S. Patagonia (& I collected every plant — flower at the season when there) would be worth comparison with the N. Patagonian collection of d'Orbigny. — I do not know anything

310

about Kings' plants, but his birds were so inaccurately habitated, that I have seen specimens from Brazil, Tierra del & the Cape de Verde Id^s all said to come from the St. Magellen. — What you say of Mr Browne is humiliating; I had suspected it, but w^d not allow myself to believe in such heresy. — FitzRoy gave him a _____ in his Preface, & made me very indignant, but it seems = much harder one had not have been wasted. My cryptogamic collection was sent to ~~London~~ Berkeley; it was not large; I do not believe he has yet published an account, but he wrote to me some years ago that he had described & mislaid all his descriptions. W^d it not be well for you to put yourself in communication with him; as otherwise some things (these soon) will perhaps be twice laboured over. — My best collection of the Cryptogam. was from the Chonos Islands. —

Would you kindly observe one little fact for me, whether any species of plant, peculiar to any isl^d. as Galapagos,

St. Helena & New Zealand, where there are no large Quadrupeds, have hooked seeds,— such hooks as if observed here would be thought with justness to be adapted to catch into wool of animals.

Would you further oblige me some time by informing me (though I forgot this will certainly appear in your Antarctic Flora) whether in isd like St. Helena. Galapagos, & New Zealand, the number of families & genera are large compared with the number of species, as happens in coral-isd, & as I believe? in the extreme Arctic land. Certainly this is case with marine shells in extreme Arctic seas. — Do you suppose the number of species in proportion to large groups, is owing to the chance of seeds from all orders, getting drifted to such new spots? as I have supposed. —

Did you collect Sea-shells in Kerguelen land, I shd like to know their character..?

Your interesting letters tempt me to be very unreasonable in asking you questions; but you must not give yourself any trouble about them, for I know how fully & worthily you are employed.

Besides a general interest about the Southern lands, I have been now ever since my return engaged in a very presumptuous work & which I know no one individual who wd not say a very foolish one. — I was so struck with distribution of Galapagos organisms &c &c & with the character of the American fossil mammifers, &c that I determined to collect blindly every sort of fact, which cd bear any way on what are species. — I have read heaps of agricultural & horticultural books, & have never ceased collecting facts — At last gleams of light have come, & I am almost convinced (quite contrary to opinion I started with) that species are not (it is like confessing a murder) immutable. Heaven forefend me from Lamarck nonsense of a "tendency to progression" "adaptations from the slow willing of animals" &c — but the conclusions I am led to are not widely different from his — though the means of change are wholly so — I think I have found out (here's presumption!) the simple way by which species become

exquisitely
adapted to various ends. — You will now
groan, & think to yourself 'on what a
man have I been wasting my time in
writing to.' — I sh^d, five years ago, have
thought so. — I fear you will also groan
at the length of this letter — excuse me,
I did not begin with malice prepense.
Believe me my dear Sir
very truly yours
C. Darwin

FROM ARTHUR C. FIFIELD, PUBLISHER,
13, CLIFFORD'S INN, LONDON, E.C.

TELEPHONE 14430 CENTRAL.

April 19 1912.

Dear Madam,

I am only one, only one, only one.
Only one being, one at the same time.
Not two, not three, only one. Only one
life to live, only sixty minutes in one
hour. Only one pair of eyes. Only one
brain. Only one being. Being only one,
having only one pair of eyes, having
only one time, having only one life, I
cannot read your M.S. three or four
times. Not even one time. Only one look,
only one look is enough. Hardly one
copy would sell here. Hardly one. Hardly
one.

Many thanks. I am returning the
M.S. by registered post. Only one M.S.
by one post.

Sincerely yours,

Miss Gertrude Stein,
27 Rue de Fleurus,
Paris,
France.

HARDLY ONE. HARDLY ONE

ARTHUR C. FIFIELD to
GERTRUDE STEIN
April 19th, 1912

Author and poet Gertrude Stein had an approach to writing that divided audiences, the unimpressed of whom found her rhythmical repetition and stream-of-consciousness style simply impenetrable and nonsensical. For others it was, and remains, a breath of fresh air; something unique, to be savoured. In 1912, having just read one of her more repetitive manuscripts, *The Making of Americans*, publisher Arthur C. Fifield rejected Stein with this wonderful, light-hearted letter that perfectly mimicked the technique for which she was famous.

JOHN LENNON SIGNED MY ALBUM

MARK CHAPMAN to A
MEMORABILIA EXPERT
April 10th, 1986

On the afternoon of December 8th 1980, outside his apartment in New York, John Lennon, one of the most famous and recognisable faces on earth, was approached by an autograph hunter who silently handed him a copy of Lennon's album, *Double Fantasy*, to sign. Lennon obliged. In roughly the same area just a few hours later, that same man, Mark Chapman, shot John Lennon four times in the back, killing him, and then waited for the police to arrive. Six years later, while incarcerated at Attica Correctional Facility in New York, Lennon's killer wrote a letter to a memorabilia expert and asked how much that signed album would be worth.

April 10, 1986
THURSDAY

Dear [Redacted]

First, I'd like you to keep this letter confidential – between us only. Thank you.

I heard you today on Andy Thomas's BUFFALO TALKS (WWKB) and felt at least from your voice, I could write you concerning a very personal matter. I also have some random questions which will follow.

On December 8, 1980 I shot and killed John Lennon. Before this, earlier in the afternoon, I had asked him to sign his <u>Double Fantasy</u> album. He did this also signing the date: 1980. I then placed this album behind the security guard's booth where it was found after my arrest. I have tried unsuccessfully for years (and 2 attorneys) to get this item back, seeking to place it at auction and donating the money to a children's charity. I felt it was the least I could do. Now, is there any way to assess the value of an item such as this? I have often wanted to write a dealer (Charles Hamilton comes to mind) concerning this but haven't. I guess listening to you convinced me I could trust you – I'm somewhat of a recluse.

<u>Is</u> there a value that could be assigned to an item like this? Is this something that could only be determined at auction? Please let me know your feelings on this.

I have an autographed Autobiography of Sophie Tucker (it's inscribed) and was wondering if this is worth anything. There is NO dust wrapper and the condition isn't that great.

Also, do you have any Stephen King <u>holograph</u> material available? What is the worth of such items?

Any J.D. Salinger letters available? I would like any holograph letters.

Could you send me any addresses of other dealers who might have any of the above items?

Thank you Kindly,

(Signed)

M.CHAPMAN
81 A 3860
BOX 149
ATTICA CORRECTIONAL FACILITY
ATTICA, NY 14011

April 10, 1986
Thursday

Dear,

First, I'd like you to keep this letter confidential - between us only. Thank you.

I heard you today on Andy Thomas's Bizarre Tales (WNCB) and felt at least from your voice, I could write you concerning a very personal matter. I also have some random questions which will follow.

On December 8, 1980 I shot and killed John Lennon. Before this tragedy in the afternoon, I had asked him to sign his Double Fantasy album. He did this also signing the date: 1980. I thus placed this album below the security guards table where it was found after my arrest. I have tried unsuccessfully for years (and 2 attorneys) to get this item back seeking to place it at auction and donating the money to a children's charity. I felt if it was the best I could do. Now, is there any way to assure the value of an item such as this? I have often wished to write a dealer (Charles Hamilton comes to mind) concerning this but haven't. I guess bottom line, to you convinced me I could trust you - I'm somewhat of a recluse.

Is there a value that could be assigned to an item like this? Is this something that could only be determined at auction? Please let me know your feelings on this.

I have an autographed photograph of Sophie Tucker (it invoiced) one time invoicing. If this is worth anything, there is no dust wrapper and the condition isn't that great.

Also, do you have any Steak Knife holograph material available? What is the worst of such items?

Any J.D. Salinger letters available? I would like my Salinger letters.
Could you send me any reference of other dealers who might have any of the above items?

Thank you kindly,
Mark David Chapman

M. CHAPMAN
81 A 3860
Box 149
ATTICA CORRECTIONAL FACILITY
ATTICA, NY 14011

SASE ENCLOSED

THINGS TO WORRY ABOUT

F. SCOTT FITZGERALD to SCOTTIE
August 8th, 1933

When he wasn't busy writing some of the most critically lauded and enduring novels of the 20th century, *The Great Gatsby* author F. Scott Fitzgerald could often be found penning the most fascinating of letters to such famous characters as his good friend Ernest Hemingway; editor extraordinaire Maxwell Perkins; and his wife and fellow author Zelda – to name but a few. However, no letters are more revealing, or indeed endearing, than those written to his daughter, Scottie, many of which see him imparting wisdom in a way only he could. This particular letter of advice, written to Scottie while she was away at camp at 11 years of age, is a perfect example.

Dear Pie:

I feel very strongly about you doing duty. Would you give me a little more documentation about your reading in French? I am glad you are happy — but I never believe much in happiness. I never believe in misery either. Those are things you see on the stage or the screen or the printed pages, they never really happen to you in life.

All I believe in in life is the rewards for virtue (according to your talents) and the <u>punishments</u> for not fulfilling your duties, which are doubly costly. If there is such a volume in the camp library, will you ask Mrs. Tyson to let you look up a sonnet of Shakespeare's in which the line occurs "<u>Lilies that fester smell far worse than weeds.</u>"

Have had no thoughts today, life seems composed of getting up a <u>Saturday Evening Post</u> story. I think of you, and always pleasantly; but if you call me "Pappy" again I am going to take the White Cat out and beat his bottom <u>hard, six times for every time you are impertinent</u>. Do you react to that?

I will arrange the camp bill.

Halfwit, I will conclude. Things to worry about:

Worry about courage
Worry about cleanliness
Worry about efficiency
Worry about horsemanship
Worry about. . .

Things not to worry about:

Don't worry about popular opinion
Don't worry about dolls
Don't worry about the past
Don't worry about the future
Don't worry about growing up
Don't worry about anybody getting ahead of you
Don't worry about triumph
Don't worry about failure unless it comes through your own fault
Don't worry about mosquitoes
Don't worry about flies
Don't worry about insects in general
Don't worry about parents
Don't worry about boys
Don't worry about disappointments
Don't worry about pleasures
Don't worry about satisfactions

Things to think about:

What am I really aiming at?
How good am I really in comparison to my contemporaries in regard to:
(a) Scholarship
(b) Do I really understand about people and am I able to get along with them?
(c) Am I trying to make my body a useful instrument or am I neglecting it?

With dearest love,
Daddy

P.S. My come-back to your calling me Pappy is christening you by the word Egg, which implies that you belong to a very rudimentary state of life and that I could break you up and crack you open at my will and I think it would be a word that would hang on if I ever told it to your contemporaries. "Egg Fitzgerald." How would you like that to go through life with — "Eggie Fitzgerald" or "Bad Egg Fitzgerald" or any form that might occur to fertile minds? Try it once more and I swear to God I will hang it on you and it will be up to you to shake it off. Why borrow trouble?

Love anyhow.

MY WICK HATH A THIEF IN IT

CHARLES LAMB to
BERNARD BARTON
January 9th, 1824

In January 1824, unable to write anything constructive after weeks of intense suffering at the hands of what he later admitted was simply "a severe cold", renowned essayist and poet Charles Lamb sent to his good friend and fellow poet, Bernard Barton, a hugely entertaining letter that contains what is surely one of the greatest, most eloquently melodramatic descriptions of a cold ever put to paper. Barton, however, completely failed to see the funny side of Lamb's comically extravagant cry for help and wrote back immediately, genuinely concerned for his wellbeing.

January 9th, 1824

Dear B.B.—

Do you know what it is to succumb under an insurmountable day-mare,— "a whoreson lethargy," Falstaff calls it,—an indisposition to do anything, or to be anything,—a total deadness and distaste,—a suspension of vitality,—an indifference to locality,—a numb, soporifical, good-for-nothingness,—an ossification all over,—an oyster-like insensibility to the passing events,—a mind-stupor,—a brawny defiance to the needles of a thrusting-in conscience. Did you ever have a very bad cold, with a total irresolution to submit to water-gruel processes? This has been for many weeks my lot, and my excuse; my fingers drag heavily over this paper, and to my thinking it is three-and-twenty furlongs from here to the end of this demi-sheet. I have not a thing to say; nothing is of more importance than another; I am flatter than a denial or a pancake; emptier than Judge Parke's wig when the head is in it; duller than a country stage when the actors are off it; a cipher, an o! I acknowledge life at all, only by an occasional convulsional cough, and a permanent phlegmatic pain in the chest. I am weary of the world; life is weary of me. My day is gone into twilight, and I don't think it worth the expense of candles. My wick hath a thief in it, but I can't muster courage to snuff it. I inhale suffocation; I can't distinguish veal from mutton; nothing interests me. 'Tis twelve o'clock, and Thurtell is just now coming out upon the New Drop, Jack Ketch alertly tucking up his greasy sleeves to do the last office of mortality, yet cannot I elicit a groan or a moral reflection. If you told me the world will be at an end to-morrow, I should just say, "Will it?" I have not volition enough left to dot my i's, much less to comb my eyebrows; my eyes are set in my head; my brains are gone out to see a poor relation in Moorfields, and they did not say when they'd come back again; my skull is a Grub-street attic to let—not so much as a joint-stool or a crack'd jordan left in it; my hand writes, not I, from habit, as chickens run about a little, when their heads are off. O for a vigorous fit of gout, cholic, toothache,—an earwig in my auditory, a fly in my visual organs; pain is life—the sharper, the more evidence of life; but this apathy, this death! Did you ever have an obstinate cold,—a six or seven weeks' unintermitting chill and suspension of hope, fear, conscience, and everything? Yet do I try all I can to cure it; I try wine, and spirits, and smoking, and snuff in unsparing quantities, but they all only seem to make me worse, instead of better. I sleep in a damp room, but it does me no good; I come home late o'nights, but do not find any visible amendment! Who shall deliver me from the body of this death?

It is just fifteen minutes after twelve; Thurtell is by this time a good way on his journey, baiting at Scorpion perhaps; Ketch is bargaining for his cast coat and waistcoat; and the Jew demurs at first at three half-crowns, but on consideration that he may get somewhat by showing 'em in the town, finally closes.

C. L.

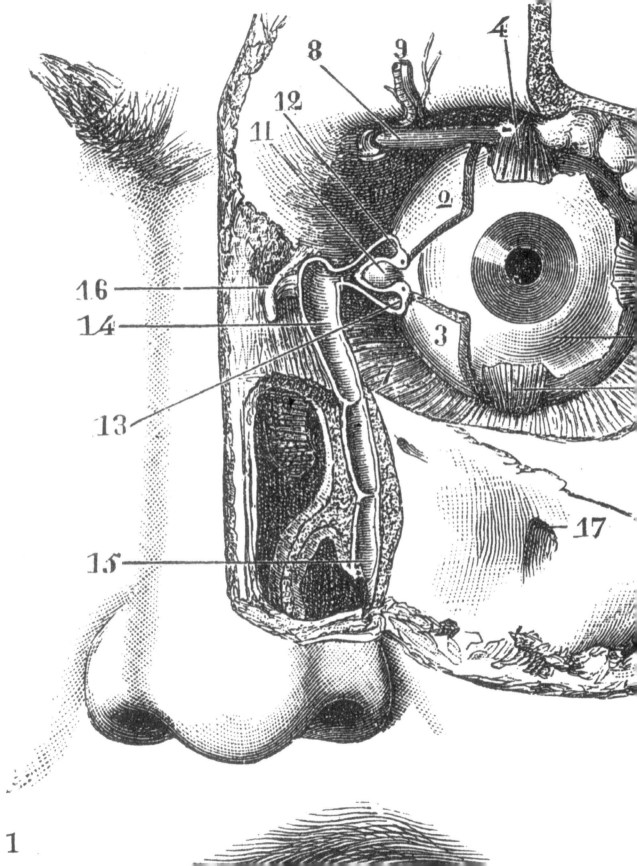

VOTE FOR ME I WILL HELP YOU OUT

JOHN BEAULIEU to US
PRESIDENT DWIGHT D.
EISENHOWER
1956

In 1956, a 13-year-old
student at Massachusetts'
Perkins School for the
Blind, the world's oldest
establishment of its kind,
wrote, in Braille, this letter
of advice to US President
Dwight D. Eisenhower. The
letter was made using a
stylus, some heavy paper,
and assistance from a
teacher who wrote out the
words above the Braille;
the letter itself contained a
short speech for Ike to use
in his bid for re-election.
The speech itself was
never used, but on October
24th, young John Beaulieu
did receive a reply from
Eisenhower in which he was
thanked for his support.

Perkins School For The Blind
Watertown 72, Mass.

Dear Ike,

I decided to write you a little speech which might help you to win the election.

Vote for me I will help you out. I will lower the prices and also your tax bill. I also will help the negroes, so that they may go to school.

Good luck in November.

John Beaulieu
Age 13 Grade Six.

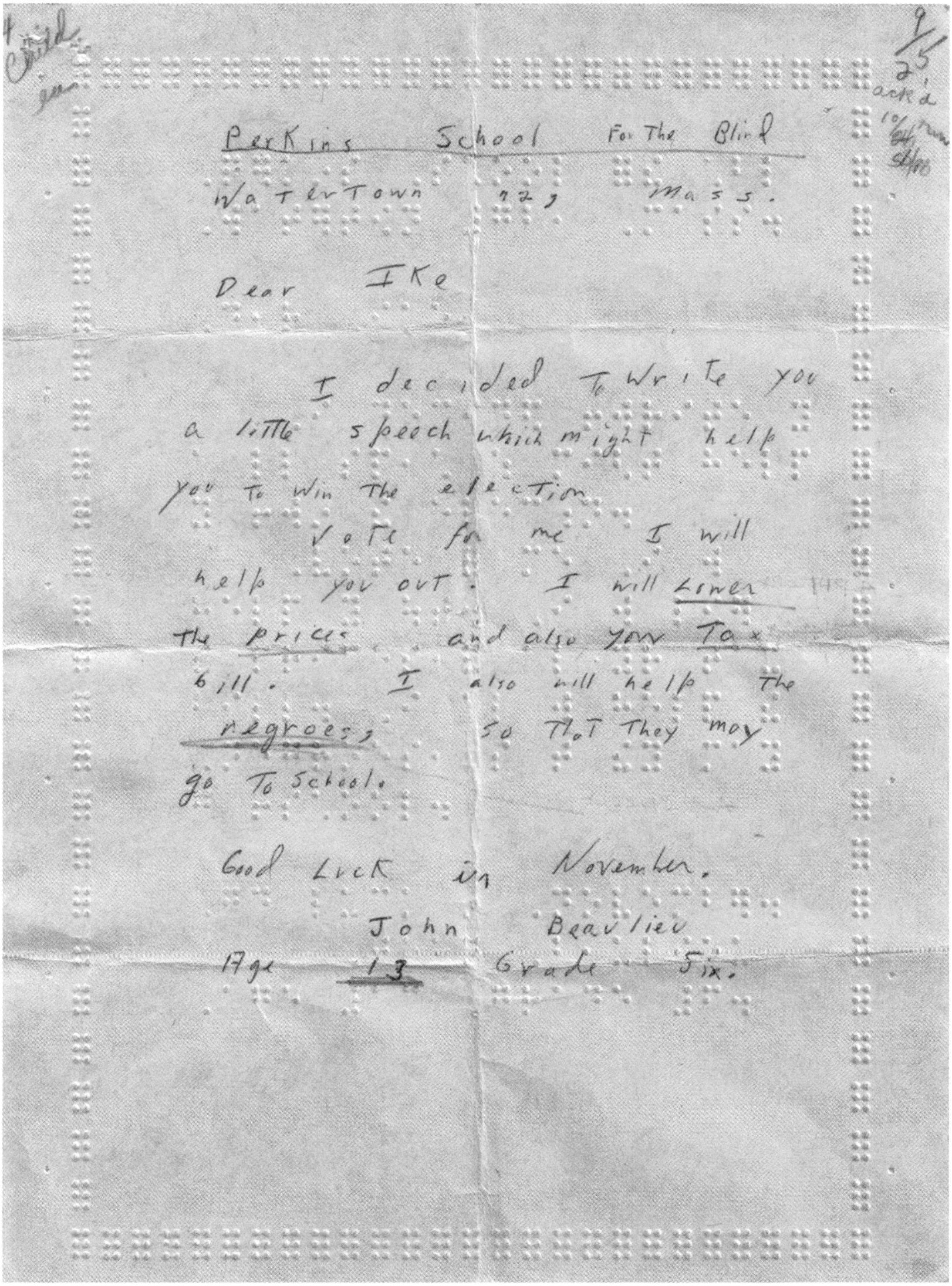

9/
25
ack'd
10/
6/
6/80

<u>Perkins School For The Blind</u>

Watertown 729 Mass.

Dear Ike

    <u>I</u> decided To Write you
a little speech which might help
you To Win The election
    Vote for me I will
help you out. I will <u>Lower</u>
the <u>prices</u> and also your <u>Tax</u>
bill. <u>I</u> also will help The
<u>negroess</u> so That They may
go To School.

Good Luck in November.
    John Beaulieu
17 ge 13 Grade Six.

October 24, 1956

Dear John:

I can't tell you how pleased I was to receive the letter you wrote me recently in Braille. I certainly admire the skill that you must have had to master such a difficult art.

It was nice of you to send me a little speech to help win the election. Your good luck wishes for November mean a lot to me too, and I am very grateful to you for them. I wish I were able to write back to you in Braille also, but I am sure that one of your teachers will be happy to read this to you.

I hope you're enjoying your schoolwork and are taking advantage of the fine opportunity that you must have in Watertown. Many thanks again for being so thoughtful.

With best wishes,

Sincerely,

(Sgd.) DWIGHT D. EISENHOWER

John Beaulieu
Mouton Cottage
Perkins School
Watertown, Massachusetts   sb/cdj

CROSS CARD FOR STAFF SECRETARY.

October 24, 1956

Dear John:

I can't tell you how pleased I was to receive the letter you wrote me recently in Braille. I certainly admire the skill that you must have had to master such a difficult art.

It was nice of you to send me a little speech to help win the election. Your good luck wishes for November mean a lot to me too, and I am very grateful to you for them. I wish I were able to write back to you in Braille, also, but I am sure that one of your teachers will be happy to read this to you.

I hope you're enjoying your schoolwork and are taking advantage of the fine opportunity that you must have in Watertown. Many thanks again for being so thoughtful.

With best wishes,

Sincerely,

(Signed)

DWIGHT D.
EISENHOWER

John Beaulieu
Mouton Cottage
Perkins School
Watertown, Massachusetts

sb/cdj

DO SCIENTISTS PRAY?

ALBERT EINSTEIN to
PHYLLIS
January 24th, 1936

As one of the world's great intellects and arguably the most famous of all scientists, Albert Einstein was regularly questioned about his views on religion. In 1954, he broached the subject with Eric Gutkind, the author of a book he had recently read, in a letter which continues to generate debate to this date and from which this snippet is often quoted:

"The word God is for me nothing more than the expression and product of human weaknesses, the Bible a collection of honorable but still primitive legends which are nevertheless pretty childish. No interpretation no matter how subtle can (for me) change this."

Eighteen years before he wrote to Gutkind, in January 1936, a young girl named Phyllis wrote to Einstein on behalf of her Sunday school class, and framed the question a little differently. She simply asked, "Do scientists pray?" Einstein soon replied.

The Riverside Church

January 19, 1936

My dear Dr. Einstein,

We have brought up the question: Do scientists pray? in our Sunday school class. It began by asking whether we could believe in both science and religion. We are writing to scientists and other important men, to try and have our own question answered.

We will feel greatly honored if you will answer our question: Do scientists pray, and what do they pray for?

We are in the sixth grade, Miss Ellis's class.

Respectfully
yours,
Phyllis

_____

January 24, 1936

Dear Phyllis,

I will attempt to reply to your question as simply as I can. Here is my answer:

Scientists believe that every occurrence, including the affairs of human beings, is due to the laws of nature. Therefore a scientist cannot be inclined to believe that the course of events can be influenced by prayer, that is, by a supernaturally manifested wish.

However, we must concede that our actual knowledge of these forces is imperfect, so that in the end the belief in the existence of a final, ultimate spirit rests on a kind of faith. Such belief remains widespread even with the current achievements in science.

But also, everyone who is seriously involved in the pursuit of science becomes convinced that some spirit is manifest in the laws of the universe, one that is vastly superior to that of man. In this way the pursuit of science leads to a religious feeling of a special sort, which is surely quite different from the religiosity of someone more naive.

With cordial greetings,
your A. Einstein

As at Wardha
C.P.
India.
23.7.'39.

Dear friend,

Friends have been urging me to write to you for the sake of humanity. But I have resisted their request, because of the feeling that any letter from me would be an impertinence. Something tells me that I must not calculate and that I must make my appeal for whatever it may be worth.

It is quite clear that you are today the one person in the world who can prevent a war which may reduce humanity to the savage state. Must you pay that price for an object however worthy it may appear to you to be ? Will you listen to the appeal of one who has seliberately shunned the method of war not without considerable success? Any way I anticipate your forgiveneas, if I have erred in writing to you.

Herr Hitler
Berlin
Germany.

I remain,

Your sincere friend

M.K. Gandhi

FOR THE SAKE OF HUMANITY

MOHANDAS GANDHI to
ADOLF HITLER
July 23rd, 1939

On July 23rd 1939, as tensions mounted in Europe following Germany's occupation of Czechoslovakia, Mohandas Gandhi, the famously non-violent leader of the Indian independence movement, wrote a letter to the man who was orchestrating what would become World War II: the leader of Nazi Germany, Adolf Hitler. As it happens, Gandhi's letter – a clear and concise plea for Hitler to avoid war "for the sake of humanity" – never reached its intended recipient due to an intervention by the British government. Just over a month later, the world looked on in horror as Germany invaded Poland, thus beginning the largest, most deadly conflict in the history of the world.

I HAVE NOT SHOT HER YET

DOROTHY PARKER to
SEWARD COLLINS
May 5th, 1927

In 1927, the year after
her first collection of
poetry, *Enough Rope*, was
published to rave reviews,
the eternally sarcastic and
rightly celebrated satirist,
critic and founding member
of the Algonquin Round
Table, Dorothy Parker,
found herself in hospital
suffering from exhaustion
– a condition brought on, in
part, by a turbulent affair
with American publisher
Seward Collins during which
they travelled to Europe
and rubbed shoulders
with the likes of Ernest
Hemingway and F. Scott
Fitzgerald. Her time in
hospital was a welcome
respite from the madness,
but also irritatingly
uneventful. On May 5th she
wrote a humorous letter
to Collins and gave him an
entertaining update on her
visit.

The Presbyterian Hospital
In the City of New York
41 East 70th St.
May 5, I think

Dear Seward, honest, what with music lessons and four attacks of measles and all that expense of having my teeth straightened, I was brought up more carefully than to write letters in pencil. But I asked the nurse for some ink—just asked her in a nice way—and she left the room and hasn't been heard of from that day to this. So that, my dears, is how I met Major (later General) Grant.

Maybe only the trusties are allowed to play with ink.

I am practically bursting with health, and the medical world, hitherto white with suspense, is entertaining high hopes—I love that locution—you can just see the high hopes, all dressed up, being taken to the Hippodrome and then to Maillard's for tea. Or maybe you can't—the hell with it.

This is my favorite kind of hospital and everybody is very brisk and sterilized and kind and nice. But they are always sticking thermometers into you or turning lights on you or instructing you in occupational therapy (rug-making— there's a fascinating pursuit!) and you don't get a chance to gather any news for letter-writing.

Of course, if I thought you would listen, I could tell you about the cunning little tot of four who ran up and down the corridor all day long; and I think, from the way he sounded, he had his little horse-shoes on—some well-wisher had given him a bunch of keys to play with, and he jingled them as he ran, and just as he came to my door, the manly little fellow would drop them and when I got so I knew just when to expect the crash, he'd fool me and run by two or even three times without letting them go. Well, they took him up and operated on his shoulder, and they don't think he will ever be able to use his right arm again. So that will stop that god damn nonsense.

And then there is the nurse who tells me she is afraid she is an incorrigible flirt, but somehow she just can't help it. She also pronounces "picturesque" picture-skew, and "unique" un-i-kew, and it is amazing how often she manages to introduce these words into her conversation, leading the laughter herself. Also, when she leaves the room, she says "see you anon." I have not shot her yet. Maybe Monday.

And, above all, there is the kindhearted if ineffectual gentleman across the hall, where he lies among his gallstones, who sent me in a turtle to play with. Honest. Sent me in a turtle to play with. I am teaching it two-handed bridge. And as soon as I get really big and strong, I am going to race it to the end of the room and back.

I should love to see Daisy, but it seems that there is some narrow-minded prejudice against bringing dogs into hospitals. And anyway, I wouldn't trust these bastards of doctors. She would probably leave here with a guinea-pig's thyroid in her. Helen says she is magnificent—she has been plucked and her girlish waist-line has returned. I thought the dear devoted little beast might eat her heart out in my absence, and you know she shouldn't have meat. But she is playful as a puppy, and has nine new toys—three balls and six assorted plush animals. She insists on taking the entire collection to bed with her, and, as she sleeps on Helen's bed, Helen is looking a little haggard these days.

At my tearful request, Helen said to her "Dorothy sends her love."
"Who?" she said.

I am enclosing a little thing sent by some unknown friend. Oh, well.

And here is a poem of a literary nature. It is called Despair in Chelsea.

> Osbert Sitwell
> Is unable to have a satisfactory evacuation.
> His brother, Sacheverel,
> Doubts if he ever'll.

This is beyond doubt the dullest letter since George Moore wrote "Esther Water." But I will write you decent ones as soon as any news breaks. And after my death, Mr. Conkwright-Shreiner can put them in a book—the big stiff.

But in the meantime, I should love to hear how you are and whatever. And if in your travels, you meet any deserving family that wants to read "Mr. Fortune's Maggot," I have six copies.

Love
Dorothy—

I promised my mother on her deathbed I would never write a postscript, but I had to save the wow for the finish. I have lost twenty-two pounds.

LETTER TO A YOUNG POET

RAINER MARIA RILKE to
FRANZ KAPPUS
February 17th, 1903

In 1902, whilst a student
at the Military Academy of
Vienna in Austria, a 19-year-
old aspiring poet named
Franz Kappus sent some
of his work to the hugely
influential Bohemian-
Austrian poet, Rainer Maria
Rilke, along with a polite
request for some feedback.
Much to his credit, Rilke
responded some months
later with the invaluable
and eloquent letter seen
here, which in essence
urged Kappus to look inward
rather than seek criticism
from others. And it didn't
end there: young Kappus
wrote again and over the
course of the next five years
Rilke continued to reply
with advice on a whole host
of subjects, of which poetry
was just one. In 1929, three
years after his idol's death,
Kappus published Rilke's
ten letters in a book, *Letters
to a Young Poet*, which has
since become a classic.

Paris,
February 17th, 1903

Dear Sir,

Your letter only reached me a few days ago. I want to thank you for its great and kind confidence. I can hardly do more. I cannot go into the nature of your verses; for all critical intention is too far from me. With nothing can one approach a work of art so little as with critical words: they always come down to more or less happy misunderstandings. Things are not all so comprehensible and expressible as one would mostly have us believe; most events are inexpressible, taking place in a realm which no word has ever entered, and more inexpressible than all else are works of art, mysterious existences, the life of which, while ours passes away, endures.

After these prefatory remarks, let me only tell you further that your verses have no individual style, although they do show quiet and hidden beginnings of something personal. I feel this most clearly in the last poem, "My Soul." There something of your own wants to come through to word and melody. And in the lovely poem "To Leopardi" there does perhaps grow up a sort of kinship with that great solitary man. Nevertheless the poems are not yet anything on their own account, nothing independent, even the last and the one to Leopardi. Your kind letter, which accompanied them, does not fail to make clear to me various shortcomings which I felt in reading your verses without however being able to specifically name them.

You ask whether your verses are good. You ask me. You have asked others before. You send them to magazines. You compare them with other poems, and you are disturbed when certain editors reject your efforts. Now (since you have allowed me to advise you) I beg you to give up all that. You are looking outward, and that above all you should not do now. Nobody can counsel and help you, nobody. Search for the reason that bids you write; find out whether it is spreading out its roots in the deepest places of your heart, acknowledge to yourself whether you would have to die if it were denied you to write. This above all—ask yourself in the stillest hour of your night: must I write? Delve into yourself for a deep answer. And if this should be affirmative, if you may meet this earnest question with a strong and simple, "I must," then build your life according to this necessity; your life even into its most indifferent and slightest hour must be a sign of this urge and a testimony to it. Then draw near to Nature. Then try, like some first human being, to say what you see and experience and love and lose. Do not write love-poems; avoid at first those forms that are too facile or commonplace: they are the most difficult, for it takes a great, fully matured power to give something of your own where good and even excellent traditions come to mind in quantity. Therefore save yourself from these general themes and seek those which your own everyday life offers you; describe your sorrows and desires, passing thoughts and the belief in some sort of beauty—describe all these with loving, quiet, humble sincerity, and use, to express yourself, the things in your environment, the images from your dreams, and the objects of your memory. If your daily life seems poor, do not blame it; blame yourself, tell yourself that you are not poet enough to call forth its riches; for to the creator there is no poverty and no poor indifferent place. And if you were in some prison the walls of which let none of the sounds of the world come to your senses—would you not then still have your childhood, that precious, kingly possession, that treasure-house of memories? Turn your attention thither. Try to raise the submerged sensations of that ample past; your personality will grow more firm, your solitude will widen and will become a dusky dwelling past which the noise of others goes by far away.—And if out of this turning inward, out of this absorption into your own world, verses come, then it will not occur to you to ask anyone whether they are good verses. Nor will you try to interest magazines in your poems: for you will see in them your fond natural possession, a fragment and a voice of your life. A work of art is good if it has sprung from necessity. In this nature of its origin lies the judgement of it: there is no other. Therefore, my dear sir, I know no advice for you save this: to go into yourself and test the deeps in which your life takes rise; at its source you will find the answer to the question whether you must create. Accept it, just as it sounds, without inquiring into it. Perhaps it will turn out that you are called to be an artist. Then take that destiny upon yourself and bear it, its burden and its greatness, without ever asking what recompense might from outside. For the creator must be a world for himself and find everything in himself and in Nature to whom he has attached himself.

But perhaps after this descent into yourself and into your inner solitude you will have to give up becoming a poet; (it is enough, as I said, to feel that one could live without writing: then one must not attempt it at all.) But even then this inward searching which I ask of you will not have been in vain. Your life will in any case find its own way thence, and that they may be good, rich and wide I wish you more than I can say.

What more shall I say to you? Everything seems to me to have its just emphasis; and after all I do only want to advise you to keep growing quietly and seriously throughout your whole development; you cannot disturb it more rudely than by looking outward and expecting from the outside replies to questions that only your inmost feeling in your most hushed hour can perhaps answer.

It was a pleasure to me to find in your letter the name of Professor Horacek; I keep for that lovable and learned man a great veneration and a gratitude that endures through the years. Will you, please, tell him how I feel; it is very good of him still to think of me, and I know how to appreciate it.

The verses which you kindly entrusted to me I am returning at the same time. And I thank you once more for your great and sincere confidence, of which I have tried, through this honest answer given to the best of my knowledge, to make myself a little worthier than, as a stranger, I really am.

Yours faithfully and with all sympathy:

Rainer Maria Rilke

WHAT GREAT BIRTHS YOU HAVE WITNESSED!

Hartford, May 24/89

MARK TWAIN to WALT WHITMAN
May 24th, 1889

Walt Whitman – "the father of free verse" – is arguably one of the most important figures in literary history and one of the great American poets. He published *Leaves of Grass* in 1855, a self-financed collection of his life's poetry which at the time was denounced by many critics due to its unconventional and "obscene" verse, but which slowly and steadily attracted praise from all manner of people and has since gone on to be immeasurably influential. In May 1889, as Whitman was approaching his 70th birthday, the great Mark Twain wrote this beautiful and suitably grand letter of congratulations to Whitman – a stunning four-page love letter to human endeavour as seen during the poet's lifetime.

To Walt Whitman:

You have lived just the seventy years which are greatest in the world's history & richest in benefit & advancement to its peoples. These seventy years have done much more to widen the interval between man & the other animals than was accomplished by any five centuries which preceded them.

What great births you have witnessed! The steam press, the steamship, the steel ship, the railroad, the perfected cotton-gin, the telegraph, the phonograph, the photograph, photo-gravure, the electrotype, the gaslight, the electric light, the sewing machine, & the amazing, infinitely varied & innumerable products of coal tar, those latest & strangest marvels of a marvelous age. And you have seen even greater births than these; for you have seen the application of anesthesia to surgery-practice, whereby the ancient dominion of pain, which began with the first created life, came to an end in this earth forever; you have seen the slave set free, you have seen the monarchy banished from France, & reduced in England to a machine which makes an imposing show of diligence & attention to business, but isn't connected with the works. Yes, you have indeed seen much — but tarry yet a while, for the greatest is yet to come. Wait thirty years, & <u>then</u> look out over the earth! You shall see marvels upon marvels added to these whose nativity you have witnessed; & conspicuous above them you shall see their formidable Result — Man at almost his full stature at last! — & still growing, visibly growing while you look. In that day, who that hath a throne, or a gilded privilege not attainable by his neighbor, let him procure his slippers & get ready to dance, for there is going to be music. Abide, & see these things! Thirty of us who honor & love you, offer the opportunity. We have among us 600 years, good & sound, left in the bank of life. Take 30 of them — the richest birth-day gift ever offered to poet in this world — & sit down & wait. Wait till you see that great figure appear, & catch the far glint of the sun upon his banner; then you may depart satisfied, as knowing you have seen him for whom the earth was made, & that he will proclaim that human wheat is worth more than human tares, & proceed to reorganize human values on that basis.

Mark Twain

"Hartford, May 24/89.

To Walt Whitman:

You have lived just the seventy years which are greatest in the world's history & richest in benefit & advancement to its peoples. These seventy years have done much more to widen the interval between man & the other animals than was accomplished by any five centuries which preceded them.

What great births you have witnessed! The steam press, the steamship, the steel ship, the railroad, the perfected cotton-gin, the telegraph, the telephone, the phonograph, the photograph, photo-gravure, the electrotype, the gaslight, the electric light, the sewing machine, & the amazing, infinitely varied & innumerable products of coal tar, those latest & strangest marvels of a marvelous age. And you have seen even greater births than these; for you have seen the application of anæsthesia to surgery-practice, whereby the ancient dominion of pain, which began with the first created life, came to an end in this earth forever; you have seen the slave set free, you have seen monarchy banished from France, & reduced in England to a machine which makes an imposing show of diligence & attention to business, ~~but~~ but isn't connected with the works. Yes, you have indeed seen much — but tarry yet a while, for the greatest is yet to come. Wait Thirty years, & _then_ look out over the earth! You shall $_{see}$ marvels

upon marvels added to these
whose nativity you have witnessed;
& conspicuous above them you
shall see their formidable Result
— Man at almost his full stature
at last! — & still growing, visibly
growing while you look.   In that
day, who that hath a throne, or
a gilded privilege not attainable
by his neighbor, let him procure
him slippers & get ready to
dance, for there is going to be
music.   Abide, & see these things!

Thirty of us who honor & love
you, offer the opportunity. We
have among us 600 years, good
& sound, left in the bank of life.
Take 30 of them — the richest
birth-day gift ever offered to

4

poet in this world — + sit down + wait. Wait till you see that great figure appear, + catch the far glint of the sun upon his banner; then you may depart satisfied, as knowing you have seen him for whom the earth was made, + that he will proclaim that human wheat is worth more than human tares, + proceed to reorganize human values on that basis.

Mark Twain

```
                                        Albert Einstein
                                        Old Grove Rd.
                                        Nassau Point
                                        Peconic, Long Island

                                        August 2nd, 1939

F.D. Roosevelt,
President of the United States,
White House
Washington, D.C.


Sir:
        Some recent work by E.Fermi and L. Szilard, which has been com-
municated to me in manuscript, leads me to expect that the element uran-
ium may be turned into a new and important source of energy in the im-
mediate future. Certain aspects of the situation which has arisen seem
to call for watchfulness and, if necessary, quick action on the part
of the Administration. I believe therefore that it is my duty to bring
to your attention the following facts and recommendations:

        In the course of the last four months it has been made probable -
through the work of Joliot in France as well as Fermi and Szilard in
America - that it may become possible to set up a nuclear chain reaction
in a large mass of uranium,by which vast amounts of power and large quant-
ities of new radium-like elements would be generated. Now it appears
almost certain that this could be achieved in the immediate future.

        This new phenomenon would also lead to the construction of bombs,
and it is conceivable - though much less certain - that extremely power-
ful bombs of a new type may thus be constructed. A single bomb of this
type, carried by boat and exploded in a port, might very well destroy
the whole port together with some of the surrounding territory. However,
such bombs might very well prove to be too heavy for transportation by
air.
```

EINSTEIN'S ONE GREAT MISTAKE

ALBERT EINSTEIN to US
PRESIDENT FRANKLIN D.
ROOSEVELT
August 2nd, 1939

On August 2nd 1939, after consultation with fellow physicists Leó Szilárd and Eugene Wigner, Albert Einstein signed this letter to then US President Franklin Roosevelt. The letter warned that the construction of an atomic bomb using uranium was indeed possible, advised the US government to invest time and money into its research and then warned that physicists in Nazi Germany had already begun similar work. As a result of the letter, President Roosevelt created the Briggs Advisory Committee on Uranium, which slowly evolved to become the Manhattan Project, an enormous research project in which the Little Boy and Fat Man bombs were developed. It was these bombs that were dropped on Hiroshima and Nagasaki in 1945, killing over 200,000 people. Einstein later described signing the letter as the "one great mistake in my life"

The United States has only very poor ores of uranium in moderate quantities. There is some good ore in Canada and the former Czechoslovakia, while the most important source of uranium is Belgian Congo.

In view of this situation you may think it desirable to have some permanent contact maintained between the Administration and the group of physicists working on chain reactions in America. One possible way of achieving this might be for you to entrust with this task a person who has your confidence and who could perhaps serve in an inofficial capacity. His task might comprise the following:

a) to approach Government Departments, keep them informed of the further development, and put forward recommendations for Government action, giving particular attention to the problem of securing a supply of uranium ore for the United States;

b) to speed up the experimental work,which is at present being carried on within the limits of the budgets of University laboratories, by providing funds, if such funds be required, through his contacts with private persons who are willing to make contributions for this cause, and perhaps also by obtaining the co-operation of industrial laboratories which have the necessary equipment.

I understand that Germany has actually stopped the sale of uranium from the Czechoslovakian mines which she has taken over. That she should have taken such early action might perhaps be understood on the ground that the son of the German Under-Secretary of State, von Weizsäcker, is attached to the Kaiser-Wilhelm-Institut in Berlin where some of the American work on uranium is now being repeated.

Yours very truly,

A. Einstein

(Albert Einstein)

COME QUICK TO ME

ZELDA FITZGERALD to F.
SCOTT FITZGERALD
September, 1920

While attending a country club dance in July 1918, and shortly after graduating from high school, 17-year-old Zelda Sayre met Francis Scott Fitzgerald, a 22-year-old second lieutenant in the US Army with aspirations to one day become a famous novelist. He was smitten; she less so. However, her doubts about his career prospects were laid to rest two years later upon publication of his wildly successful debut novel, *This Side of Paradise*, and she soon agreed to become his wife. Instantly a celebrity couple in New York in "The Roaring Twenties", they quickly began to drink to excess and argue regularly, thus setting a routine for what would become one of the most tempestuous marriages in literary history.

This particular letter was written by Zelda in 1920, post-quarrel, just six months after their wedding. They parted ways in 1934.

I look down the tracks and see you coming—and out of every haze & mist your darling rumpled trousers are hurrying to me—Without you, dearest dearest I couldn't see or hear or feel or think—or live—I love you so and I'm never in all our lives going to let us be apart another night. It's like begging for mercy of a storm or killing Beauty or growing old, without you. I want to kiss you so—and in the back where your dear hair starts and your chest—I love you—and I cant tell you how much—To think that I'll *die* without your knowing—Goofo, you've *got* to try [to] feel how much I do—how inanimate I am when you're gone—I can't even hate these damnable people—nobodys got any right to live but us—and they're dirtying up our world and I can't hate them because I want you so—Come Quick—Come Quick to me—I could never do without you if you hated me and were covered with sores like a leper—if you ran away with another woman and starved me and beat me—I would still want you *I know*—
    Lover, Lover, Darling—
    Your Wife

ART IS USELESS
BECAUSE...

OSCAR WILDE to BERNULF
CLEGG
1891

In 1891, shortly after
reading the great Oscar
Wilde's *The Picture of Dorian
Gray*, a puzzled young man
named Bernulf Clegg wrote
to its author and politely
asked him to explain the
assertion that "All art is
quite useless", as printed in
the novel's preface. To his
surprise, Wilde soon replied
with exactly that.

16, TITE STREET,
CHELSEA. S.W.

My Dear Sir

Art is useless because its aim is simply to create a mood. It is not meant to instruct, or to influence action in any way. It is superbly sterile, and the note of its pleasure is sterility. If the contemplation of a work of art is followed by activity of any kind, the work is either of a very second-rate order, or the spectator has failed to realise the complete artistic impression.

A work of art is useless as a flower is useless. A flower blossoms for its own joy. We gain a moment of joy by looking at it. That is all that is to be said about our relations to flowers. Of course man may sell the flower, and so make it useful to him, but this has nothing to do with the flower. It is not part of its essence. It is accidental. It is a misuse. All this is I fear very obscure. But the subject is a long one.

Truly yours,

Oscar Wilde

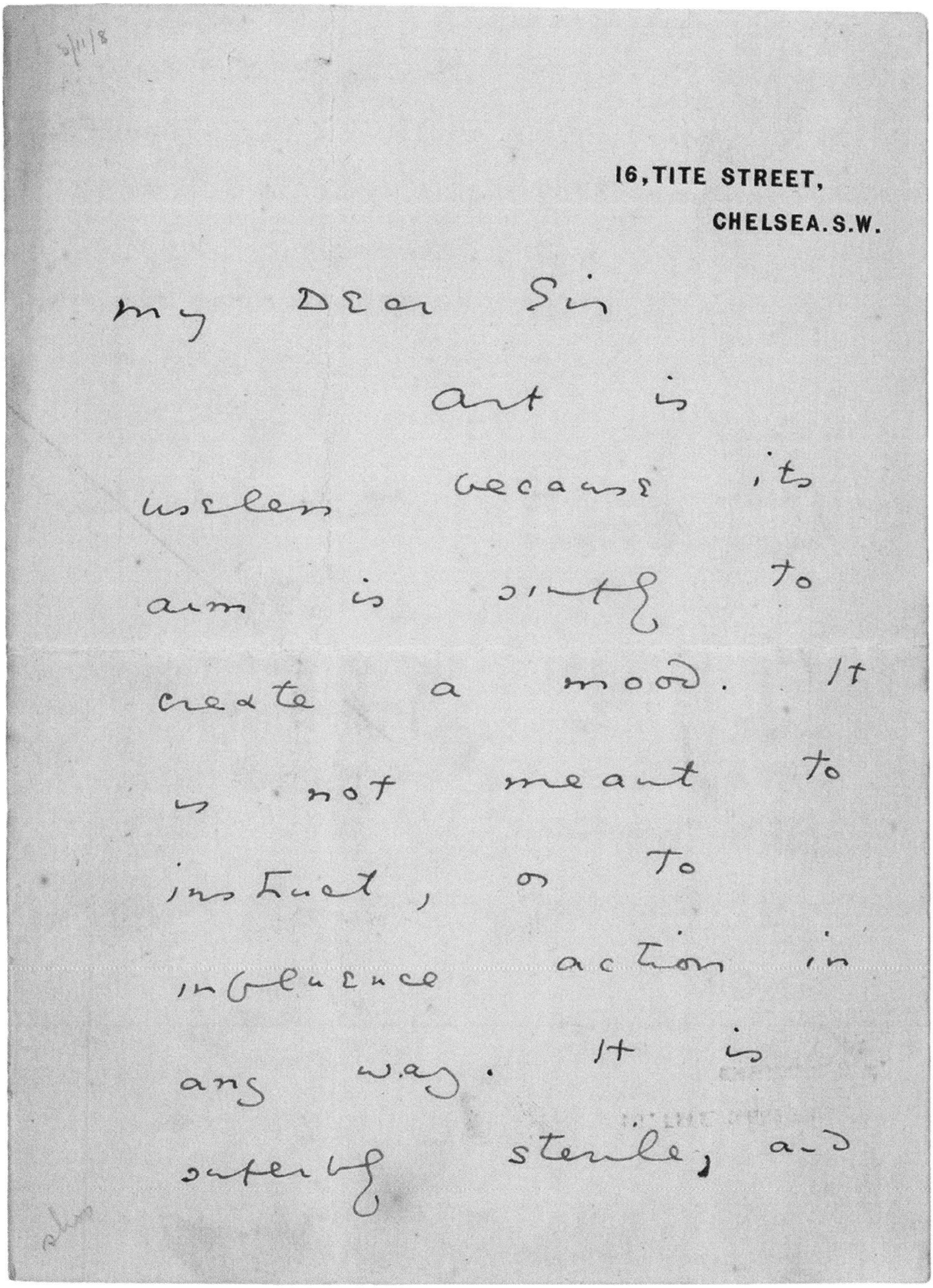

16, TITE STREET,
CHELSEA. S.W.

My Dear Sir

Art is
useless because its
aim is simply to
create a mood. It
is not meant to
instruct, or to
influence action in
any way. It is
superbly sterile, and

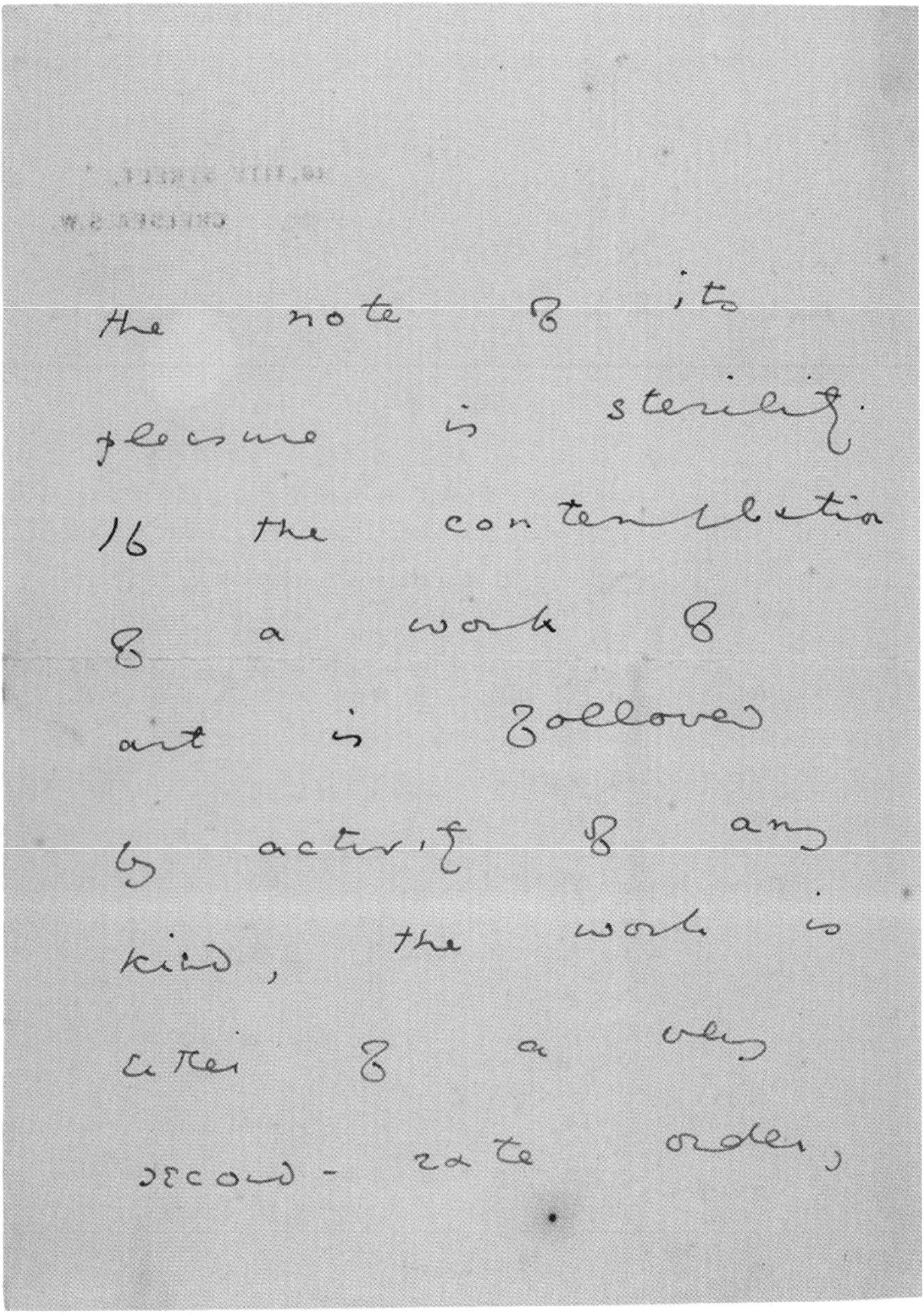
the note of its
pleasure is sterility.
If the contemplation
of a work of
art is followed
by activity of any
kind, the work is
either of a very
second-rate order,

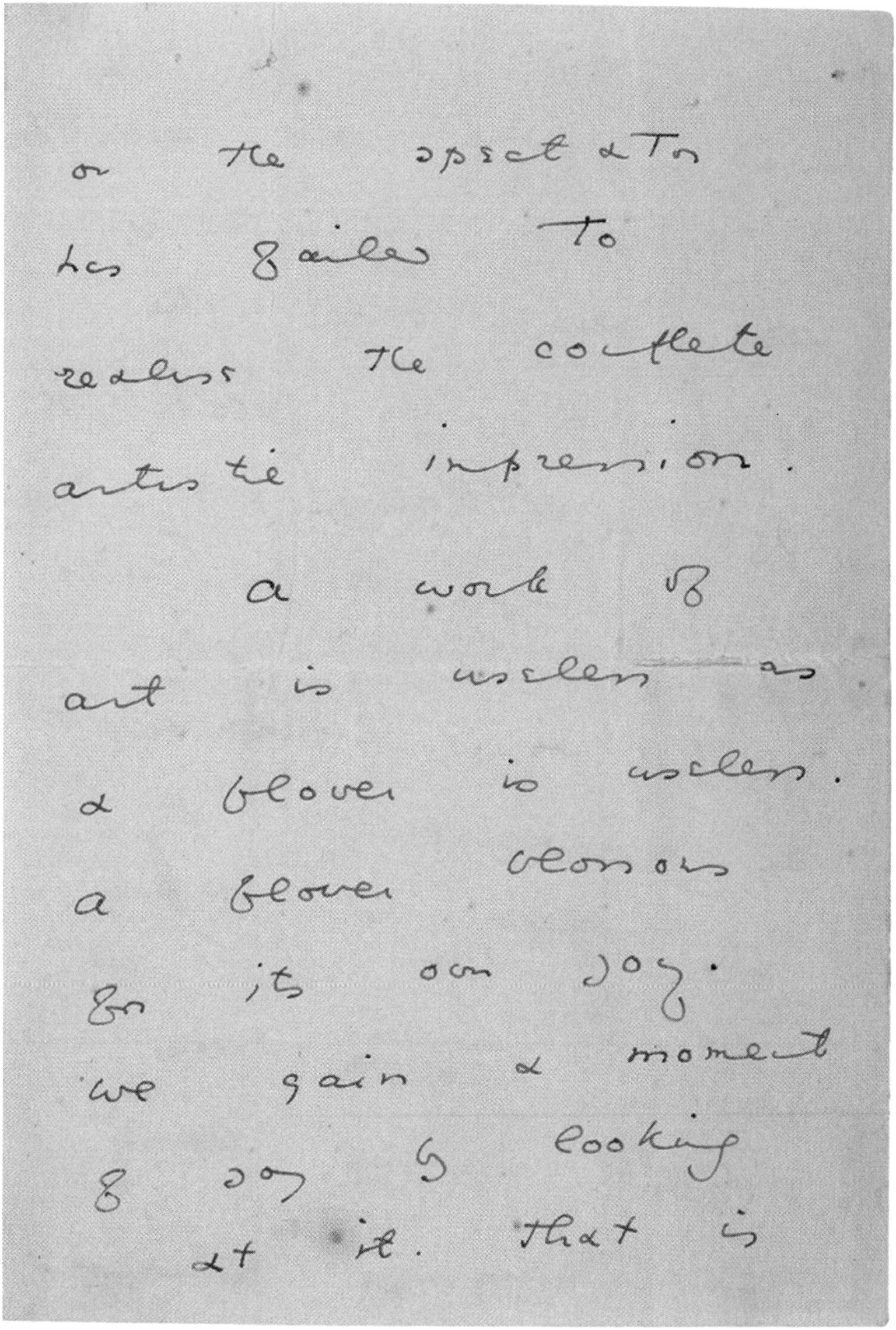

or the spectator

has failed to

realise the complete

artistic impression.

a work of

art is useless as

a flower is useless.

a flower blossoms

for its own joy.

we gain a moment

of joy by looking

at it. that is

all that is to be said about our relations to flowers. Of course man may sell the flower, & so make it useful to him, but this has nothing to do with the flower. It is not part of its essence. It is accidental. It is a misuse. All this is / fear very obscure. But the subject is a long one.

Oscar Wilde

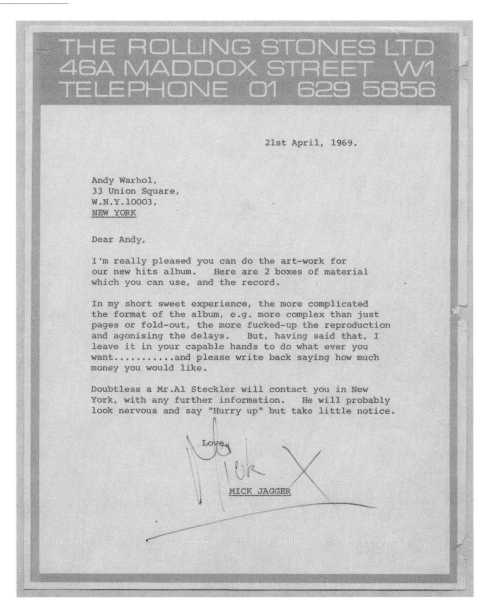

THE ROLLING STONES LTD
46A MADDOX STREET W1
TELEPHONE 01 629 5856

21st April, 1969.

Andy Warhol,
33 Union Square,
W.N.Y.10003,
NEW YORK

Dear Andy,

I'm really pleased you can do the art-work for
our new hits album.   Here are 2 boxes of material
which you can use, and the record.

In my short sweet experience, the more complicated
the format of the album, e.g. more complex than just
pages or fold-out, the more fucked-up the reproduction
and agonising the delays.   But, having said that, I
leave it in your capable hands to do what ever you
want..........and please write back saying how much
money you would like.

Doubtless a Mr.Al Steckler will contact you in New
York, with any further information.   He will probably
look nervous and say "Hurry up" but take little notice.

Love,

MICK JAGGER

I LEAVE IT IN YOUR CAPABLE HANDS

MICK JAGGER to ANDY WARHOL
April 21st, 1969

In 1969, as they worked on their ninth studio album, *Sticky Fingers*, The Rolling Stones approached one of the world's most influential artists, Andy Warhol, and asked him to design its sleeve. Warhol agreed and quickly received this letter from Mick Jagger – a wonderfully relaxed brief that included a polite warning not to make the cover too complex so as to avoid problems during production. His advice was completely ignored. Warhol went on to produce an unforgettable cover that featured a close-up shot of Warhol superstar Joe Dallesandro's jean-clad crotch, complete with a working zip that resulted in countless problems, including, most notably, scratched copies of the record itself.

SLAUGHTERHOUSE-FIVE

KURT VONNEGUT, JR to
KURT VONNEGUT
May 29th, 1945

In December 1944, while
behind enemy lines during
World War II's Rhineland
Campaign, 22-year-old
Private Kurt Vonnegut was
captured by Wehrmacht
troops and subsequently
became a prisoner of war. A
month later, Vonnegut and
his fellow PoWs reached a
Dresden work camp where
they were imprisoned
in an underground
slaughterhouse known
by German soldiers
as 'Schlachthof Fünf'
(Slaughterhouse Five). The
next month – February –
the subterranean nature
of the prison saved
their lives during the
highly controversial and
devastating bombing of
Dresden, the aftermath of
which Vonnegut and the
remaining survivors helped
to clear up.

In May, by which time he
was at a displaced persons
camp, Vonnegut wrote to his
family and described both
his capture and survival –
an ordeal that went on to
inspire his classic novel,
Slaughterhouse-Five.

TO:

Kurt Vonnegut,
Williams Creek,
Indianapolis, Indiana.

Dear people:

I'm told that you were probably never informed that I was anything other than "missing in action." Chances are that you also
failed to receive any of the letters I wrote from Germany. That
leaves me a lot of explaining to do -- in precis:

I've been a prisoner of war since December 19th, 1944, when our
division was cut to ribbons by Hitler's last desperate thrust through
Luxemburg and Belgium. Seven Fanatical Panzer Divisions hit us and
cut us off from the rest of Hodges' First Army. The other American
Divisions on our flanks managed to pull out: We were obliged to
stay and fight. Bayonets aren't much good against tanks: Our
ammunition, food and medical supplies gave out and our casualties
out-numbered those who could still fight - so we gave up. The 106th
got a Presidential Citation and some British Decoration from Montgomery for it, I'm told, but I'll be damned if it was worth it. I
was one of the few who weren't wounded. For that much thank God.

Well, the supermen marched us, without food, water or sleep to
Limberg, a distance of about sixty miles, I think, where we were
loaded and locked up, sixty men to each small, unventilated, un-
heated box car. There were no sanitary accommodations -- the floors
were covered with fresh cow dung. There wasn't room for all of us
to lie down. Half slept while the other half stood. We spent
several days, including Christmas, on that Limberg siding. On
Christmas eve the Royal Air Force bombed and strafed our unmarked
train. They killed about one-hundred-and-fifty of us. We got a

little water Christmas Day and moved slowly across Germany to a large
P.O.W. Camp in Muhlburg, South of Berlin. We were released from the
box cars on New Year's Day. The Germans herded us through scalding
delousing showers. Many men died from shock in the showers after ten
days of starvation, thirst and exposure. But I didn't.

Under the Geneva Convention, Officers and Non-commissioned
Officers are not obliged to work when taken prisoner. I am, as you
know, a Private. One-hundred-and-fifty such minor beings were
shipped to a Dresden work camp on January 10th. I was their leader
by virtue of the little German I spoke. It was our misfortune to
have sadistic and fanatical guards. We were refused medical attention and clothing: We were given long hours at extremely hard labor.
Our food ration was two-hundred-and-fifty grams of black bread and
one pint of unseasoned potato soup each day. After desperately trying
to improve our situation for two months and having been met with bland
smiles I told the guards just what I was going to do to them when the
Russians came. They beat me up a little. I was fired as group
leader. Beatings were very small time: -- one boy starved to death
and the SS Troops shot two for stealing food.

On about February 14th the Americans came over, followed by the
R.A.F. their combined labors killed 250,000 people in twenty-four
hours and destroyed all of Dresden -- possibly the world's most
beautiful city. But not me.

After that we were put to work carrying corpses from Air-Raid
shelters; women, children, old men; dead from concussion, fire or
suffocation. Civilians cursed us and threw rocks as we carried bodies
to huge funeral pyres in the city.

When General Patton took Leipzig we were evacuated on foot to
Hellexisdorf on the Saxony-Czechoslovakian border. There we remained

until the war ended. Our guards deserted us. On that happy day the
Russians were intent on mopping up isolated outlaw resistance in our
sector. Their planes (P-39's) strafed and bombed us, killing fourteen.
but not me.

Eight of us stole a team and wagon. We traveled and looted our
way through Sudetenland and Saxony for eight days, living like kings.
The Russians are crazy about Americans. The Russians picked us up in
Dresden. We rode from there to the American lines at Halle in Lend-
Lease Ford trucks. We've since been flown to Le Havre.

I'm writing from a Red Cross Club in the Le Havre P.O.W. Repat-
riation Camp. I'm being wonderfully well feed and entertained. The
state-bound ships are jammed, naturally, so I'll have to be patient.
I hope to be home in a month. Once home I'll be given twenty-one days
recuperation at Atterbury, about $600 back pay and -- get this --
sixty (60) days furlough!

I've too damned much to say, the rest will have to wait. I can't
receive mail here so don't write.   May 29, 1945

                          Love,
                          Kurt - Jr.

INDEX

ACKNOWLEDGEMENTS

The kind efforts of a large number of people have enabled me to compile and write this book, beginning with the most important and unending source of support: my wife, Karina. I would like to thank them all for helping, but especially Karina for not despairing of me to the point where I noticed. I am also indebted to the following people for various reasons related to the project, all of whom deserve special mention: the book's subscribers; all at the mighty Unbound, particularly John Mitchinson and Cathy Hurren; Frederick Courtright; Caz Hildebrand; Andrew Carroll; James Cameron; Sam Ward; Nick Hornby; Patrick Robbins; Robert Gibbons; Amir Avni; Frank Ciulla and family; Margaret and Hugh Connell; Bob Mortimer; Jim Temple; Moose Allain; Nigel Brachi; Bob Meade; Denis Cox; Lauren Laverne and all at the BBC; Jason Kottke; Leslie Barany; Graham Linehan; Roger Launius; Henry McGroggan; John Johnson; TinyLetter; Anna Neville; and, last but by no means least, my friends and family.

SUBSCRIBERS

Unbound is a new kind of publishing house. Our books are funded directly by readers. This was a very popular idea during the late eighteenth and early nineteenth centuries. Now we have revived it for the internet age. It allows authors to write the books they really want to write and readers to support the writing they would most like to see published.

The names listed below are of readers who have pledged their support and made this book happen. If you'd like to join them, visit: www.unbound.co.uk.

Kevin Abbott
Joe Abley
Ron Ackland
Raúl Acuña
Carole Adams
Chris Adams
Geoff Adams
Tim Adams
Gail Affleck Ward
Sajjad Afzal-Woodward
Evangeline Agass
Steve Ager
Phil Agius
Louise Agley
Habiba Ahmed
Khadijah Ahmed
Elia Ajram
Hamza Alawiye
Bruce Alcorn
Patricia Alderhout
Naomi Alderman
Andy Aldridge
Alison Alexander
Ahmed Alfi
Lena Alfi
Manal Alfi
Omar Alfi
Zainah Alfi
Heather Alford
Cory Ali
Peter Alison
Moose Allain
Lynne Allan
Ebonie Allard
Errol Allcock
Catherine Allen
Kathryn Allen
Rachel Allen
Tracey Allen
Simon Allison
Alexandria Allsop
Shiroq Al-Megren
Fatima Al Sulaiti
Abigail Amey
Hani Anani
Heath Anderson
Liam Anderson
Tom Anderson
Emily Anderton
Victoria Andrew
James Andrews
Alex Andronov
Danny Angel
Michael Angus
Graham Annaly
Andy Annett
David Annett
John Annett
Anon
Anonymous from KY

Jo Anyon
Isabelle Appleyard-Yong
Jenny Aranha
Cheryl Arany
Joe Arasin
Dawn Armfield
Peter Armstrong
David Arnold
Mary-Kim Arnold
Miranda Arnold
Uriel Arnon
Adrian Arratoon
Penny Arrowood
Robert Arthur
Jon Asbury
Amelia Ashton
Nesher Asner
Debbie Aspery
At the end of the day you're either
    sound or you're not
Oye Atilade
Michael Atkins
Sally Atkinson
Pram Attale
Lorna Attia
James Austin
Roby Austin
Ave
Ava Patricia Avila
Eleni Azarias
Nikolay Bachiyski
Kevin Bachus
Captain Badbeard
Signe Bahrt
Bryan Bailey
Helen Bailey
Paul Bailey
Sam Bailey
Alice Baillie
Helen Bain
David Baird
Abbie Baker
Chris Baker
Danny Baker
David Baker
Frank Baker
Signe Gyrite Balch
Brian Baldi
Lesley Balkham
Rob Ball
John Band
Ray Banks
Thomas U. Banner
Karen Banno
Heather Barber
Julia Barbosa
Isabel Barbosa
Connor Barclay
Andrew Bardsley
Lisa Barfoot

Ali Barker
Wendy Barker
Victoria Barnard
Kim Barnes
Kate Barnett
Sharon Barnett
Gordon Barr & Jenny Bann
Jim Barr
Mark Barrett
James Barrett-Bunnage
Jane Barrett-Danes
Abi Barrington
Cecil Barrington III
Marvin Barron
Charles Barry
Carolina de Bartolo
Matt Barton
Arpinder Baryana
Sarah Bastress
Helen Bates
Becky Batt
Meg Bauer
Carole Bawden
David Bawden
Juliet Bawden
Chrissy Baxter
Mia Baxter
Richard Baxter
Walter Bayer
Emma Bayliss
Rachael Beale
Carol Beasmore
Eric Beaulieu
Lynne Bebout
Choucri Bechir
Drew Beck
Tim Beeker
Donovan Beeson of the Letter Writers
    Alliance
MT Begley
Rachel Belden
Allie Bell
Emma Bell
Rachel Bell
Gareth Bellamy
Jo Bellamy
Martin Bellamy
Tracey Bellow
Geoff Bemrose
Ben and Annie
Federico Benedetto
Terry & Margaret Benjamin
Brett Bennett
Jessica & Jonathan Bennett
Catherine Benson
Elinor Bentley
Frances Bentley
Jill Bentley
Terri Ellen Bentley
The Berjikly Family

Scott & Miranda Berridge
Katrina Berry
Paula Best
E. J Betz
Stephen Beynon
Kathleen Bibbins
Heather Bibby
Martha Marie Bicket
Lisa Binnie
Hannah Bird
Nick Birtwistle
Christopher Bishop
Matt Biskobing
Paul Bissett
Emily Bitterlich
Rosemary B K
David Black
Judy Blackett
Rachel Blair
Billy Blanco-Usher
Maarten Bleijerveld
Christiane Bligh
Innes Blight
Sarah Blincoe
Josh Blinston
Robbert Bloem
David Boal
Julie Bobikevich
James Bock
Ingrid Boeck
Peter Boer
Greg Boguslavsky
Bill Bold
Jessica Bolger
Shaun Bolt
Karen Boncher
Nicky Bond
Nickie Bonn
Brian Bonnar
Sophie Charlotte Bonner
Thomas Bonnick
Elizabeth Bonsor
Gregory Boone
Fiona Booth
Robert Bordoli
Ruth Bordoli
Jacques Bossonney
Nicola Bossuyt
Ian Botterill
Caroline Bottomley
Alanna Bottrell
Wendy Boucek
Muriel Bouvier
Karl Bovenizer
Robert Bowers
Jules Bowes
Helen & John Bowness
Kate Boydell
Hannah Boylan
Geoff Boyle

Carrie Boysun
Adam Bradley
Emma Bradley
Mark and Susan Bradley
Stephanie Bradley
James Bradshaw
Sacha Brady
Ledio Braho
Mark Braley
Dan Bramall
Michelle Brannan
Scott Brant
Francesca Branthwaite
Margaret Branton
John Brassey
Richard W H Bray
Deborah Brazendale
Andrew Brearley
Lindsay Brechler
Leo Breebaart
Linda Breedlove
Sherry Brennan
The Brenner Ladies' Reading Group
Tanya Breshears
Ronan Breslin
Una Breslin
Charlie Briar
Vicki Brideau
Andy Bridges
Jon Bridgewater
Louisa Briggs
Kevin Bringuel
Barnaby Britton
Joanne Brockington
Matt Brockwell
Sarah Broderick
Robert Brook
Melissa Brookes
David Brooks
Anne & Joe Brophy
Jade Broughton
Bob & Kim Brown
Neil Brown
Richard Brown
Seanna Brown
Sharon Brown
Steven Brown
Sue Brown
Vicky Brown
Kala Brownlee
Kristine Bruneau
Hal Bryan
Andrew Bryant
Philip Bryer
Gareth Buchaillard-Davies
C. Tapscott Buchanan
Paul Buchanan
Colm Buckley
Helen Buckley-Hoffmann
Lia Buddle
Gabrielle Bullard
Chris Bullick
Andrew Bullock
Kate Bulpitt
Anthony Bunge
Genna Burchell
Jason Burgess
Robert Burk
Ann Burke
Lucie Burnett
Shelley and Joe Burnham
Chris Burns ('Wee Chrissie B')
Iain Burns
Sarah Burrell
Jake Burrows
Elizabeth Jean Margrain Burton
Jon Busby
Maurizio Bussi
Marcus Butcher
Mike Butcher
Steve Butcher
Michael Butera
Vikkie Buxton

Jodie Byrne
Trish Byrne
James Cadman
Ed Caesar
Ana Caetano
Michael Cahill
Keith Calder
Emma Callagher
Elliot Callard
Auriel Camacho
Joseph Camann
Lia Camargo
Claire Cameron
David Cameron
Lachlan Cameron
Peter Cameron
Raphael Campardou
Andrew Campbell
Nathan Campbell
Stuart Campbell
Nick Campion
Debra Campise
Andy & Joy Candler
Stefano Canducci
Phillipa Candy
Xander Cansell
Peter Capel
Shawn Capistrano
Gareth Cardew-Richardson
Chris Careford
Helen Carey
Wharton Caroline
Martin Carr
Amy Carroll
Kelly Carroll
Paul Carroll
Brad Carson
Greg & Chloe Carter
James Carter
Rob Carter
S. R. Carter
Suzanne Carter
Stuart Cartwright
Laura Carus
Ellie Cary
Leslie Casse
Steve Casteel
Anna Castleton Simmons
Kelly Cates
Val Catlin
Stephen Caulfield
Wanda Caulfield
Cathy Cavanagh
Emma Cawley
Elizabeth Caygill
Christian Cederfjärd
Richard Chalu
Bridget Chamberlain
Mark Chambers
Minal Champaneri
Sharon Chan
Evelyn Chan & Paul Leong
Dhruv Chanchani
Aaron Chandra
Tristen Chang
Dan Chapman
Jack Montgomery Baxter Chapman
Jonathan Chapman
Matt Chapman
Emily Chappell
Farley Chase
Lea Chayes
Dan Cheesbrough
Jonathan Cheetham
Kenneth I Chenault
Nita Cherry
Virginia Cherry
Helen Chesshire
Martin Childs
Caroline Chilley
James Chilvers
Chloe Chittenden
Ana Victoria Chiu

Ho Jae Choi
Dhruv Chopra
Katherine Chowdhary
Regina Choy
Oliver Christeller
Julian Christopher
Dominic Christophers
Nathaniel Chua
Chika Chukwujekwu
Ogo Chukwujekwu
Shelly Chung
Ade Churchett
Autumn Clack
Richard Clack
Paul Clancy
Brian Clark
Murray Clark
Sarah Elizabeth Clark
Angela Clarke
Danny Clarke
Gareth Clarke
Nicholas Clarke
Susan Clarke
Kath Clayden
Jenny Clayden
Sam Cleasby
Alex Cleave
Brenda Clerkin
Emma Clifford
Nick & Carey Clifford
Daniel Clifton
Matt Clifton
Vivienne Clore
Nic Close
Caroline Coady
Roxanne Coady
Sarah Coakley
Bronte Coates
Nick Cobley
Josh Cockcroft
Matthew Cocking
Jason Cohen
Sally Coker
Emma Coldicott
Claire Coleman
Peter Coleman
Vanessa Coleman
Pamela Collett
Maide Collin
Catherine Collins
Gavin Collins
Harley Collins
Kevin Collins
Melissa Collins
Samantha Collins
Mhari Colvin
Martin Colyer
Ryan Concannon
Michelle Conceison
Tara Condell
Ros Conisbee
Liz Conlan
Charles Connolly
Justin Connolly
Pete Connolly
Stephen Conrad
Joanne Conroy
Joy Conway
Karl Conway, Kate Nowak
Caitlan Cook
Cissy Cook
Conan Cook
James & Lindsey Cook
Lewis Cook
Melinda Cooke
Dean Cooney
Nathan Coons
Andrew & Emily Cooper
Charles and Deborah Cooper
Dennis Cooper
Gaynor Cooper
Glenda Cooper
Marcia Cooper

Suzy Cooper
Jessica Coppin
Kaelee Corcoran
Valentina Cordelli
Natalie Corfield
Jesse Corinella
David Cornish
Patrick Cornwell
Sarah Corrice
Michael Cosby
Bryony Cosgrove
Alan Coss
Rosanne Cousins
Ben Couture
Mike Coventry
Bob Covey
Andrew Cowley
David Cox
Elizabeth Cox
R.M Cox
Jerry Coy
Sarah Coyne
Adrian Crabtree & Debbie Blanchard
Helen Craddock
Cristin Craig
Daniel Craig
David and Judith Craig
Julia Craik
Wayne Crampton
Alex Crawford
John Crawford
John Crawley
Stuart Crawley
Anthony Creagh
Sarah Creed
Daisy Cresswell
Marion Cromb
Paula JE Crook
Sarah Crook
Jennifer Crossland
John Crowe
Louise Crowe
Jessica Crowell
Niall Crowley
Emma Crump
Shane Cullinane
Heather Culpin
Bethan Cunnane
Forbes Cunningham
Matthew Cunningham
Matthew E. Cunningham
Alessandra Curci
Lee Currie
Richard J. Currie
Anita Curry
Jennifer Curtis
Vickie Curtis
Mia Cusack
Daan
Sonal Dack
Chrysa DaCosta
Anthony Dagnall
Aaron Dail
Bruce Daisley
Jacqui D'Alessandro
Dominic Dalgliesh
Peter Dalling
Jo Dally
Andrew Dalmahoy
John Dalton
Teddy Daly
Valerie Daly
Benn & Megan Dance
Michael 'nomadiqueMC' Dangalaba
Duncan Danger
Saskia Daniel
Anne-Marie Dao
Richard Dare
Maria Dasios
Andrew Daum
Teresa Daum
Dave, Debbie, Faye, Ronan, Bibi, Wyll
 & Rees

Alexander Davie
Chris Davie
Louise Davies
Ashley Davies
Jean Davies
Jesse Davies
Jolène Davies
Jonathan Davies
Liam Davies
Rhiannon Davies
Clea Davis
Holly Davis
Philip Davis
Tom Dawkins
Emma Dawson
Jeffrey Day
Phil Day
Harriet Deacon
Gary Deans
Lindsey Dear
Marjan Debevere
Jonathan K Debrick
Oscar de Cruz
Rachel Deeson
Andrew De Gabriele
Brad DeHond
Martijn de Jong
Hannah Dell
Forrest DeMarcus
Jamie Dempster
Jak Denny
Marcus Denny
Nicky Denovan
Sonia Depa
Sean Derbyshire
Steph Derbyshire
Meaghan Derrick & Nathan Fine
destroyevil.com
Stephen Deuters
Tomash Devenishek
Tricia Dever
Michelle de Villiers
Gina Devivo
Donna DeWick
John Dexter
Slesha Dhakal
Rosa M Diaz
Uliana Dic
Mark DiCristina
Jill Wisniewski Dietrich
Caroline Diezyn
Roland Dillon
Emily Dimmock
Joel Dimmock
Mark Dixon
Natalie Dixon
Ritchie Djamhur
Ramona D'Mello
Tina Doan
Lynnette Dobberpuhl
Thomas Docker
Rebecca Dodd
Michael Dodds
Chris Doherty
Cullen Domaracki
Kim Domican
Jo Dommett
Emma Dones
Bill Donnelly
Patrick Donovan
Bathsheba Doran
Natalie Dorey
Molly Dorkin
Peter Doughty
Christopher Douglas
Jack Douglass
Nina Douglas
Paul Douglas
Doug Dowling
Eoin Dowling
Jeff Dowling
Sarah Downes
Willie Downs

Deborah Doyle
Niamh Doyle
Katy Drake
Claire Draycott
Tyler Drosdeck
Sue Ellen Duchene
Andy Dudley
Stuart Duncan
Philippa Dunjay
William Dunleavy
Vivienne Dunstan
Jack Dyson
Liam Dyson
Rebekah Eagle
John Earls
Cornelia Eberhardt
Karyn Eberle
Chris Eccles
James Edmondson
Chiara Edwards
Daniel Edwards
Daryl Edwards
James Edwards
Jenny Edwards
Paula Edwards (Pukka)
Rhys Edwards
Matthew Egglestone
Jon Ehrenfeld
Fredrik Ekman
Meghan Elayne
Lynsey Ellard
Andrew Elliott
Bill Elliott
Lisa Elliott
Tim Elliott
Wendy Elliott
Jonathan Ellis
Rob Ellis
Sophie Ellison
Jerry Emanuel
Matthias Embid
Stephanie Emila
Nick Emmel
Jonathan England
Johanna English
Sean Ennis
EO & KK
Emma Eratt
Jennie Erdal
Christian Eriksen
Elizabeth Eschete
Christopher Esposito
Ashleigh Evans
Cath Evans
Charles Evans
Simon Evans
Ian Evetts
Jo Ewan
Pete Faint
Peter Falconer
James, Michelle & Rosalie Falla
Mitchell Family
Florian Fangohr
Liberty Fannon
Maximus Fannon
Pamela Farias-Martin
Kia Farokhi
Sherri Farris
Conal Farry
Ewan Farry
Benedict Farse
Eleanor Fast
Timothy Faught
Declan Fay
Christopher Fedak
Alison Fellows
John Fellows
Pamela Fellows
Adam Fenn
David Fennell
Russell Fenwick
Chris Ferebee
Lorena Fernandez Oviedo

Gavin Fernback
Engemi Ferreira
Joshua Fidler
Seth Fiegerman
James Fielden
Reid Finlayson
Paul Fischer
Andi Fisher
Fiona Fisher
Jon Hernes Fiva
Pål Hernes Fiva
Taylor Fleet
Kyle Flemister
Rhian Fletcher
Lizzie Flew
Chris Floyd
Da Fluff
Rich & Charlie Flynn
Brian Focarino
Yin Ling Fock
Gregory Fodero
Erin and John Foff
Aidan Fogarty
Victoria Foord
Susan Foote
Greig Forbes
Chris Ford
Jude Ford
Kevin Ford
Ruth Ford
Doug Forrest
Jaime Forson
Gareth Forster
Jonas Forth
Roselyn Fortuna
Rosalie Foss
Marco Fossati-Bellani
Ali Foster
Melanie Foster
Paul Foster
J S Fowler
D G Fowlie
Katie Fowlie
Bob, Jacky, Thomas, Aidan and
    Oliver Fox
Ilana Fox
Neil Fox
Francis Foyle
Nancy Fracasse
Mark Franich
Katie Frank
Michael Franke
Isobel Frankish
Sarah Frankish
Maxyne Franklin
Kyle Frazer
Sophie Freeland
Sara Freeman
Sasha Frere-Jones
Helen Marie Frosi (SoundFjord)
Nick Frost
Victoria Frostis
Tom Frusher
Katy Fry
Karen Fu
Marta Fuchs
Katharine Fuge
Nathan Fulwood
Travis Funk
Simon, Hannah and Ella Funnell
Katherine Furman
Simon Gadd
Winston Gallagher
Hilary Gallo
Tracey Gamble
Kimberly Gamboa
Sai Ganesh
Beth Gardiner
Penny Gardiner
Sarah Gardiner
Rosemary Gardner
Kate Gardoqui
Richard Garnett

Francesca Garrett
Mike Garvey
Daniel Garwood
Gabrielle Gascoigne
Patrick "MH" Gatenby
Ben Gatewood
Tamsin Gatewood
Emma Gawen
Karen Gearhart
Amro Gebreel
Raf Geens
Sean Geer
Noah Geldberg
Saunders Gemma
Andrew Gemmell
Josie George
Paul George
Rachel Gerber
Emma Giacon
Michelle Gianatti
Eric Gibbons
Jack & Ellie Gibbons
Joanne Gibbons
Rob Gibbons
Butch Gibbs
Paul Gibbs
Will Gibbs
Chris Gibson
Sueli Giesler
Cyrus Gilbert-Rolfe
Adam Gilder
J. Gildner
Kimberley Gill
Sharan Gill
Aaron Gilmore
Jessica Gilmour
Dominic Gittins
Chris Gladman
Matthew & Aubrie Glanville
Ben Glass
Michael Glass
Barry Glinister
Richard Goddard
Gemma Godfrey
Mark Goerlich
Joe Goh
Alexandra Roumbas Goldstein
Sophie Goldsworthy
Alicia Gomez
Yo Gomi
Carmen Gonzalez
Jessica Gooch
James William Jack Good
Philip Goodman
Kristie Goote
Smita Gopinath
Alistair Gordon
Catherine Gordon
Charlie Gordon
John Gordon
Sarah Gorman
Ceri Gorton
Jo Gostling
Benjamin Gott
Roberta E. Gottlieb
Bonnie and Claire Gough
Denise Gould
Akshay Govind
Virginia Gow
Samantha Gower
David Graham
Deborah Graham
Gillian & Alan Graham
Justine Graham
Tom Graham
Gernot Grassl
Gavin Gray
Karen Gray
David Green
Nick, Jacob & Dan Green
Matthew Greenall
Jessica Greenwood
Kate Gregory

Wendi Gregory
Jessica Grehan
Meredith Greiling
Ellen Gremmen
Lucy Greswell
Cecilia Greyson
Harriet Griffey
Charmian Griffin
Mark Griffin
Craig Griffiths
Nichola Griffiths
Scott Grimes
Alyssa Grisham
Thomas Groat
Carol Grocott
Darragh Groeger
Dan Groenewald
Jon Groten
Julia Grove
Jude Groves
Tina Groves
Ian Grunig
Sebastián Guadarrama
Bertie Guard
Frank Guerra
Nick Guerra
Katie Guest
Ruchika Gupta
Tom Gurney
Kim Haack
Eleni Hack
William Hackett-Jones
Jenny Haddon
Philip Haddon
Lothar Haeger
Christa Hafemann
Carolyn Haggar
Robert Haines
Elaine Hake
Rachael Hale
Aaron Haley
Alfie Hall
Kevin Hall
Wes Hall
J.C. Hallman
Niamh Hamill
Catherine Hamilton
Darren Hamilton
Jacinta Hamilton
Jan Hamilton
Stuart A Hamilton
Colin Hammond
Alun Hamnett
David Hancock
Roisin Hancock
Melanie Hancox
Daniel Hand
John Handley
Sarah Handyside
Des Hanrahan
John Hansa
Marie Hanson
Reda Haq
Stephanie Harcrow
Tanya Harding
Mr and Mrs Hardy
David Harford
Sean Harkin
Ruth Ann Harnisch
Aaron Harnly
Andrew Harper
Jordan Harper
Susan Harper
Tina Harper
Aleta Harris
Elisa Harris
Josephine Harris
Linda K. Harris
Michael Harris
Nick Harris
Shelley Harris
Steve Harris
Ashley Harrison

Greg Harrison
John Harrison
Kris James Harrison
Martin Harrop
Scott Hartig
Craig Hartley
Steve Hartley
Amanda Harvey
Arabella Harvey
Caitlin Harvey
David Harvey
Anneli Harvie
Sara Hassan
Joanne Haswell
Susanna Hauru
Paul Hauser
Jess Have
Irma Havlicek
Christina Hawley
Michael Haydock
Rob Haye
Andy Hayes
Matt Hays
Susie Hayward
Cain Michael Tiberius Hay-
    ward-Hughes
Elspeth Head
Gareth Headon
Cat Heath
Jolie and Chris Heath
Jeff Hebert
Emma Hebron
Liz Hedgecock
Jolyon Hedges
Mary Heffernan
Deborah Hefter
Mark Hegarty
Emma Helenius
Victoria Hellon
Chris Helsen
Neil Hemmings & Lesley Duke
Brian Henderson
Will Henderson
Kylie Hendy
Ruud Hennequin
Pierre Henner
Caroline Hennessy
Kevlin Henney
Victor Henriquez
Henry and Syma
Susan Hensley
Liz Hensor
Kirstie Hepburn
Mary-Ellen Hepworth
Michael Herbert
Lewis Heriz
Dominic Herlihy
Hannah Herman
Robin Heron
David Hess
Jason Hesse
Beverly Hetherington
Renee Hetter
Jason Hewitt
David Heyman
Anthony Hibbert
Patricia Hickey
James Higginson
Davida Highley
Colin Hill
Gregory Hill
Lisa Hill
Richard Hill
Victoria Hilliard
Lisa Hilton
Thomas Hilton
David Hiltscher
Ruth & Klaus Hiltscher
Christian Hindemith
Julia Hines
Holly Hinton
Sigi Hirschbeck
Richard Hiscutt

Henry Hoare
Leland Hodgkins
Cheryl Hodgkinson
Dan Hoffman
Mike Hoffman
Steve Hoffman
Ingo Hofmann
Anders Hofseth
CMT Hogan
Tyler Holcomb
Jill Louise Holdcroft
Joanna Holland
Alan Holloway
Paul Holloway
Jonathan Holt
Sarah Holt
Stefan Holtemeier
Tarje Holtvedt
Oliver Holworthy
Jackie Homer
Paul Homer
Bill Hominuke
Melanie Hondros
Hongelong & Boefer AS
Joshua Hood
Andreas Hooftman
Celeste Hoover
Roger Horberry
Kate Horler
Alex Horne
Susan Hornidge
Andy Horton
Lesley Hossner
Sara L. Hough
Brian House
Liz Houston
Todd Hovis
Ross Howard
Catherine Howard-Dobson
Tracy Howarth
Rich Howell
Sarah Howells
To my dearest son Hridhaan with love
    from Rajendra Belvalkar
David Hsu
Eric Hsu
Shirley Huang
Tara Huddleston
Nathalie Hudson
Sue & Colin Hudson
Laura Huggett
Elizabeth Huggins
Matt Huggins
Alexander Hughes
Alison Hughes
David Hughes
Deirdre Hughes
Jean Hughes
Stephanie Hughes
Stuart Hughes
William Hughes
Michael Hulme
Jeroen Hulscher
Simon Hultgren
Derek Humphries
Lisa Hunt
Sonia Hunt
Julie Hunter
Giselle C.W. Huron
Cathy Hurren
Lee Hurst
Amy Hurt
Kariem Hussein
Renate Hussein
Syahril Hussin
Edward Huxley
Sylvia Huynh
Abraham Hyatt
Saud iAspire
Scott Inglis
Simon Ings
Yulya Ippolitova
Kirsty Irvine

Alanna Evelyn Irwin
Erin Rachel Irwin
Lee Isaacsohn
Natalija Isajenko
Michael Islip
Julie Carpenter Isom
Avi-Yona Israel
Kaushik Iyer
Garth, Katie, Coel & Lorelei Jackson
Hilary Jackson, Ben Golding
Jim Jackson
Pete Jackson
Roy Jackson
Stephanie Jackson
Tammy Jackson
Michael Jagger
Sarah Jakes
Janet Jakobe-Gray
Holly Jakobs
Fadi Jameel
Becca James
Neil James
Jamie and Ben
David Janes
Natalie Jarian
Gemma Jeeves
Alex Jefferies
Mark Jefferson
Laura Jellicoe
Laura Jenkins
Heather Jenkinson
Leonie Jennings
Charles Joels
Simon Johansson
Trinity John
Alex Johnson
Anne Johnson
Ben Johnson
Daniel Johnson
David Johnson
Mrs Gemma Johnson
Georgie Johnson
Nimet Johnson
Sandra Johnson
Alex & Abbie Johnston
Callum Johnston
Kimberley Johnston
Andrew Johnstone
Alyson Jones
Ceri Jones
Cheryl M. Jones
Gail Jones
Glynis Jones
Rebecca Jones
Robert Jones
Ross Jones
Simon R Jones and Kate Jones
Stephanie Jones
Terri Jones
Tim Jones
Francois Jordaan
Christine Jordan
Jillian Jordan
Jordan & Priya
Michelle and Stuart Jordan-Smith
Robert Joselow
Elizabeth Joseph
Michael Josephson
George Julian
Rachel Julis
Cornelia Junge
Milan Juza
Susanne Kahle
Jalil Kamaruddin
David Kane
Martin Kane
Michelle Kane
Eric Kanner
Ron Kaplan
Karen loves Nelson T.
Peter Karpas
Darius Katz
Janine Kaufman

Rhi Kavok
Linda Kaye
Daisy Kay-Taylor
Deborah Kee Higgins
Helen Keenlyside
Opemipo Kehinde
Steven Kehoe
William Kellar
Jeff Kelley
Andrew Kelly
Nicola Kelly
Stephen Kelly
Jo Kemp
Lee Kemp
Alex Kennedy
Barbara Kennedy
Christopher Shane Kennedy
Heather Kennedy
Janis Kennedy
Scott Kennedy
Simone Kenny
John Kent
Peter Kenyon
Cailan Kern – 'Big Bear'
Christian Kern & Tati Otaka
Nicola Alice Kerr
Marion Kerry
Maria Kerschen
Lewis Kershaw
Jack Kessler
Maika Keuben
James Key
Marcel Khan
Rajesh Khatri
Daniella Khosid
Mike Kidson
Sarah Kidson
Dan Kieran
James Kilford
Edward King
Jen J King
Kiara King
Rhys King
Simon King
Teri Kingdon
Judith Kinghorn
Jordan King-Lacroix
Meg Kingston
Laura Kiralfy
Katrina Kirkby
Laura Kirkpatrick
Steve Kirtley
Fiona Klomp
India Knight
Katie Knight
Nicole Knight
Roger Knight
Melanie Knott
Lynsay Kobelis
Robert J. Kohlmeyer & Hilary C.
    Woodward
Nicola Kohut
Juha Kolari
Alexis Konevich
Olga Kortanová
Gabe Krabbe
Joseph Kuah
Janet Kubalak
Jonas Kuehl
Eric Kuhne
B.J. Kunkel
Stephan Kurz
Ann Laatsch
Lenanne Labrusciano
Qiana La Croix
Bunny La'flare
Zhenyu Lai
Shannon Lail
Jeremy Laird
Miss Erica Lally
Mark Lambert
Jill Lambeth
Daniel Lanciana

Camille Landau
Ruediger Landmann
Jenny Landreth
Christina Lang
Nicholas Lang
Valerie Langfield
Tom Langsford
Jason Lankow
Klare Lanson
Ian LaPoint
Matthew Lardner
Alaine Large
Stephen & Kathryn Larkin
Elizabeth Larsen
Oliver Latham
Adam Latty
Andrew, Donna-Marie and Georgina
    Lawrence
Matt Lawson
Zoe Lawson
Alfie Lay
Wendi Le
Grace and Anna Lea
Matt Lea
Paul Leahy
Ian Leak
Johnny Leathers
Daria Lebedeva
Ciara Lee
Kevin Lees
Craig Le Grice
Steven Leigh
Viktor Leijon
Sam Leith
Andrew Leman
Mark Lennox
Bethany Leong
Gerry Leonidas
Eva Lesiak
Reuben Levine
Benjamin Levitt
Ashley Lewis
Elen Lewis
Jessica Lewis
Matthew Lewis
William Lewis
Richard Leyton
Yin Li
Claire Liddle
Karen Liff
Charles Light
Adrian Lightly
Ben Lillie
Ailsa Lindop
Laura Lindsay
Paul Lindsay
Eric Linge
David Linke
Joonas Linkola
Matt Linsenmayer
Liane Linstead
Robert Lischke
Elizabeth Litchfield
Deborah Little
Steve "thesliu" Liu
Sally Llewelyn-Jones
James Lloyd
Chau-Yee Lo
Seth Lobree
Barbara Lodge
Michael Logan
Karen Lollis
Kari Long
Nate Long
Nick Longhurst
Cindy Lonita
Kyle Lonsdale
Sara López Cayero
Dara Lorentzson
Isabell Lorenz
Dave Loverink
Stuart Lowbridge
Alison Lowe

Andrew Lowe
Jonathan Lowe
Dianne Lowry
Flora Penrose Loxley
Olivia Loxley
Adam Lucas
Kathryn Lucas
Jim Lucht
Amanda Lucier
Martina Luisetti
Sarah Luke
Magdeline Lum
Tina Wittorff Lund and Martin Lund
Tim Lusher
Zachary Lute
Steve Lynch
Mike Lynd
Robert Lynem
Derek Lynn
Christine Lynskey
Nancy Lyons
Doc M.
Alice Ma
MA Creative Writing @ Edinburgh
    Napier
Anne McAllister
Kirsty MacAlpine
David McAsey
Jon McAuliffe
Katie McCandlish
Bennett McCardle
Brian McCarthy
Jim McCauley
Steeve McCauley
Tara McCausland
Charlotte McClean
Claire McClean
Claudine McClean
John McCloskey
Cameron McClure
Pauline & Séamus Mac Conaonaigh
Ewan McCowen
Claire McCoy
Bess McCulloch
Laura McDonagh
Anne Macdonald
Iain MacDonald
Lucy McDonald
Rob McDonald
Cara MacDowall
Fred McElwaine
Lee Macey
Mo McFarland
Annie Macfarlane
Orla McGann
Luke McGarrity
Bridget McGing
Shona McGinlay
Philip McGinley
Eoin McGonigle
Caimin McGovern
Ana Machado da Silva
Andrew Macheta
Sharon Machin
Rebecca McHugh
Richard McIlroy
William McInerney
Pete MacIntyre
Carole McIntosh
Vi McIntosh
Anne McIntyre
Alistair Mackay
Katherine McKay
Stuart Mackay-Thomas
Doug McKee
Mark McKellier
Kiershen MacKenzie
Madeline McKeon
Maureen McKerrall
Emma Mackintosh
Kevin McLaughlin
Fiona Maclean
Leanne MacLeod

Will McLoughlin
Rachel McMaster
Bryan McNamara
David McNicoll
Olivia Maconie
Emma Macphail
Calvin Mcphaul
Christy McSpadden
Alana McVerry
Holly Louise McWalter
Jennie Maria McWalter
Marie Therese McWalter
Alan Maguire
Kate Mahady
Steven Maher
Daniel Maier
MailChimp
Francesca Main
Russ Main & Sarah Gorlov
Claire Mairs
Kayce Maisel
Elinor Maizels
Nolan Majors
Sharoz Makarechi
Malhotra
Debra Malouf
Andy Malt
Rashida Mangera & Hady Bayoumi
Peter Mangold
Hannah Manktelow
Tara Manning
Kim Mannion
Hannah March
Heather Marchant
Elizabeth Maren
Lynell French Marianetti
Tiffiny Mariha
Jeanne Markel
Audrey Marks
Caro Marks
Kieran (Kieranties) Marron
Rhodri Marsden
Steve Marsden
Jane Marshall
Louise Marston
Sean Martelli
Cally Martin
Ciara Martin
Ian Martin
Rafael Martin Delatorre
Abigail Martone
Kimberley Marvell Curry
Alexander Mason
Lynsey Mason
Patrick Mason
Rosalind Mason
Beth Mathiowetz
Stephanie Mathisen
Thomas E. Matlock
Gigi Matthews
Jessica Matthews
John Matthews
Susie Matthews
Caroline Mauger
Claire and Jolyon Maugham
Christian May
James May
Stephen May
Norman Mayer
Alex Mayes
Walter Mayes
Sarah Mayfield
Helen Mayson
Keaton Mazurek
Caryl Mead
James Medd
Rob Medford
Rik Meier
Shana Meier
Melanie
Kay Matlock Melcher
Judith Mellor
Bryan Melville

Michele Menditto
Ann Menke
Agnes Merat
Doug Merrett
Sid Merrett
Jenni Merson
Allie Lassar Meyer
Alice Meynell
Elliott Michelsen
Roger Miles
Naomi Miller
Shannon Miller
Tracy Miller
Andrew Milligan
Caroline Milligan
Susan Milligan
Adam Mills
Robert Mills
Christopher Milne
Esther Milne
Jennie Milne
Philip Milner
Kay Minchington
E. Susan Minder
Tim Minogue
Jane Mitchell
MaryLou Mitchell
John Mitchinson
Jorge Miyares
James Moakes
Gordon Moar
Deirdre Molloy
Joe Molloy
Kevin Molloy
Danny Molyneux
Jimmy Monger
Andrew Monk
Paul Monk
Nuno Monteiro
Kevin Montuori
Alex Moody
Tom Moody-Stuart
Adrian Moore
Christopher Moore
Jim Moore
Laura Moore
Lizzie Moore
Rose Moore
Steve Moores
Hattie Morahan
Martina Moran
Dominic Morgan
James Morgan
Joanne Morgan & Pete Kelly
Clothilde Morgan de Rivery
Paul Morin
Rose Morley
Daniel Moroz
Neil Morrill
Clair Morris
Jenny Morris
Luke Morris
Nancy Morris
Hope Morrissett
Paul Mortimer
Richard Morton
Chailee Moss
Harry Moss
Julia Mottram
Bryan Mouat
Nick Moult
Esther Mourits
Haydn Mowbray
Niall Muckian
Christopher Mudiappahpillai
Alexander Muhr
Victoria Muir
Ciara Muldoon
Peter Mullen
Wesley Mullen
Happy Birthday Mum! Love Joe
Judy Munday
Faye Murfet

Margaret Anne Murgatroyd
Brendan Murphy
Colm Murphy
David Murphy
Deirdre Murphy
Laura Murphy
Phil Murphy
Andy Murray
Beatrice Murray
Beth Murray
Claire Murray
Ewen Murray
Kevin Murray
Lee & Christine Murray
Sharon Murray
Kai Muxlow
Sarah N
Michelle Nagashima
Hana Nakamura
Nalini Arti Narayan
Erica Nardello
Stuart Nathan
Katharine B. Neary
Ruth Nederveen
Leigh Neithardt
Jessica Nelson
John Nelson
Scott Allan Gordon Nelson
Andrew Neve
Keith Neville
Richard Neville
Paul New
Peter Newbould
Eric Newcomb
Tara Newell
Li Ann Ng
Min Ann Ng
Kim Ngo
Viet Nguyen
Síle Nic Chonaonaigh
Andy Nichol
Vic Nicholas
Matt Nicholls
Lisa Nicholson
Emily Nicol
Nick Nieman
 Nigel & Ruth
Alex Nightingale
Marijn Nijenhuis
Keyvan Nilforoushan
Carolyn Nisbet
Sarah Ní Shúileabháin
Samantha (Sami) Noble
Wilhelm Noeldeke
Anthoula Nolan
Eamonn Nolan
Paul Nolan
Sara Nolan
Stewart Nolan
Tara Noonan
Marianne Ø. Nordgård
Den Norland
Greg Norman
Laura Norton
Bettye Nothmann
Conor Nugent
Ethna Nugent
Mark Nunn
Kristen Nyberg
Jacqui Oakley & Jamie Lawson
Catarina (Obelhinha)
Damian O'Broin
Martin O'Byrne
Kerrie O'Callaghan
Laura O'Connor
Sarah O'Connor
Lauren O'Dam
Tim O'Dea
Aude Odeh
Eden Odell
Matthew Odell
Amanda O'Donnell
Barry O'Donoghue

Angela O'Farrell
Andy Offor
Tessa Ogilvie Thompson
Jenny O'Gorman
Maryanne Ohara
Sinead O'Keeffe
Molly Oldfield
Hannah Oldman
Sharon Olevano
Ben Oliver
Juliana Oliver
Marina O'Loughlin
Vincent Olson
Chatrina O'Mara
Nikki O'Neill
Sophie O'Neill
Kees Oosterholt
Colm O'Regan
Susan O'Reilly
Jennifer Orton, Susan Hammond
Eileen Osborne
John O'Shea
Greg O'Toole
Patrick Ottery
Anne Ovenden
David Overend
Matthieu Oviedo
Richard Owen
Barb Owens
Jonny Owens
Phoebe Pacheco
Lea Sio Pacis
Asa Packer
Tom Pacy
Louise Paddock
Sarah Page
Vincent Pagnard-Jourdan
Catherine Paine
Ellen Paine
Fernand Pajot
Juliet Palfrey
Samuel Palin
Richard Palmer
Kim Paniagua
Pauline Pannier
Laarni Paras
Linley Park
Andrew Parker
Eleanor Parker
Kevin Parker
Steve Parker
Sally Parker Mitchell
Neil Parkinson
Samantha Parnell
Rebecca Parsons
John Pascale
Sherri Pasian
Diana Passy
Rima Patel
Jonas Paterno
Flora Paterson
Robbie Paterson
Craig Patrick
Andrea Patterson
Sharelle Patterson
Lise Pavich
Dave Pawson
John Leslie Peake
Richard Pearce
Ben Pearson
Ewan Pearson
Karen Pearson
Peter Pearson
Simon Pearson
Joy Pecknold
Pedro Pedroso
Caroline Pegram
Maria Pekurovskaya
Jessica Pellegrin
Joy Pencilina
Bella Pender
Alison Penton-Harper
David Percival

Robert Peretson
Karen Perez
Guillermo Pérez-Hernández
Anna Perkins
Jethro Perkins
David & Karen Perry
Michael Perry
Kate Pert
Vicky Pert
Sarah Peters
Svend Aage Petersen
John H. Petrey
John Petrie
Susan Petrie
Ernst-Jan Pfauth
Phil & Carmel
Darren Phillips
Jennifer Phillips
Ollie Phillips
Rose Phillips
Amy Phung
Rachel Pictor Roberts
Cynda Pierce
Mary Pierce
Mike Pilkington
Daniel Pimley
Jane Pink
Sacha Dielle Pinto
Tina & Tomasz Pirc
Candice Pires
Pauline Pires
Michael Pittuck
Marco Piva-Dittrich & Solveig
    Dittrich-Piva
David Platonoff
Thomas Pluck
Glenn Pohs
Justin Pollard
Alex Pollock
Cressida Pollock
Michael Pollock
Stefanie Pont
Claire Poore
James Porteous
Samuel Porter
Lauri Portz
Donna Potter
Louise Potter
Elspeth Potts
Adam Powell
Alison Collison Powell
Amy Powell
Kevin Powell
Naomi Powell
Jean Power
Diana Pray
Lucy Prebble
Leon Prescod
Julie Press
Richard Preston
Gavin Pretor-Pinney
Mike Price
Nick Price
Sara Price
Tom Price
Joshua Prince
Arthur Prior
Sharon Prior
Johnny Pritchard
David Pritchard
Emma Probst
Catherine Procter
Kristel Proctor
James Proud
Jenny Pryer
Rebecca Pugh
Doug Purcell
Helen Purves
Martin Quested
Megan Quinn
QuizQuizQuiz
Saad Qureshi
Andrew Radcliffe

Pamela Radley
Tom Rafferty
Brady Rafuse
Mariano Raigón
Emma Raine
Jason Ramapuram
Cynthia Claire Ramirez
Mark Ramirez
James Ramsay
Michael Ramsay
Edward Randell
Michelle Ransom-Hughes
Lane Rasberry
Michele Howarth Rashman
Jonathan Ratcliff
Malcolm Raven
Michael Ravnitzky
Rauf Rawson
Gary S. Ray
William Read
Mark Reading
Aline Reed
Katie Reed
Amy Rees
Sarah Reeson
Carlene Chittenden Reeves
Guy Reeves
Margaret Reeves
Phillip Reeves
Rebecca Regan
Philip Reid
Scott Reid
Elizabeth Reilly
Joyce Reingold
Chris Remo
G Rendle
Lesley Rennie
Ruby Rennie Panter
Siddharth Rewari
John Reynolds
Malcolm Reynolds
Nick Reynolds
Diana Rhoten
Lowri Rhys
Allyson Rice
Jennifer Rice
Hugh Richards
Peter Richards
Kath Richardson
Terri Richardson
Erica Richman
Simon Ricketts
Helen Ridgway
Sally Rigg
Candy Riley
James Riley
Tim Riley
Gareth Rimmer
Robert Ristroph
Phillippa Ritchie
Jim & Jackie Robbins
Malcolm & Christine Robbins
Colin Roberts
Michelle Colleen Roberts
Rachael Roberts
Wyn Roberts
Hamish Robertson
Iain Robertson
Cassandra Naomi Robinson
Dave Robinson
Ed Robinson
Elaine Robinson
J.C. Robinson
Jean Robinson
Kiera Emily Robinson
Lindsey Robinson
Paula Robinson
Simon Robinson
Jeffrey Roche
Gabriel Rockefeller
Barbara Roddam
Charlotte Roden
Wendy Roden

Cristina Rodriguez Meneses
Charles Rogers
Kate Rogers
Kevin Rogers
Simon Rogers
Trevor Rogers
Greg Rolan
Michaela Rolph
Mike Rook
Daniel Roper
Anna Rosenberg
Howard E. Rosenman
John Rosensweig
Ben Rosenthal
Emma Ross
Sabrina Ross
Rowan Rosser
Catherine Rossi
Laurie Roth
Michael Rothchild
Matt Rotheram
Chip Rowe
Tracey Rowe and Alan Teixeira
Catherine Rowlands
Marcel Roy
Sonny Ruff
Sebastian Rumberg
Michael Runyan
Toni Ruotsalainen
Clare Rushforth
Anastasiya Ruskykh
Allan Russell
Gary Russell
Lynne Russell
Simon Russell
Stephen Russell
Stuart Rutherford
Jenny Ryan
Fiona Ryan-Clark
Lykara Ryder
Dean Rylander
Rolande Saam
Margretl Sabine
Hesham Sabry
Monica Saksena Joye
Amy Sakurai
Adam Sales
Stefano Salis
Natasha Salwan and David Mayo
Any Salyer
Jorge Sanchez
Alejandro Sánchez Vaca
Christoph Sander
Christian Sandino-Taylor
Nina Sankovitch
Val Santiago and Marie Chan
Manik Sarkar
John-Paul Sarni
Sarah Sarni
Shrikant Sawant
Callum Sawdy
Garry Sawdy
Olivia Sawdy
Peter Sawdy
Josh Sawislak
Tim Scanlin
John Schebeck
Judith Schenck
Bonnie Schepers
Martin Scherer
Andrew Scheuber
Charles Schilb
Joel Schimchak
Cathleen Schine
Shelley Schmidt
Matthias Schmitt
Henriette Schoemaker
John Schoenbaum
Chuck Scholla
Scott Schonberger
Jillian Scott
Kaz Scott
Kevin Scott

Lisa Scott
Paul Scott
Stephanie Scott
Sarah Scougal
Hetty Scrope
James Scudamore
Alexandra Sedrowski
Katja Seebohm
Miranda Seed
Lizzie Seetharaman
Will Sefton
Beth Serota
Aline Severi
John Shale
Sophie Shanahan-Kluth
Alex Shapowal
Daniel Shaq
Neil Sharma
Kate Sharp
Miriam Sharrad
Andy Shaw
Deb Shaw
Natalie Shaw
Magnus Shearer
Margaret Sheer
Chris Sheffield
Jacqui Sheldon
Dinesh Shenoy
Jen Shenton
Lloyd Shepherd
Steven Shepherd
Hannah Sheppard
Lyn Sherburne
Arthur Sheriff
Jonathan (Jasper) Sherman-Presser
Gary Shewan
Nicky Shiell
Anna Shipman
Nadia Shireen
Kate Shires
Cynthia Shore
Ben Short
Justin Shorten
Sarah Shulman
Richard Sickinger
Bill Silverio
Carole Sim
Andy Simm
Emma Simmons
John Simmons
Joseph Simpson
Julian Simpson
Duncan Sims
Debarati Singh
Tony Singh
Thomas Singlehurst
Natalie Fatima Morales Sio
Michelle Sissons
Alex Sitaras
Jan Skakle
Jeremy Skillington
Mat Skinner
Susan Skipper
Agneta Skoog Svanberg
DawnMarie Skora
William Slack
John Slater
Harry Smail
Olivia Smales
Christo Smallwood
Nick Smee
Sally Jane Smeretsky
Roger Smethurst
Dennis Smit
Andrew Smith
Baxter Smith
Ben Smith
Catriona R Smith
Christopher Smith
Derek Smith
Derek Smith (and Kelsie too!)
Don Smith
Iain Smith

Leonie Smith
Megan Smith
Nichola L. Smith
Owen Smith
Scott Smith
Adam Smithson
Paul Smithson
Simon Smundak
Sara Smylie
Jason Smyth
Margaret Snape
Matt Soar
Stephen Sobol
The Society Club
Lili Soh
Rachel Sommerville
Laura Sommo
Robin Sommo
Edward Song
Valerie Sonnenthal
Joann Soon
Andrew Sorcini
Julie Sorge Way
Mate Soric
Alan Sorohan
Kristina Sostarko
Eduardo Sousa
Oliver South
Tom Southam
James Spackman
Jennifer and Brian Spaid
Marcia and David Spaid
Kerri J Spangaro
Louise Speak
Lesley Spence
Florence Spencer
Lesley Spencer
Emily Spencer-Rigby
Ellie Spicer
Robbie Spicer
Susie Spicer
Leigh Spriggs
Robyn Squyres
Kylee St George
Diane St John
Jane St. Pier
Nate St. Pierre
Aidan Stacey
Jennie Stacey
Svetlana Stafeeva
Johannes Staffans
Tim, Sarah & Penny Stainthorpe
Judith Staley
Jason B Standing
John Stanfield
Kelly Stanford
Laura Stanning
Dana Stanton
Katrina Stats
Karen Steed
Nigel Steggel
David Stelling
Mo Stemen
Ian Stevens
Katherine Stevens
LeAnne Stevens
David Stevenson
Jennifer Eileen Stevenson
Kathie Marie Stevenson
Rachel Stevenson
Cianna Stewart
Deb Stewart
Jennifer Stewart
Tabatha Stirling
Renee Stock
Alexandra Stockley
Naomi Stocks
Sarah Stokely
Alan Stoll
Jennie J. Stoltz
David A Storey
Katie Stowell
Simon Strachan

Erik Straub
Cara Strickland
Suky Stroud
Robert Stutts
Matthew Stylianou
Julia Ross Suits
Colin Summers
Carol Sumner
Joanne Sumner
Neil James Sumner
Yonga Sun
Mark Suret
Suzana & Ricardo
Danielle Swain
David Swartz
EstherMaria Swaty
Debi Symonds
Nick T
Bronágh Taggart
Kana Takahashi
Morgan Tanswell
Soulla Tantouri Eriksen
Tan Zhi Wen Hazel
Beverly Tapper
Margarita Tartakovsky
Ezra Tassone
Jo Tate
Arthur Taylor
Helen Taylor
Isobel Taylor
James Taylor
Leanne Taylor
Maria Taylor
Jennifer Teagle
Mike Teare – happy 60th love J,S&S x
Howard Teece
Erin Tehee
Sitar Teli
Corinne Lozzio for Gregg Temner
Will Thames
Darren Theakstone
Jim TheSchoolgirl
Daniel Thirion
Christine Thirlwell
Martine Thiry-Greff
Garry Thom
Alan Thomas
Glenn Thomas
Greg Thomas
Jason Thomas
Jayne Thomas
Jessie Thomas
Joseph Thomas
Perry Thomas
Tania Thomas
Amanda Thompson
Andrea Thompson
Cathryn Thompson
Jolly Thompson
Judith Thompson
Philip Thompson
David Thomson
Jon Bryan Thomson
Roy Thomson
Graham Thorley
Sharon Thresher
Amanda Thurman
Nicholas Tims
@tinapievergara
Jon, Cara and Porter Tinning
Isabela Titze
Alice Tjiu
Frances Tobin
James Tobin
Todd and Mark
Hayley Tolley
Victoria Tomlinson
Bryan Tookey
Andy Tootell
Keith Tootell
Hernan Toro
Helen Towns
Daniel Townsend

Victoria Traube
Chloe Travers
Patrick Treacy
Jody Tresidder
James Trigg & Ro Taylor
Melissa Trinh
Ma. Angela Tripon
Tjarda Tromp
Mari Troskie
Robert I. Trunley
Arturo Gio Tsuchida
Matt Tubb
Darla Tucker
Fiona Tucker
Shelley Tule
Linda Tulett
Belinda Turffrey
Kathleen & Neville Turley
Paul Turley
Colin Turner
Jane Turner
Leah Turner
Ryan Turner
Neil Turton
Byron R. Tuyay
Karen Twible
Georg Uecker
Oyvind Ultvedt Stenersen
Gus Unger-Hamilton
Atilla Murat Unver
John and Lindsay Usher
Sarah Usher
Mehmet Emir Uslu
Maria Valencia
James Vallance
Anna Vallesteros
Gordon J. Van De Water
Christiaan van der Woude
Wieland Van Dijk
Martha van Drunen
Kathleen van Geete
Jan Van Hoef
John Van Lue
Kathleen van Mourik
Michiel van Ruitenbeek
William Vaughan
Heleen Veerman
Ville Vehmanen
Jack Vening
Mark Vent
Andrew Ventura
Paul Verhaeghen
Anne Verrept
Linda Verstraten & Pyter Wagenaar
Dave Verwer
Sarrah Vesselov
Nick Veys
Terry Vickers
Prashanthy Vigneswaran
Sanjay Vijayanathan
Ian Vincent
James Vincent
Laura Vincent
Normandy Vincent
Rhodri Viney
Catherine S. Vodrey
Dhara Vyas
Jo W
Alex Wade
Laura Wade
Seren Wade
Nick Wadlow
Matia Wagabaza
Jonathan Wakeham
Gregory Waldorf
Richard Wales
Claire Walker
George Walker
Joel Walker
Julie Walker
Steve Walker
Matt Wallace
Kathy Wallis

Jamie Walsh
Lisa Walsh
Lucy Walsh
Maureen Walsh
Mike Walsh
Mike J Walsh
Rob & Liz Walsh
Tom Walsh
David Walshe
Martin Walton
Richard Walton
Rod Wampler
Shao Wang
Yuhong Wang
Emma Wardle
Adam Warn
Ben Warren
Emma Warren
Rebecca Warren
Nicole Warwick
Madeleine Waterford
Nichola Waterhouse
Kat Waterman
Zoë Waterman
Richard Waters
Colin and Jane Watson
Graham Watson
Yvonne Watterson
Natalie Watts
Simon Watts
Owen Way
Susan Rachael Weaver & Gaynor
  Jones
Nick Webb
Paul Webb
Vicky Webb
Frank Webster
Rosie Weeks
Erica Weiner
Daniel Weir
Jason J. Weir
Jörn Weisbrodt
Ryan Weiss
Courtney Welsh
David Welsh
Annie West
Jayne West
Marcel Westhoff
Tom Wexler
Pearl Wheeler
Mary Lotis Whelan
Paul Whelan
Levin Wheller
Louise Yvonne White
Paul Wayne White
Rosemary White
Simon White
Stephen White
Taylor White
Tom White
Jennifer Whitehead
Jacob Whitlow
Emma Whitten
David Whittle
Sharon Whooley
Daniel Wiborg
Hayley Wickens
Michelle Wickman
David Widdick
Rebecca Wiegand
Christoph Wiesenack
Hans-Guenter Wiesenack
Ali Wiff
Gabrielle Wight
Thomas Wigley
Diana Elizabeth Wilbur
Beth Wilde
Naomi Wildey
Tilly Wilding Coulson
Kimberly Wilkerson
Cary Wilkins
Adam Wilkinson
David Wilkinson

Kate Wilkinson
Olly Wilkinson
Samantha Wilkinson
Jane Wilks
Kimberly Willardson
Rod Willcox
Anna Williams
Betty Sarah Amelia Williams
Chris Williams
Daniel Williams
David Williams
Fiona Williams
Jeremy Williams
Julie Williams
Laurence Williams
Nick Williams
Paul Williams
Ronald A. Williams
Samuel Williams
Sean Williams
Better Better Willis
Jim Willis
Jennifer Wills
Alexa Wilson
Angela Invincibile Wilson
Iain Wilson
Lauren Wilson
Leslie Wilson
Lisa Windsor
Dan Wise
Charlotte Wissett
Steven Wolfson
Dar Wolnik
Debbie Wood
Julie Woodgate
George Woodhouse
Ryan Woodward
Carrie Wright
David Wright
Deborah Wright
Emma Wright
Huckleberry Wright
Rhiannon Wright
Steve Wright
Tom Wright
Will Wrightson
Tom Wrobel & Sara Morgan
Debbie Wythe
Michael Yamartino
Nicholas Yates
Elhaam Yavari
Riana Yeates
Denise Yeo
Lainie Yeoh
David Yllanes
Hattie Yolland Quartermaine
Julia Yong
Daniel Yoo
Carol Young
Fraser Young
Judy Young
R I Young
Sarah Young
Susan Young
Ayca Yuksel
Hye-Young Yune
Jane Zara
Henrietta Zeffert
Rebecca Zemunik
Jennifer Ziembo
Jeff Zimmerman
Ned Zimmerman
Mike Zipsin
Samer Zureikat

PERMISSION CREDITS

A NOTE ABOUT THE TYPEFACES

The introductions to the letters are set in DIN, a sans serif font defined in 1931 by the Deutsches Institut für Normung (the German Institute for Standardization). It is the typeface used on German road signs and on all kinds of technical documents. For a long time it was regarded as the classic example of a corporate typeface (the German Green party rejected its use on a proposed new logo in 2006), but it was clearly influenced by the geometric typeface experiments of the Bauhaus school, and research by the Dutch designer Albert-Jan Pool suggests that it wasn't just the work of a committee. He identifies the designer as Siemens engineer Ludwig Goller (1884–1964) who was chairman of the DIN committee for design. Pool himself went on to design a full family of DIN fonts in the mid-1990s. Its clarity and legibility mean it remains one of the most popular sans serif fonts. Type historian Evert Bloemsma attributes its success to the following formula: 80% hi-tech, 10% imperfection (which equates with charm) and 10% static.

The transcripts of the letters are set in Ehrhardt, a typeface developed in 1937 by Stanley Morison while at the Monotype Corporation. Morison was responsible for making modern versions of many antique faces, including Bembo and Baskerville, and designed the now ubiquitous Times New Roman. The creator of the original Ehrhardt typeface is unknown but it is named after the late 17th-century Ehrhardt foundry in Leipzig and is similar to some Dutch typefaces of that period produced by the Amsterdam printer Anton Janson. The typographical historian Robin Nicholas believes Ehrhardt was Morison's take on Janson, 'made a little heavier and narrower to give improved legibility and economy'.